RENEWALS 458-4574
DATE DUE

WITHDRAWN
UTSA Libraries

INTERNATIONAL HUMAN RESOURCE MANAGEMENT IN JAPANESE FIRMS

International Human Resource Management in Japanese Firms

Their Greatest Challenge

Timothy Dean Keeley

palgrave

© Timothy Dean Keeley 2001

All rights reserved. No reproduction, copy or transmission of this publication may be made without written permission.

No paragraph of this publication may be reproduced, copied or transmitted save with written permission or in accordance with the provisions of the Copyright, Designs and Patents Act 1988, or under the terms of any licence permitting limited copying issued by the Copyright Licensing Agency, 90 Tottenham Court Road, London W1T 4LP.

Any person who does any unauthorized act in relation to this publication may be liable to criminal prosecution and civil claims for damages.

The author has asserted his right to be identified as the author of this work in accordance with the Copyright, Designs and Patents Act 1988.

First published 2001 by
PALGRAVE
Houndmills, Basingstoke, Hampshire RG21 6XS and
175 Fifth Avenue, New York, N.Y. 10010
Companies and representatives throughout the world

PALGRAVE is the new global academic imprint of
St. Martin's Press LLC Scholarly and Reference Division and
Palgrave Publishers Ltd (formerly Macmillan Press Ltd).

ISBN 0-333-96506-X

This book is printed on paper suitable for recycling and made from fully managed and sustained forest sources.

A catalogue record for this book is available from the British Library.

Library of Congress Cataloging-in-Publication Data
Keeley, Timothy Dean, 1956–
    International human resource management in Japanese firms: their greatest challenge/Timothy Dean Keeley.
        p. cm.
    Includes bibliographical references and index.
    ISBN 0-333-96506-X
    1. International business enterprises—Management. 2. International business enterprises—Personnel management. 3. Organizational change—Management. 4. Industrial Management—Japan. I. Title.
HD62.4 .K435 2001
658.3'00952—dc21

2001036091

10 9 8 7 6 5 4 3 2 1
10 09 08 07 06 05 04 03 02 01

Printed in Great Britain by
Antony Rowe Ltd, Chippenham, Wiltshire

Library
University of Texas
at San Antonio

Contents

List of Tables	vi
List of Figures	vii
Acknowledgements	viii
Abbreviations	ix
Glossary of Japanese Terms	x
1 The Challenge	1
2 Cross-Cultural Management Issues	15
3 Japanese Culture and Organizational Behaviour	32
4 International Human Resource Management	98
5 Communication and Decision-Making	141
6 A Study Clarifying HCN Integration in Japanese MNCs	172
7 Conclusions Concerning HCN Integration in Japanese MNCs	202
Appendix: List of Questions in Scales	222
References	225
Bibliography	237
Index	252

List of Tables

6.1	Correlation matrix, means and standard deviations for HCN data	194
6.2	Multiple regression reporting standardized coefficients for HCN data	196
6.3	Decomposition for final empirical path model	197
6.4	Correlation matrix, means and standard deviations for PCN managers	199
6.5	Standard multiple regression reporting standardized coefficients for PCN data	200

List of Figures

1.1	Conceptual model of factors affecting HCN integration	13
6.1	Conceptual model of factors affecting HCN integration	195
6.2	Final empirical path model for HCN respondents (standardized coefficients)	197
6.3	Final empirical path model for PCN respondents (standardized coefficients)	198

Acknowledgements

The findings presented in this book are primarily based upon research carried out while I was at the Australian Centre for Strategic Management (ACSM) at Queensland University of Technology (QUT). First of all, I would like to thank Mark Shadur for inviting me to carry out this research at ACSM. I would also like to express my appreciation to the entire faculty at Kyushu Sangyo University (KSU) who allowed me to take a year's sabbatical so I could concentrate on this research. The financial support for the first phase of the research was covered by a grant from the Industrial Management Research Institute at KSU. The funds for the second phase were provided by the ACSM along with the Faculty of Business at QUT.

I greatly appreciate all the time and energy spent by all the parent company national and host country national managers who completed questionnaires and participated in interviews. Without their co-operation this research could not be successfully carried out. In addition, there are numerous individuals who assisted me in this research. In particular, I would like to express my sincere gratitude to Mark Shadur, who contributed to the development of the model and the statistical analysis presented in this book, and Kazuo Doi, who was an excellent partner in the first phase of the research.

TIMOTHY DEAN KEELEY

Abbreviations

The following is a list of the abbreviations that appear *repeatedly* throughout the text:

FDI	foreign direct investment
HCN	host country national
HRM	human resource management
IHRM	international human resource management
MITI	Ministry of trade and industry (Japan)
MNC	multinational corporation
PCN	parent company national
SME	small and medium size enterprises
TCN	third country national
UNCTC	United Nations Center on Transnational Corporations
UK	United Kingdom
US	United States

Glossary of Japanese Terms

Though the Japanese terms used in the text are all defined when introduced, for ease of reference a summary of the terms with brief explanations are offered below: (Note: the romanization of Japanese words used is without distinction between short and long vowels.)

ba: place (frame)
bucho: department chief
endaka: high value of the yen
gaijin: foreigner
hi-yatoi: day labourers
ie: household, often used in reference to companies as households
gaman: endurance, sufferance
genchi-ka: localization
jinji-bu: personnel department
jinmyaku: human network
kao: face
jirei: assignment notice
kacho: section chief
kaisha: company
kazokushugi: familism
kigyo-betsu rodo kumiai: enterprise-based unions
keiretsu: (sangyo keiretsu) industrial grouping (*kinyu keiretsu*) grouping centred on a main bank
kokoro: mind, heart, soul
mado-giwa zoku: window tribe, employees with nothing to do but look out the window
Monbu-sho: Ministry of Education
nanpo boke: tropical amnesia
nemawashi: lay the groundwork for obtaining one's objective mainly through informal discussions (part of Japanese typical decision-making process)
nenko joretsu: Japanese-style seniority system
nihonjinron: a school of thought that stresses Japanese uniqueness
omikoshi management: a metaphor referring to the teamwork involved in carrying a portable shrine
omote-ura: front and back
onjo-shugi: paternalism

Glossary of Japanese Terms xi

oyabun-kobun: the boss or leader and the subordinate or follower (derived from parent-child)
ringi: the process of obtaining the sanction to a plan by circulating the draft prepared by a person in charge of a matter
ringi-sho: the written proposal (draft of a plan)
rinji-shain: temporary employees
saiko keiei sekininsha: position of highest managerial authority
sei-shain: a regular or full-time employee
shain: an employee (member)
shain ryoko: company trip
shataku: company housing
shikaku: attribute (used in conjunction with *ba*)
shiteiko seido or *tokuteiko seido*: system of recruiting exclusively from a selected number of elite universities
shokumu kijutsu-sho: job description
shushinkoyo: long-term or lifetime employment
sogo-shosha: general trading company
soto-uchi: outside versus inside
soto no hito: outsiders
tan-i kumiai: unit union to which workers are affiliated individually and directly
tan-itsu kumiai: single union to which individual members affiliate directly
tansan: industrial federations
tanshin funin: living away from the family while on assignment in some far away location
tatemae-honne: something stated for public consumption versus the real thought or feeling
uchi no hito: insiders
wa: harmony
wa: used in compound words to refer to Japanese things
wa-shoku: Japanese food
wa-shitsu: a Japanese style room
yo: (character for ocean) used to refer to foreign, usually Western, things
yo-fuku: Western-style clothing

1 The Challenge

Perhaps the greatest challenge Japanese companies face in expanding their foreign direct investment (FDI) is how to integrate host country national (HCN) managers into the management process of their overseas subsidiaries as well as that of the parent companies themselves. I examine the problems associated with HCN integration in Japanese companies and seek to clarify the extent to which HCN managers are actually integrated. As an integral part of this process I explore a number of important related topics such as: Japanese management in general, the transferability of Japanese management practices to their foreign subsidiaries, international human resource management (IHRM) issues, as well as cross-cultural management and multinational management issues. Investigating the role of HCN managers provides insights into Japanese IHRM through the eyes of the HCN managers themselves and reveals how Japanese multinational corporations (MNCs) actually manage their foreign subsidiaries. I also address numerous misunderstandings concerning Japanese management in general and the management of Japanese foreign subsidiaries in particular.

There are four underlying assumptions that substantiate the importance of effective integration of HCNs. First, globalization of human resource management policies and practices is a positive and prevailing trend among the world's MNCs and those MNCs that do not effectively globalize their operations may find themselves at a competitive disadvantage. Second, effective IHRM offers competitive advantages that are only fully exploited by employing the talents of HCN managers. Third, MNCs must learn to develop and retain talented HCN managers in order to enjoy long-term prosperity. Fourth, HCN managers should play a key role in the management of foreign subsidiaries in their country, at the parent company, or in a third country when the talents they possess warrant such arrangements.

Employing HCNs in management positions offers numerous advantages for the MNC and benefits to the host country. HCN managers usually have an inherent understanding of the local language(s) and culture(s). They are more likely than a parent country national (PCN), on his/her first assignment in the host country, to be familiar with the local business and regulatory environment. The costs associated with employing HCNs are usually much lower than those associated with employing PCNs. Employing HCN managers creates greater opportunities for HCN white-collar workers. In addition, it bestows more benefits to the host country through the transfer of management know-how and experience, as well as improving public relations in terms of the MNC being viewed as a good corporate citizen.

On the other hand, failure to successfully integrate HCN managers in the management process of foreign subsidiaries may have substantial negative outcomes for the parent company. These problems include high turnover, low morale, internal strife, and poor productivity (Kopp, 1994b:10). In addition, not offering fair opportunities for qualified HCNs to assume positions of managerial responsibility and/or discrimination against HCNs may lead to problems with the host country government authorities. Japanese companies have become infamous for their transgressions in this area and have been suffering the consequences.

In the USA, the Employment and Housing Subcommittee of the House Committee on Governmental Operations held hearings in 1991 to investigate claims that Japanese MNCs were discriminating against US HCN employees. Likewise, in Malaysia, though Prime Minister Mahathir Mohamad promoted FDI investment by Japanese companies in order to speed up the industrialization of his country, he later complained that Malaysians were not being given adequate opportunities to advance in the managerial ranks of the Japanese subsidiaries. The successful integration of HCN managers in Japanese MNCs is imperative if Japanese MNCs are to attract and retain top local talent. Former US Secretary of Labor Robert Reich (1991:81), a former Harvard University professor, made this point in an article appearing in *Harvard Business Review*:

> In the competition for global talent, corporations that are reluctant to consider foreign nationals for top management positions will lose out; the most talented people simply will not join an organization that holds no promise of promotion. Japanese-owned companies that have been notoriously slow to open their top executive ranks to non-Japanese will operate at a competitive disadvantage.

1.1 INCREASING FDI AND THE GROWING IMPORTANCE OF IHRM

In recent years, the importance of developing effective IHRM policies and practices has received greater recognition. This increased interest in effective IHRM is a natural outcome of the spectacular growth of FDI during the post-war period. Prior to the Second World War, the number of firms involved in FDI was relatively small and the majority of firms in the United States as well as many other countries concentrated on their domestic markets. However, during the post-war period FDI by MNCs from around the world greatly increased. A report by the United Nations Center on Transnational Corporations (UNCTC) estimated the world stock of FDI to have reached 1.7 trillion US dollars by the end of 1990 (UNCTC, 1992). Furthermore, since 1983, direct investment outflows have increased at the unprecedented compound annual rate of 29 per cent a year, three times faster than that of the growth of exports (at 9.4 per cent) and four times that of the growth of world output (UNCTC, 1991).

The free trade movement has gained considerable strength over the past few decades and has expedited the growth of international business. Negotiations under the General Agreement on Trade and Tariffs (GATT) opened up markets for exports and facilitated FDI. The institution of GATT led to the creation of the International Trade Organization (ITO) and the trend towards greater trade and FDI world-wide is continuing. As tariff and non-tariff barriers continue to fall and the philosophy of free trade gains more proponents, there are fewer protectionist barriers behind which inefficient industries and firms can hide. International competition is now a significant factor in most industries and in most countries throughout the world. The orientation of most major corporations has shifted from domestic markets to global markets and firms of all sizes are expanding their international operations.

As MNCs expand their overseas operations they are confronted with the problem of how to effectively manage international human resources. The management of human resources internationally is complicated by the fact that all the human resource decisions that are normally made in a domestic environment must be made in a foreign environment. Human resource practices dictated by customs and regulations vary from country to country. Dealing with local customs is usually the greatest challenge. It is difficult for MNCs to understand and deal with abstract IHRM issues such as how to motivate employees, what are the appropriate relationships between superiors and subordinates, how to effectively communicate, and how best to involve HCN managers in decision-making. Furthermore, there are additional important IHRM issues that must be dealt with, such as to what extent should HCN managers be allowed to run the foreign subsidiary and should they be considered as global human resources available to work in other foreign subsidiaries or at the parent company.

Managers in companies new to FDI are often uncertain how to adjust HRM policies and practices to foreign environments. As will be discussed in Chapter 4 on IHRM issues, most firms tend to follow ethnocentric policies when they first become involved in FDI. The managers either tend to believe that the way the parent company is run is the best way to run the foreign subsidiary and/or it is the only way they know. As MNCs gain more experience they tend to adopt a more global approach to the management of all their operations both domestic and international (Dowling and Schuler, 1990). It is understood that certain industries or markets may require a more local (polycentric) or regional (regiocentric) approach to management. Nevertheless, following ethnocentric management policies is usually a sign of immature IHRM that may lead to chronic human resource problems (Kopp, 1994a).

The view that effective IHRM is a key to the success of international operations was recognized in the development of MNCs as early as in the 1970s. For example, Desatnick and Bennett (1978) in their study of managing MNCs concluded that the primary causes of failure in multinational ventures stem from a lack of understanding of the essential differences in managing human resources, at all levels, in foreign environments. Though certain management philosophies and techniques have proved successful in the domestic environment, their application in a foreign environment too often leads to frustration, failure and under-achievement. They assert that consideration given to IHRM policies and practices is as important as the financial and marketing criteria upon which so many decisions to undertake multinational ventures depend.

Globalization has brought about a cultural transformation in many of today's MNCs. Evans *et al.* (1989) noted that the cultures of many of the large MNCs were created in the relatively stable, nationally focused era of post-war growth and prosperity. They, and other researchers (for example: Mishra, 1994; Pucik, 1992), view this cultural transformation in terms of a shift towards recognizing the importance of IHRM as a competitive tool. Evans *et al.* (1989:3) remark that some scholars view the task of developing managers who can provide leadership in the face of ever increasing complexity as such a major challenge that the basis for competitive advantage of the multinational firm has shifted from its material and financial resources to the capabilities of the organization of its people. This view is strongly supported by Pucik (1992:61) who asserts that the human resource function as a competitive tool in an environment of global competition is replacing the traditional sources of competitive advantage:

> In today's business environment, the traditional sources of competitive advantage cannot provide a sustainable edge. Low production cost, technology, or access to capital have become necessary, but not sufficient, conditions for success. Instead, contemporary approaches to global business strategies point to core competencies, invisible assets, and organizational capabilities as key factors influencing long-term success in global markets. Thus, we are witnessing a renewed interest in human resource management as a major strategic tool that can uphold the competitive position of a global firm.

The research undertaken for this book seeks to understand how well Japanese MNCs are dealing with IHRM issues they confront as a result of their great increase in FDI to expand overseas production and related activities. In particular, the focus is on how effectively are Japanese MNCs employing the talents of HCN managers at their foreign subsidiaries in Southeast Asia and Australia. The primary data presented in this book is gathered from this region. However, the literature indicates that the findings may be extrapolated to most geographical and cultural environments where Japanese companies have overseas subsidiaries. Furthermore, a colleague of mine employed the questionnaire I developed for this research in investigating Japanese subsidiaries in the US and obtained very similar results to those I obtained in Southeast Asia and Australia.

1.2 THE GLOBALIZATION AND LOCALIZATION ISSUE

The trend among MNCs in recent years is to seek to be global and local at the same time. On the one hand, MNCs should seek global efficiencies and competitive power by integrating to the greatest degree possible its diverse activities around the globe. They must consider how to use all their resources, both material and human, in the most efficient and effective manner possible. Such a goal implies that a firm will have a global perspective on the acquisition and utilization of resources (including human resources) and ignore the national origin factor. On the other hand, MNCs should strive to be sensitive and responsive to local situations, considering the needs and desires of the local population as much as feasible in balance with a global integration strategy. Bartlett and Ghoshal (1989) espouse this concept in *Managing Across Borders: The Transnational Solution*.

Changes in the international environment during the last two decades are forcing Japanese firms to consider globalization and localization issues more seriously. Factors such as the high value of the yen and trade friction have led Japanese firms of all sizes to establish or expand foreign manufacturing facilities. The large-scale expansion of overseas operations by Japanese firms during the 1980s and 1990s has brought about a shortage of qualified Japanese PCN managers to fill management positions at foreign subsidiaries. The high cost of maintaining so many PCN managers at foreign subsidiaries and complaints by HCN employees and local authorities underline the importance of integrating HCNs into the management process.

There is a significant body of research (which includes: Yoshihara, 1996; Kopp, 1994a and 1994b; Sethi *et al.*, 1984; among others), suggesting most Japanese MNCs have a long way to go before reaching such a stage in their organizational development. Wingrove (1997) argues that Japanese corporations are going global in the sense that they are engaging in extensive FDI but at the same time they are not going local, as US and European companies have tended to do. She bases her conclusions on a study of well-known Japanese companies operating in Britain, including: Mitsubishi Electric, Hitachi Power Tools, Kobe Steel and Mitsui and Co.

Wingrove (1997) found that Japanese expatriates fill practically all the senior managerial posts, a finding that is common among numerous studies reported in Chapter 4. Furthermore, Wingrove contends that even when decision-making is delegated to managers in the European markets, the Japanese practice of consensus still requires thorough consultation with head office in Japan. She asserts that the Japanese parent companies tightly control the operation of their foreign subsidiaries and that many Japanese foreign manufacturing subsidiaries have not moved beyond the screwdriver-plant stage. She also reported that Shoichiro Irimajiri, senior managing director at Honda, stated Japanese firms are 10–20 years behind in internationalization.

It appears that the majority of Japanese MNCs are still stuck in an ethnocentric mode. Recently, however, Japanese firms have become keenly aware of the need to move away from their ethnocentric approach to management to a more global approach. This issue has really come to the forefront during the past 15 years or so with the sudden surge in FDI in manufacturing autos and electronics in America, Europe, and Southeast Asia. There have been calls for greater localization of not only procurement of material and components but also localization of the management of the subsidiaries. The issue has become so important that the Japanese equivalent for localization, *genchi-ka* is now another popular slogan promoted by the Japanese government. Bartlett and Ghoshal (1989:8) assert that this was a serious issue from the late 1970s:

> By the late 1970s, the impact of localizing forces was being felt with increasing urgency, particularly by many Japanese companies. Indeed, if the strategic implications of globalization have dominated management thinking in the West, localization has become the preoccupation of top-level executives in Japan.

1.3 IHRM, THE ACHILLES' HEEL OF JAPANESE MNCs?

Since the late 1970s Japanese corporations have succeeded in greatly increasing their market share in the major world markets, particularly in the automotive and electronic industries. In the minds of many consumers, 'made in Japan' has become synonymous with quality. The global proliferation of Japanese products may give the impression that Japanese companies must be adept at all aspects of management. However, the research carried out by various scholars and the results of the study presented here paint a different picture.

IHRM, in particular the management of non-Japanese HCN white-collar employees, may in fact be the 'Achilles' heel' of Japanese MNCs. Bartlett and Yoshihara (1988) made this assertion in an article on organizational adaptation of Japanese MNCs to foreign environments. They were examining the evidence of their own work as well as the work of other researchers. Their assertion is examined in detail in this book using a rich amount of quantitative as well as qualitative data.

The manner in which MNCs manage international human resources is related to many factors including national culture, organizational culture, international experience, administrative heritage, and organizational structure. All these factors in relation to Japanese MNCs are examined thoroughly in the following chapters in this book.

At this point it is useful to broadly introduce these factors to provide an overview. On the one hand, the present difficulties Japanese MNCs experience in IHRM appear to be related to their relative inexperience in operating large scale operations abroad and their tendency to operate with a centralized management structure based at headquarters in Japan (discussed in Chapter 4). On the other hand, Japanese culture, language and business practices have also inhibited smooth internationalization (examined in Chapters 2 and 3). There have been numerous reports of conflicts between PCN and HCN employees at Japanese overseas subsidiaries due to cultural dissonance, both organizational and national, as reflected in individual values and behaviour (Marshall, 1993; Klein, 1992; Kleinberg, 1989; Iida, 1985; Ishida, 1990, 1986, and 1985).

Though various books and articles have praised traditional Japanese HRM practices (Tung, 1984a; Ouchi, 1981; Rohlen, 1974; among others), there are many constraints to the effective implementation of these traditional Japanese HRM practices in Japanese foreign subsidiaries. Beechler and Yang (1994:448) conclude from their study of Japanese subsidiaries in the US that the effective implementation of Japanese HRM practices at their foreign subsidiaries is constrained by both the local environment (for instance: labour market conditions, alternative job opportunities for employees, host-country regulatory conditions) and the internal environment of the Japanese MNCs (such as: administrative heritage, corporate culture, organizational structure, and employee characteristics). In addition, the relationship between the employee and the company in Japan (in particular managerial employees) tends to be a more central part of the employee's self-concept than it does in many other countries. There are demands made on Japanese employees in the domestic environment that few non-Japanese at foreign subsidiaries would tolerate, especially since they do not benefit from the same support system that exists at the parent company. Bartlett and Yoshihara (1988:20) argue that ethnocentrism, the organizational structure of Japanese MNCs, and Japanese culture may represent major impediments to the global restructuring of their operations:

> Even in companies that are at the vanguard of the Japanese invasion of overseas markets, there often seems to be a remarkable lack of understanding about the international operating environment and little sophistication in the management of the newly evolving world-wide organization. In many ways, their current problems are

similar to those of their American counterparts when they were building their international organizations in the immediate post-war decades. But, in addition to limitations of an ethnocentric perspective, the Japanese manager must also overcome the huge obstacle presented by an organizational system that is strongly rooted in Japanese culture, and in many ways is ill suited to the newly imposed task.

A key point here is that the Japanese system of management is so culture-dependent that it is difficult to incorporate non-Japanese into the system making internationalization of their organizations problematic. This argument is introduced here and explored further in Chapters 2 and 3. The difficulties Japanese experience in integrating HCN managers into the management system of their foreign subsidiaries is closely linked to the ethnocentric nature of Japanese culture and society. This strong ethnocentrism is found in Japanese social organizations such as business enterprises. Japanese organizations strongly reflect the unique characteristics and patterns of communication, human relations, decision-making processes, and logic of the relatively homogeneous national culture. Thus, Japanese organizations tend to function best when behaviour patterns of group members are uniform. On the other hand, they tend to be weak in handling cultural diversity.

Yoshino (1976) correctly predicted that Japanese management practices would impede the internationalization of Japanese organizational systems. Yoshino demonstrated strong support for the above argument when he described the Japanese system as being closed and too tightly bound to Japanese culture, indicating it is not well suited for the international environment of the foreign subsidiary (1976:164–5):

> Japanese management is a closed, local, exclusive, and highly culture-bound system, and the *ringi* system epitomizes it. Compared with the Japanese, the American system is less culture-bound, has greater flexibility, and has a considerable degree of tolerance for heterogeneous elements.

Thus, even though certain Japanese management practices are successful in Japan, it is often difficult to transfer these practices successfully to foreign subsidiaries. In support of this view Sasaki (1981:111) stated:

The style of management and the decision-making mechanism in Japan can claim to be unique. As long as they are confined to the activities within Japan, they do not cause serious problems. When they go abroad, however, they often make trouble because of their uniqueness.

A review of various empirical studies and other research indicates that Japanese subsidiaries are facing numerous human resource related problems in the management of their foreign subsidiaries (for example: Yoshihara, 1996; Kopp, 1994a and 1994b; Thome and McAuley, 1992; Pucik *et al.*, 1989; Sethi *et al.*, 1984). Problems include centralized decision-making at the parent company and a corresponding lack of autonomy at the foreign subsidiary, domination of top-level management positions by Japanese PCN managers, low confidence in HCN managers' abilities, low level of trust in HCN managers, lack of clearly formulated human resource policies for local employees, ceiling on promotion for HCNs, problems with labour unions and equal employment regulations. Most of these problems are associated with ethnocentric management approaches and a lack of localization of management. Fernandez and Barr (1993:90) argue that Japanese companies are strongly hindered in their internationalization by their ethnocentrism:

> Japanese view the homogeneity of their society as a key to their success and see any threat to that homogeneous state as negative. This attitude leads to racist and ethnocentric policies that exclude and discriminate against foreigners and minorities on Japanese soil, as well as discriminate against non-Japanese employees in Japanese companies throughout the world.

Though Japanese MNCs have experienced various degrees of success with HCN blue-collar workers in Japanese subsidiaries, they have not had the same success in effectively utilizing the talents of HCN managers. Linguistic and cultural barriers represent a greater obstacle when dealing with HCN white-collar employees since effective communication and good working relationships are necessary for joint decision-making. The contrast in terms of success between Japanese IHRM practices dealing with white-collar HCN employees versus those involving blue-collar HCN employees is well illustrated by an American manager of a Japanese subsidiary quoted in Bartlett and Yoshihara (1988:26):

The Challenge

It is ironic that the very factors that have made this company's management of its production workers abroad so successful (participation in decision-making, job security, and advancement opportunities, and an egalitarian attitude) all seem to be missing from their treatment of management. I am becoming doubtful that I can look forward to a satisfying career.

1.4 WHY ANOTHER BOOK ON JAPANESE MANAGEMENT?

Japan's post-war economic growth has led to a fascination with Japanese business practices, culture, industrial relations, industrial structures, government–business relations and other factors considered to be the principal elements of Japan's economic success. A plethora of books and articles have been written in both academic and popular literature on these subjects. Explaining Japan to the outside world has become an industry in and of itself that occupies the minds and efforts of academics and consultants of many nationalities. However, there is a lot of disagreement amongst the so-called Japan experts, so much so that there is still a lot of confusion concerning Japan, Japanese culture, Japan's economy, and the management of Japanese firms.

In this book I critically review the literature related to Japanese management with a focus on IHRM in Japanese MNCs. In this task, I draw on my proficiency in written and spoken Japanese; experience in business dealings with over 200 Japanese companies and their foreign subsidiaries in North America, Mexico, Europe and Asia as an employee of two major US MNCs; and ten years' teaching management at a Japanese university. I believe that I have read most of the pertinent literature in both English and Japanese in order to obtain a balanced understanding. In addition, my extensive experience in Japan has allowed me to develop a well-rounded understanding of Japanese management policies and practices within the social and cultural milieu in Japan.

Though a number of non-Japanese authors have greatly contributed to the understanding of the issues dealt with in this book, some of the so-called 'Japan experts' often offer an unbalanced mythical view of Japanese management practices. Woronoff (1992), a Western author who has written extensively on Japan argues that such authors are rarely familiar with the daily workings of the Japanese system and their books do not portray the true state of affairs. He claims that many Western books on Japanese management merely portray a collection of myths bearing little relation to reality (Woronoff, 1992:5):

> For anyone familiar with the Japanese attitude toward Japanese management, the success of this myth making is even stranger. For, in Japan, where people have a first-hand acquaintance with the system there is plenty of criticism. In fact, there is an almost unending round of censure of one sort or another from one quarter or another. There, Western 'experts' would be scorned if it were not assumed that they simply did not know what they were talking about. As it happens, most Western books on Japanese management elicit more laughter than applause.

On the other hand, excellent works of some Japanese authors have not been translated into English. Perhaps this is because, obviously written with a Japanese audience in mind, they assume a great deal of contextual knowledge. However, even in the works written in Japanese that discuss the role of HCN managers there is a lack of empirical data concerning important issues such as HCN managers' participation in decision-making. The primary data gathered for this book address the gaps in the body of research on this subject and some of the many misunderstandings concerning Japanese IHRM. The data contribute to clarifying the IHRM problems experienced by Japanese MNCs. These data highlight particular areas of concern that need to be addressed. In addition, the development and application of the Conceptual Model of Factors Affecting HCN Integration (presented below) adds to the practical and theoretical understanding of the issue as well as such related issues as the transferability of Japanese human resource practices.

In light of the benefits to be gained by successfully integrating HCN managers and ramifications of failing to do so, the findings of this research should be meaningful to the human resource managers of Japanese MNCs as well as MNCs of other nationalities, labour organizations, and government policy makers. The operation of Japanese MNCs as genuinely global organizations might be enhanced if our understanding of HCN managers' role in Japanese subsidiaries is improved. In summary, I hope that the critical review of the related literature and the primary research presented in this book offers a unique well-founded understanding, not available in any single work at this time, of Japanese IHRM policies and practices and how they

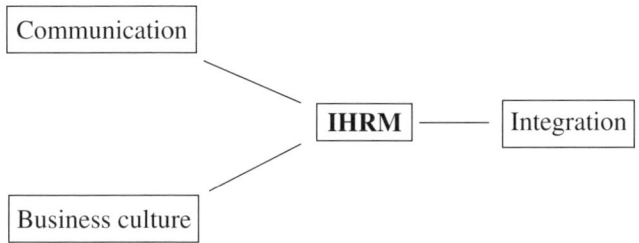

Figure 1.1 Conceptual Model of Factors affecting HCN integration

affect HCN managers employed at Japanese subsidiaries. In the end, it will be the readers who shall make this judgment.

1.5 CONCEPTUAL MODEL OF FACTORS AFFECTING HCN INTEGRATION

The Conceptual Model of Factors Affecting HCN Integration in Figure 1.1 presents three factors that are postulated to predict integration of HCN managers in Japanese overseas subsidiaries. Integration is understood to be the degree to which HCN managers participate in the process of making management decisions. Though perhaps there are numerous factors that might be included in the model, IHRM policies and practices, communication, and business and culture issues were chosen as the most important three factors after an extensive review of related literature discussed in Chapters 2–5.

First, IHRM is deemed to be the most important factor affecting integration. The model indicates a direct relationship between IHRM and integration. IHRM policies and practices such as the staffing of management positions in foreign subsidiaries with PCNs or HCNs as well as the positions that HCNs hold in the parent company as a whole should logically be a major factor in determining HCN integration. Second, communication is an integral part of the decision-making process. Without effective communication, HCNs would not receive the necessary information to be involved in the decision-making process. The model suggests that communication should directly affect IHRM policies and practices since Japanese firms are likely to consider problems related to communication between the subsidiary and the parent company in making their staffing decisions. Finally, the variable business culture deals with the challenges of cross-cultural management. The literature indicates that non-Japanese experience difficulties in adapting to Japanese business practices and cultural peculiarities. Likewise, it appears that Japanese experience difficulties in dealing with non-Japanese managers within their organizations. The model also suggests a direct relationship between the variables, business culture and IHRM since, as in the case of communication, Japanese firms are likely to consider problems related to business culture in making their staffing decisions.

The variables in the model are discussed in detail in Chapters 2 to 5. These are examined in the context of other salient issues that impinge on HCN integration in Japanese firms. The relationships between these factors and the integration of HCN managers in the model are expressed in terms of three hypotheses that are tested using regression analysis as part of the presentation and analysis of the data in Chapter 6. The discussion of the findings and conclusions appears in Chapter 7.

2 Cross-Cultural Management Issues

The discussion of the variable business culture in the Conceptual Model of Factors Affecting HCN Integration is covered in two chapters. First, this chapter focuses on general cross-cultural management issues in order to set the stage for a discussion of the specific characteristics of Japanese culture and business practices covered in the following chapter. This chapter stresses the importance of culture as a factor determining the effectiveness of IHRM policies and practices. The definition of culture in the context of this research emphasizes the predictive power and understanding of human behaviour, particularly work related behaviour, gained through understanding culture. It is argued that culture is an important factor in determining the effectiveness of IHRM policies and practices and must be considered. The national culture versus organizational culture debate is examined in order to assert that MNCs should avoid IHRM policies and practices that conflict with the national culture of the host country.

Cultural synergy in organizational settings is discussed in relation to Japanese MNCs. It is argued that the nonreciprocal causal model corresponding to the international firm best describes most Japanese MNCs, since in most Japanese MNCs there is limited organizational learning and transformation through cross-cultural interaction. In addition, one of the most important aspects of culture in connection with work behaviour is examined in relation to Japanese organizational behaviour; namely, the collectivism–individualism dichotomy. In order to understand Japanese organizational culture, it is essential to grasp how collectivism or 'groupism' describes Japanese social behaviour and how it shapes the functioning of its social institutions.

2.1 DEFINING CULTURE

The word culture can be used in a variety of ways ranging from a very narrow context in connection with subjects such as art and music, to a very broad context concerning the total psychological and social behaviour determinants or patterns of groups of individuals. There are various levels on which culture may be analysed. For example, Hayashi (1989:34) views culture on five different levels:

1. national culture belonging to the members of the nation in general;
2. organizational or corporate culture which shapes collective will and work methods;
3. material culture which includes styles in food clothing and shelter;
4. spiritual culture which subsumes values and normative systems; and
5. individual culture which governs a person's attitudes and tastes.

However, the most common levels of analysis in dealing with management issues are organizational and national culture.

Arriving at a common definition of culture has always troubled scholars. Ajiferuke and Boddewyn (1970:154) remarked: 'culture is one of those terms that defy a single all-purpose definition, and there are as many meanings of culture as people using the term.' Erez and Earley (1993:41) reviewed definitions of culture proposed by various scholars and among the definitions they reported, three definitions in particular indicate that behaviour patterns may be predicted by understanding culture:

1. Kluckhohn, and Strodtbeck (1961): Culture consists of patterned ways of thinking, feeling and reacting, acquired and transmitted mainly by symbols, constituting the distinctive achievements of human groups, including their embodiments in artefacts; the essential core of culture consists of traditional ideas and especially their attached values.
2. Hofstede (1980): Culture consists of a set of mental programmes that control an individual's responses in a given context.
3. Shweder and LeVine (1984): Culture is a set of shared meaning systems wherein members of the same culture are likely to interpret and evaluate situational events and practices in a similar way.

As a working definition or understanding of culture for the purposes of this study, the predictive elements of the definitions of culture proposed by the above scholars are embraced. It is essential to understand culture in terms of its manifestations in individual and group behaviour which can be observed and formulated into patterns useful for predictive purposes, in particular, for predicting the efficacy of IHRM policies and practices. In utilizing the predictive and explanatory powers obtained through understanding cultural factors in relation to IHRM issues, there is a fine line between cultural reductionism and lucid understanding. Adler *et al.* (1986:299) maintain that the idea of culture as a mind-state raises the problem of reductionism and an explanatory cul-de-sac, whereas using social patterns for explanation removes the understanding of their determinants. They argue that progress may be made and more predicted with culture being accepted as an observable aspect of human behaviour, manifest in social interaction and tangible objects like organizations, but resting on symbolic frameworks, mental programmes, and conceptual distinctions in people's minds.

2.2 IMPORTANCE OF CULTURE IN IHRM

Human resource management is the process of managing people or influencing their behaviour in order to obtain desired results. Thus, it is necessary to comprehend the values, needs, motivators, and other determinants of behaviour of the people one wishes to manage. Though these behaviour-determining factors may be considered on an individual level, they are usually viewed at the group, ethnic, or national level and expressed as aspects of the respective culture. There are numerous cultural influences on the institutional and organizational levels of human endeavour. Culture shapes the type of organizations that evolve and the nature of social structures as they grow and adapt (Hofstede, 1980). Societies shape their collectives and social aggregates according to the rules implied by culture.

The argument being put forth here is that organizational behaviour is best understood within the social and cultural context in which it has developed. Erez and Early (1993) point out that the potential contribution of various managerial practices and motivational techniques depends on cultural values and norms since employees interpret the meaning and value of various managerial techniques in relation to their own well-being. Thus, successful managerial techniques in one culture may lose effectiveness in a different cultural setting. Erez and Earley (1993:13) also argue that it is possible to understand and predict the effectiveness of management practices and policies by examining them on the basis of cognitive models of organizational behaviour, and such models should be useful in dealing with cross-cultural management issues.

The cognitive model Erez and Earley (1993) developed is based on a metacognitive approach to self-regulatory processes. This approach enhances our understanding of how different contextual stimuli are selected, processed, and interpreted by the individual. First, the self processes information, interprets it in line with internalized criteria and activates the response patterns accordingly. Second, self-concept is a composite view formed through direct experience and evaluations adopted from significant others. When significant others share the same value system and norms of behaviour, it can be argued that the self is modified by culture. Since it is reasonable to expect different selves to emerge in different cultures, different managerial approaches are required to satisfy needs for self-enhancement. Thus, cultural criteria are used to evaluate managerial practices and motivational techniques for their potential to satisfy personal goals and self-generated needs.

Central to the study of the integration of HCN managers in the management process of Japanese subsidiaries is how effectively Japanese firms adapt their management techniques to the local cultural environment of their foreign subsidiaries and likewise how well HCN managers adapt to Japanese-style practices. As discussed in more detail in Chapter 3 concerning the origin of Japanese management practices, proponents of the structuralist approach (for example: Koike, 1988; Dore, 1973) de-emphasize the importance of culture as a factor determining the transferability of Japanese management techniques. It may be possible to ignore cultural effects when examining HRM within a single homogeneous cultural system; however, transferring managerial techniques across cultures has not always been successful (for example: Morris and Wilkinson, 1995; Beechler and Yang, 1994; Kinoshita, 1992; Sethi *et al.* 1984; England, 1983; Hofstede, 1980; Johnson, 1977). Erez and Earley (1993) maintain that failures in transferring methods of HRM across cultures confirm that culture acts as a moderator in the relationship between managerial techniques and employee behaviour.

In addition, Hayashi (1989) reported that a survey of Japanese, Korean and Taiwanese employees indicated that management methods vary by culture, so that just as there is a Japanese-style management, there is also a South Korean style, and a country X style. Hayashi concluded that sufficient knowledge about the factors peculiar to each culture is necessary for effective cross-cultural management. As T. Fujisawa, the co-founder of Honda Motor Corporation (quoted in Adler *et al.*, 1986:295) stated: 'Japanese and American management is 95 per cent the same, and differs in all important aspects.'

In summary, this section contends that cultural factors affect the success or failure of IHRM practices and policies. Thus, it is important to understand how Japanese culture shapes the organization and functioning of Japanese firms and their overseas subsidiaries. In addition, it is useful to examine how culture affects the individual behaviour and attitudes of Japanese managers towards HCN managers.

Chapter 3 seeks to provide a sufficient basis for understanding the salient aspects of Japanese culture and their relationship to Japanese organizational and individual behaviour. Though it is not practical to offer a detailed analysis of the cultures and the cognitive aspects of the cultures in the host countries included in my study presented in Chapter 6, the general cultural and business environment of the host countries is discussed in Chapter 4 in order to suggest areas of possible cultural dissonance. The next section deals with the national and organizational cultural influences on group and individual behaviour and it is reasoned that the organizational culture of foreign subsidiaries should not conflict with the host country national culture.

2.3 THE RELATIONSHIP BETWEEN NATIONAL CULTURE AND ORGANIZATIONAL CULTURE

Organizational culture, a popular concept in organizational theory of management since the 1970s, refers to a company's underlying assumptions, shared values, and the norms that determine outlook and behaviour (Deal and Kennedy, 1988; Schein, 1987). Organizational and national cultures are important factors in determining work attitude and behaviour. However, in international management situations national culture and organizational culture may be in conflict. Thus, the question arises whether or not organizational culture can overcome national culture when the two are in conflict.

There is a long-standing debate concerning the relative strength of national and organizational culture in determining employee behaviour and attitudes (for example: Berry *et al.*, 1992; Adler, 1991; Schneider, 1988; Laurent, 1986; Ray, 1986). This debate has important ramifications for MNCs since the winning argument should determine a firm's approach to IHRM. That is to say, if the behaviour of HCN employees can be significantly influenced by values of the organizational culture of the foreign subsidiary, top management may seek to replicate the organizational culture of headquarters. However, if national culture is always of greater influence, then headquarters systems and structures should be modified to fit with local values.

Organizational culture serves as a behavioural control, instilling norms and values that result in the employees following a certain way of doing things. US and Japanese companies with well-known strong organizational cultures include IBM, GM, GE, Toyota, Honda, and Matsushita, to name a few. These companies succeed in instilling the organizational culture through such methods as recruiting like-minded individuals (individuals who share the same values), socialization through training and personal interaction, and developing strong organizational commitment through various other HRM policies such as long-term employment, stock option plans, recreational and housing facilities, and managerial rotation (Schneider, 1988).

On the one hand, there is evidence of the potential strength of organizational culture in shaping the values of employees. Hofstede *et al.* (1990:312) researched the values of members of 20 different organizations in Denmark and the Netherlands and concluded that organizational culture differences are composed of elements other than those that make up national culture differences. Thus, Hofstede's conclusions indicate the possibility of organizational culture instilling values in employees that may not be representative of national cultural norms, however it does not necessarily mean that this is possible when organizational values are in conflict with prevailing national values. Burack (1991:89) believes that values in the organizational culture are deeply ingrained and that they give rise to uniformity in behavioural patterns and underlying values among organizational units regardless of geographic, functional or business boundaries. In addition, Schein (1987:14) represents organizational values as a basic set of implicit assumptions about how to behave, and states that these organization values have a similar degree of influence as the values of the national culture.

On the other hand, there are indications that national culture has greater influence than organizational culture on the values and work behaviour of employees. Berry *et al.* (1992) make a brief review of the literature on national and organizational culture. They argue that there is little evidence collected indicating major differences in values between employees of various organizations within a more or less culturally homogeneous country. They contend that the differences that have been mentioned in the literature are not so much cultural values or meanings, but, more superficially, a matter of style (Berry *et al.*, 1992:312). This assertion has some important implications concerning the relative influence of national culture versus organizational culture. According to Mead (1994:156), accepting Berry *et al.*'s assertions imply:

1. The organizational culture of an existing organization reflects the national culture in strong focus.
2. Members of the organization will tend to resist plans to impose a culture that does not reflect their national values.
3. A significant lack of correspondence between organizational and national values may lead to conflict between employees and top management.

In addition, Laurent (1986:91) maintains that organizational culture is unlikely to modify national cultural values and when national and organizational cultures come into conflict, the first is likely to override values in the second. Furthermore, Ray (1986:295) doubts whether even the best efforts by top management have any significant effect on their employees' behaviour patterns at least so far as American corporations are concerned. Finally, Adler *et al.* (1986:300) believe that an organization's culture has a relatively weak influence on an individual's core beliefs and values. If these beliefs and values are threatened by organizational practices, dysfunctional work behaviour or maladjustment will result. They maintain that the culture that enters the organization through employees limits the influence of management-created organizational culture and structure.

No matter which side of the debate one supports, it is important to recognize the need to reconcile the organizational culture of the MNC with the host country's national culture(s). Furthermore, it is important to understand how national culture shapes organizational culture. Enz (1986) argued that organizational culture should be understood as a product of national culture as well as other forces such as the personalities of the organizational leaders. In addition, Hofstede (1985) indicated that national culture and the values contained therein are usually the strongest force shaping corporate culture.

This view is also supported by Berry *et al.*'s analysis of the literature as discussed above. At the same time, it is difficult to deny that organizational culture can instill values in employees. However, implementing management practices that are in direct conflict with national values and beliefs is extremely problematic and usually only possible given a charismatic leader and exceptional circumstances. Japanese PCN managers are unlikely to demonstrate such charisma in the alien environment of the foreign subsidiary. Thus, Japanese MNCs should avoid espousing organizational values and managerial practices at their foreign subsidiaries that strongly conflict with national cultural values and beliefs.

Before concluding this section a few comments concerning the degree of similarities between management policies and practices among Japanese MNCs are warranted. As discussed in this section, organizational culture is strongly shaped by national culture, however, variations in a given national culture as well as the influences of other factors such as charismatic leaders often lead to differences in organizational culture among companies sharing the same general national culture. These variations can be observed even in relatively homogeneous societies such as Japan where there are discernible differences between Tokyo and Osaka based companies (Miyamoto, 1977). Thus, while the view that Japanese MNCs all have the same organizational cultures is mistaken, that is not to say there is not a definite imprint of Japanese culture on all Japanese MNCs and generalizations cannot be made.

When observed from an international comparative standpoint, the similarities in the IHRM policies and practices among Japanese MNCs far outweigh the differences. Thus, pointing out salient characteristics of Japanese national and organizational culture and referring to them in the analysis of IHRM at Japanese MNCs is not necessarily simplistic cultural determinism or reductionism. If done with circumspection, creating analytical paradigms based on perceived generalities may increase understanding as well as explanatory and predictive power. As with all generalizations and paradigms, there will obviously be exceptions but that does not mean they are not useful analytical tools.

Finally, as MNCs expand their international operations, various national cultures may influence the development and evolution of the overall organizational culture. Thus, MNCs with a long history of operating subsidiaries in many countries may develop a more cosmopolitan corporate culture that accepts and thrives on heterogeneity. As discussed in the following section, such a company is global in its approach and may be described by the morphogenetic causal-loop model. However, it is argued in the next section that few Japanese MNCs fit this type of model.

2.4 CULTURAL SYNERGY IN ORGANIZATIONAL SETTINGS AND JAPANESE MNCs

Maruyama (1984, 1982, 1980, and 1973) has researched cultural synergy in organizational settings and proposes four metatypes of causality: nonreciprocal causal models, independent event models, homeostatic causal-loop models, and morphogenetic causal-loop models. The four correspond respectively to the organizational approaches of intentional, multidomestic, multinational, and global firms. The categories are quite similar to Perlmutter's (1969) categories (ethnocentric, polycentric, regiocentric, and geocentric) with the exception that Maruyama's focus is more on organizational learning through cross-cultural interaction. In this section a summary of these concepts is presented utilizing Adler's (1986) analysis of these concepts in relation to cultural homogeneity and heterogeneity. The purpose of the discussion is to clarify which model best describes the majority of Japanese MNCs.

The nonreciprocal causal model corresponds to the international firm. In such a firm homogeneity is considered natural, desirable and good while heterogeneity is viewed as an abnormality and a cause of friction and conflict. The culture of the head office in the parent firm is assumed to apply universally and management believes that there exists one best way to manage the corporation regardless of location and cultural differences. The culture of top management dominates all parts of the organization and there is a strong distinct organizational culture for international as well as domestic operations.

Independent event models are characteristic of multidomestic firms. Events are perceived as random and thus the question of causality lacks explanatory power. Management views the firm as an aggregate of individuals who think and act independently. Multidomestic firms recognize cultural differences and are at the opposite extreme to international firms since they do not seek to impose a single organizational culture for all domestic and international operations. Each foreign subsidiary is regarded as independent and autonomous. Thus, multidomestic firms recognize cultural diversity among their operations but do not seek to gain synergy from it.

Homeostatic causal-loop models characterize the multinational firm. In sociological terms, homeostasis refers to the maintenance of normal, internal stability within a social group by co-ordinated responses of the group that automatically compensate for environmental changes. In these models, causal relations form stable loops. Organizational structures or patterns of heterogeneity are maintained in equilibrium by causal loops. Homogeneity is the source of competition and conflict. While on the other hand, cultural diversity or heterogeneity is seen as a positive attribute that leads to appropriate organizational adaptation to changes in the international environment.

The global firm is one evolutionary step beyond the multinational firm and is characterized by morphogenetic causal-loop models. In morphogenetic causal-loop models, causal relations form loops, but heterogeneity goes beyond homeostasis and generates new patterns of mutually beneficial relations among the interacting elements, thus raising the level of sophistication of the whole system. Unlike homeostatic models, in which external forces cause change, morphogenetic models can internally generate their own evolution. Heterogeneity is seen as essential and indispensable for the global firm to generate new patterns through international interaction.

Considering the elements of each of Maruyama's models, most Japanese MNCs appear to fit the description of the nonreciprocal causal model corresponding to the international firm. The main reason is that in most Japanese firms homogeneity is definitely considered natural, desirable and good, while heterogeneity is usually avoided. Furthermore, the heterogeneous environment of the foreign subsidiary seems to have little effect on the homogeneous environment of the parent company in Japan. That is to say, even though Japanese firms may internationalize in terms of establishing foreign subsidiaries, few firms actually internationalize the outlook of the managers working at the parent company in Japan (Yoshihara, 1989a). Evidence supporting these contentions is provided in more detail in Chapters 3 and 4.

It is not that no Japanese firms have evolved along the continuum from international to global. However, it is pointed out repeatedly in the literature examined in Chapters 3 and 4 that the majority of Japanese firms experience substantial difficulties in dealing with the cultural heterogeneous environment of the foreign subsidiary. The next section examines the influence of collectivism on Japanese organizational and work behaviour. This discussion also assists in explaining the managerial environment HCN managers face at Japanese parent companies and their overseas subsidiaries.

2.5 INDIVIDUALISM VS. COLLECTIVISM

One of the most central dimensions of culture is the individualism/collectivism dichotomy. More so than other cultural dimensions, the individualistic versus collectivistic orientation of a society has profound implications for how individuals work (Triandis, 1989:506). Individualism vs. collectivism captures the dimension by which the members of one culture relate to each other. It accounts for most of the variance in the ecological cross-cultural value data collected by Hofstede (1980). This section contrasts the individual's relation to the group in collectivist and individualist societies with a focus on the characteristics of collectivism in Japanese society. One of the most distinguishing and important characteristics of collectivism in Japanese society is the tightness of Japanese culture stemming from a high degree of homogeneity and the resulting low tolerance of deviation from standard or 'proper' behaviour. The discussion in the final subsection concludes with a description of the effects on Japanese organizational behaviour and IHRM of the individualism/collectivism dichotomy.

2.5.1 Individuals' Relation to Groups in Collectivist/Individualist Societies

The major themes of individualism are self-definition as an entity that is distinct and separate from the group, emphasis on personal goals, and less concern for emotional attachment to the in-group. Collectivism, in contrast to individualism, conveys self-definition as part of the group, subordination of personal goals to group goals, concern for the integrity of the group, and intense emotional attachment to the in-group. People in collectivistic cultures stress similarities with other group members that strengthen their group identity. Thus, self-identity is strongly tied to the individual's relationship with key groups. Or as Markus and Kitayama (1991:227) stated: 'The interdependent self entails seeing oneself as part of an encompassing social relationship, recognizing that one's behaviour is determined, contingent on, and, to a large extent organized by, what the actor perceives to be thoughts, feelings, and actions of others in the relationship.'

In addition to subordinating personal to collective goals, members of collective societies tend to be concerned about the results of their actions on members of their in-groups, tend to share resources with in-group members, feel interdependent with in-group members, and feel involved in the lives of in-group members (Hui and Triandis, 1986). They emphasize the integrity of in-groups over time and de-emphasize their independence from in-groups. Triandis (1989) stresses the important role in-groups play in shaping behaviour in collectivist cultures (Triandis, 1989:509):

> Social behaviour is a function of in-group norms to a greater extent in collectivist than individualist cultures. In collectivist cultures, role relationships that include in-group members are perceived as more

nurturant, respectful, and intimate than they are in individualistic cultures. Relationships that include out-group members are perceived to be more manipulative and exploitative in collectivist than individualistic cultures.

Individualism and collectivism are prototypic American and Japanese patterns, respectively. Japanese culture is rooted in collectivism, whereas American culture is rooted in individualism. Of course, any organized society requires that people co-operate together in groups in order to accomplish certain goals. Thus people in both societies take part in co-operative group activities; however, there are basic differences between the typical American and Japanese concerning the characteristics of the individual's relation to the group. For example, Sethi *et al.* (1984:234) claim that Japanese have less freedom to select their groups and will join particular groups that are prescribed for them. They describe the group in a collectivist society like Japan as a living organism whose existence is quite independent of its current membership.

On the other hand, in the US an individual's association with a particular group activity is contingent on the individual's perception of the benefits to be derived from such participation. That is to say, in the US people will associate with a given group as long as the benefits derived from associating with the group outweigh the loss of individual freedom suffered from such association. Thus, the individual's group loyalty in the US is comparatively weak. Moreover, from the standpoint of an observer from an individualistic society, the egalitarianism in Japanese groups results in perverse inequalities by standardizing rewards that give little consideration to individual contributions or preferences. While the egalitarianism in US groups is in the form of equality of opportunity, which results in different outcomes for individuals based on their individual contributions and preferences of rewards (Sethi *et al.*, 1984:234).

2.5.2 Japan's Tight Collectivist Culture and Acceptance of HCN Managers

There are cultural-specific elements directly related to the degree of homogeneity or heterogeneity in a society. In relatively homogeneous societies, the norms and values of in-groups are similar, while heterogeneous societies have groups with dissimilar norms and values. Triandis (1989: 511) describes tight collectivist cultures as homogeneous cultures that are often rigid in requiring that in-group members behave according to the in-group norms. In such cultures, little deviation from normative behaviour is tolerated and severe sanctions are administrated to those who deviate. On the other hand, he claims that heterogeneous cultures and cultures in marginal positions between two major cultural patterns are flexible in dealing with in-group members who deviate from in-group norms. Triandis considers Japan to be an example of a tight culture that is relatively homogeneous, while he sees Thailand as a loose collectivist culture. Triandis states that in Thailand, with its marginal position between the major cultures of India and China, people are pulled in different directions by sometimes contrasting norms, and hence they must be more flexible in imposing their norms.

Thus, it may be asserted that the tight/loose aspect of collectivism determines the degree of tolerance towards deviation from the accepted norms in collective societies. This explanation may help in interpreting Hayashi's (1989:36–9) claim that the strong collectivist trait of the Japanese is by no means universal among Asians. He claims that his studies have shown that organizational behaviour in Korea and China is far more individualistic in nature. However, Hofstede's (1991:53) interpretation of his data indicates greater collectivism in Korean and Chinese (Taiwanese) societies than in Japanese society. Nevertheless, the degree of tolerance for individual expression or deviation from the norms is different for Japan, Korea, and China. Therefore, Hayashi is probably measuring the degree of tightness/looseness among these societies indicating that Japanese society is considerably tighter.

Since tight cultures are less tolerant of non-conforming behaviour than loose cultures, it follows that there is greater conformity and less acceptance of different thought and behaviour in Japanese organizations than in organizations created in loose cultures. Therefore, it is prudent to suggest that HCN managers face greater cultural barriers to integration in the management system of Japanese MNCs than those created in relatively loose cultures. Though the same degree of conformity required at the Japanese parent company is probably not expected at the foreign subsidiary, the 'tight culture' factor is still important. It may lead to exclusion of HCNs from core in-groups since it is difficult for Japanese PCNs to predict their behaviour.

The above argument is supported by Yoshimura and Anderson (1997), who explain that predictable behaviour and culturally transmitted implicit understanding of what is expected are important aspects of Japanese organizational behaviour. This concept is also related to the emphasis of Japanese companies on culturally based control systems discussed in Chapter 4. In addition, Japan ranks near the top (number seven out of 50 countries) in 'uncertainty avoidance' according to Hofstede's (1991:113) data. Hofstede explains that a high ranking in uncertainty avoidance indicates a low degree of tolerance for unpredictable behaviour ('what is different is dangerous'). The next section provides a more concrete understanding of how management practices are shaped by the individualism/collectivism dichotomy.

2.5.3 Management Practices Shaped by Collectivism/Individualism

There is hardly any facet of management that is not in some way affected by the striking contrast between collectivism and individualism (Whitehall, 1991:52). This is because the pattern of responses with which individuals relate to their groups reflects their degree of individualism and collectivism, while the degree of the person's individualism or collectivism affects their performance within a group. Earley (1987) demonstrated this concept in an experiment in which his collectivist subjects (Chinese and Israelis) performed less effectively when working in an individual or out-group context, whereas individualists (Americans) who thought they were working in either an in-group or out-group performed less well than when working alone. Furthermore, in relation to the impact of cultural collectivism on reward allocation, studies by Leung and Bond (1984) supports the notion that collectivists are oriented towards maintaining harmony in well-defined in-groups and behave in a sharply different way toward out-group members.

In Japan the key unit of organizations is the group and not the individual since the predominant pattern in most corporate organizations is teamwork. The work group is the basic building block of Japanese organizations. Owing to the central importance of group efforts in their thinking, the Japanese are extremely sensitive to and concerned about group interactions and relationships. For the Japanese, independence in an organizational context has negative connotations; it implies disregard for others and self-centredness (Pascale and Athos, 1981:123–5). Sethi *et al.* (1984:234) maintain that many of the well known Japanese management techniques are based on the strong collectivism in Japanese society: lifetime employment, involvement of every member in decision-making, consensus decision-making or *ringisei*, and fair distribution of group earnings according to a seniority-based and life-style-oriented wage and bonus system. They claim that the system has survived and flourished because its underlying premise, operating conditions, and distribution of social rewards conform to cultural norms and social expectations that endow it with a strong sense of legitimacy.

Hayashi (1989) maintains that on the one hand individualism facilitated the development of capitalist-industrial societies in Europe and the United States. While on the other hand, Japan caught up with the West by skilfully using communal patterns such as paternalism and worker loyalty. There is no indication that one group should mimic the other. Indeed, Hayashi (1989:169) states: 'If Japan had adopted Western values, it could not have modernized so rapidly.' The point he is making is that management practices must fit the individualism/collectivism dichotomy. Erez and Earley (1993:35) assert that management practices such as goal setting, incentives, and performance appraisal tend to be group-based in collectivist societies and individual-based in individualistic societies. In addition, in collectivist societies job design tends to be ambiguous and there is a high emphasis on socialization. On the other hand, in individualistic societies job design tends to be specific and there is a lower emphasis on socialization

Contrasting the influence of individualism on US MNCs with that of collectivism on Japanese MNCs may serve to clarify the above assertions. Cascio (1989) describes a typical model of HRM in the US as consisting of three groups of factors:

1. strategic objectives: productivity, quality of work life, profits;
2. environmental characteristics: competitive, legal, and social issues;
3. and functions such as employment, development, compensation, management, support, evaluation, and international implications.

Such a model is clearly tailored for an individualistic-competitive culture. The HRM functions tend to be oriented toward the individual employee. For example, selection of individual employees is based on individual difference characteristics; performance appraisal is centred on the individual and his/her personal achievements; and jobs are designed for the individual employee.

In contrast to American models of HRM based on individualism, familism *(kazokushugi)* is a basic value for the model of managerial practices and motivational techniques used in Japanese companies. The model advocates mutuality between management and employees, strong ties between employees and their corporation, and the responsibility of management for the employees' well-being. Other characteristic practices often include lifetime or long-term employment *(shushinkoyo)*, a reward system stressing years of accumulated service *(nenko joretsu)*, a strong emphasis on interpersonal communication, group participation in decision-making, and team development. Individual performance appraisal is less important than it would be at US firms since employees are often evaluated on the basis of their contribution to the group organizational unit as well as their general attitude.

Without more quantitative and qualitative data, it is not possible to definitively state whether the motivational techniques and managerial practices of Japanese firms would be more difficult to transfer to foreign subsidiaries than those of US firms would be. However, judging from the work of other researchers and the results of my research, it is possible to infer that certain Japanese practices would be difficult to transfer to foreign cultural environments. HCN managers in many countries, regardless of the degree of individualism or collectivism in the local society, are more likely to prefer individual rewards based on merit rather than be subjected to the same group-oriented rewards and seniority system as practised in many firms in Japan. In order for satisfaction to be derived from the group-oriented reward system and the seniority system, there needs to be not only a strong cultural orientation towards collectivism but also strong psychological ties to the company and the understanding that one's job is secure until retirement. It may be argued that at most Japanese foreign subsidiaries these conditions are usually not present to an extent great enough to overcome HCNs' preference for the more immediate concrete rewards associated with the individual reward system based on merit.

Moreover, in Japan the self-identity and the self-worth of the individual tend to be strongly tied to the main group or organization to which they belong. Allison (1989) argues that Japanese employees feel incomplete by themselves and always view themselves fundamentally in relation to others and, in an important sense, always feel dependent on others. For most Japanese the company is usually the main reference group moulding individuals' identity. The human resources practices at Japanese companies are developed with an implicit understanding of this relationship between the self and the main group. Since most Japanese individuals feel a strong tie to the company there is an expectation of loyalty. More may be demanded of the Japanese employee without the immediate tangible rewards that are expected by people whose self is not so closely tied to the company. However,

HCN managers at Japanese foreign subsidiaries will usually not develop the same relationship between self and the company due to differences in culture as well as the attitude of the Japanese parent company itself towards the HCN. Thus, HCN managers will usually have an attitude of a 'hired gun' and require a different evaluation and reward system than that practised at the Japanese parent company.

3 Japanese Culture and Organizational Behaviour

This chapter, along with Chapter 2, deals with the variable business culture in the Conceptual Model of Factors Affecting HCN Integration. The previous chapter demonstrated the importance of culture in determining the effectiveness of IHRM policies and practices. This chapter focuses on Japanese culture and organizational behaviour issues. The scope of this research necessarily includes understanding Japanese HRM policies and practices and their transferability or application at Japanese foreign subsidiaries. I shift through the jungle of literature on Japanese management to clarify the actual HRM policies and practices at the majority of Japanese MNCs as well as examine how they might affect the integration of HCN managers.

As argued in Chapter 2, HRM practices are shaped by the culture and society in which they develop and this is particularly true in the case of Japan where HRM practices strongly reflect characteristics of the relatively homogeneous Japanese culture. Thus, this chapter explores prominent Japanese management practices and attributes of Japanese culture that are often associated with these practices. Terms in English for HRM practices developed in the West may not always correspond well to Japanese practices. Therefore, the original Japanese terminology is used along with the closest English equivalent.

3.1 INTRODUCTION TO JAPANESE HRM PRACTICES

There are three HRM practices that have taken on an almost mythical nature both inside and outside Japan in terms of their supposed efficacy and prevalence, namely: lifetime or long-term employment *(shushinkoyo)*, a seniority-based wage system *(nenko joretsu)*, and company-dominated enterprise unionism *(kigyo-betsu rodokumiai)*. These aspects are often referred to as the pillars of Japanese management. According to Okada (1984), a leading sociologist from Tokyo University, Japanese-style HRM also includes such attributes as: employment of the total person, standardized training for all employees, respect for interpersonal harmony, the *ringi* system (see Chapter 5), *omikoshi* management (an allegory for teamwork), collective responsibility, participative management which is authoritarian and democratic, and womb-like concern for the individual both at work and at home. In describing this ideal of Japanese-style management Okada (1984:1) wrote:

> When Japanese-style management is practiced in its purest ideal form, the individual employees are welded together to share common fate and common goals. The organization assumes responsibility for the total employee, providing him regular training to update job skills, rotating him among jobs to develop well-rounded expertise, and gradually assigning him to positions of greater responsibility as he grows older, such that both the individual and his family feel themselves to be lifelong members of a caring corporate community. Based upon respect for the person, these Japanese-style management practices have been very effective in fostering strong employee loyalty, ensuring labor stability, and creating productive workplaces.

In the following sub-section, the origin of Japanese-style management is examined. The discussion provides insights into the arguments concerning the uniqueness of Japanese management policies and practices as well as their transferability to an overseas environment. Thereafter, the discussion focuses on the need for a balanced perspective of the efficacy of Japanese-style management.

3.1.1 The Development of Japanese-Style HRM

Though there are numerous schools of thought regarding the development of the Japanese-style HRM, they can be categorized under two principal schools of thought: the culturalist school (includes the theory of immutability) and the structuralist school (includes the internal labour market and rationalistic schools). The culturalist school (for example, Abegglen, 1958) argues that Japanese HRM practices are the result of combining Western techniques with traditional Japanese attitudes and behaviour. On the other hand, the structuralist school (for example, Koike, 1988) argues that the seemingly paternalistic labour-management system in modern large Japanese corporations is rooted in an economically rational response of employers to severe shortages of desired types of labour. That is to say, management strategies developed by large firms are more a pragmatic response to prevailing economic conditions than decisions based on cultural values.

Many of the proponents of the structuralist school believe that modern Japanese management practices were developed in response to needs that arose during the post-war period's rapid industrialization and growing domestic/international competition. Therefore they believe that these practices may be transplanted to other modern industrial countries facing similar conditions (for example, Dore, 1973). On the other hand, proponents of the culturalist school usually argue that the practices are difficult to transfer because they are closely tied to Japanese culture (for example, Hofstede, 1983b). Though the structuralist school recognizes the importance of developing management practices that are in synchronization with cultural values, it discounts the relationship between existing cultural values with traditional attitudes and behaviours. The structuralist school probably developed to counter-balance the cultural reductionism trends in the culturalist school. The two schools of thought have elements that can be synthesized to yield an appropriate understanding of the development of Japanese HRM. That is to say, Japanese HRM practices were influenced by Western thought, shaped and modified by traditional cultural and behavioural traits and at the same time evolved in response to prevailing economic conditions.

3.1.2 The Need for a Balanced Perspective

A lack of a balanced understanding of the contribution of Japanese HRM to the successful development of the Japanese post-war economy often leads to erroneous assumptions concerning the effectiveness of Japanese HRM. There are numerous management 'miracle cures' based on these erroneous assumptions. The aim of the argument here is not to disregard unfairly the contribution of Japanese HRM to Japan's post-war economic development but to caution that proper perspective and interpretation is necessary. More importantly, this discussion is also intended to demonstrate that HCN managers in Japanese overseas subsidiaries should not expect an exceptional environment conducive to high productivity from the practice of Japanese HRM.

The factors contributing to Japan's post-war economic success are numerous. However, some books focusing on Japanese management (for example, Ouchi, 1981) give excessive credit to the contribution of Japanese HRM practices and ignore the importance of the great sacrifices during the post-war period made by the people of Japan in order to speed industrial and economic development. They suffered from overcrowding in urban industrial centres, poor housing, the ravages of pollution, long working hours, lack of leisure time, inflated domestic prices, and non-production economic inefficiencies. It is true that Japan is relatively poor in natural resources and thus strong emphasis has been placed on the development and management of her human resources. Nevertheless, some authors stress the contribution of Japanese HRM practices that are not even actually practised in the majority of Japanese companies.

The views in books praising the contribution of Japanese HRM tend to be myopic in that they fail to comprehend the importance of many other essential elements of Japan's economic development within the context of the domestic and international post-war environment. By way of illustration, if the Korean War had not stimulated the automotive, steel, and other industries in Japan, would Japanese firms still have become leaders in these industries? If there had not been the threat of the spread of communism, would the US have been so keen on assisting Japan's economic development? Sethi *et al.* (1984:vi) argued that the successes of the Japanese business and management system have been mainly due to its favoured position as the principal recipient of political and government support, often at the expense of other societal interests in Japan. Likewise, Okada (1984:8) stated:

> Japan's economic success was also due to other factors almost completely unrelated to Japanese management practices. It is the accumulative effect of all these factors that accounts for Japan's success. The myth, however, holds that the positive effects of Japanese management – the employment stability, employee loyalty, and the strong sense of corporate self-identity – were mainly responsible.

Shimada (1986) claims that books like *Theory Z* by Ouchi, *Japan As Number One, Lessons for America* by Ezra Vogel and *The Art of Japanese Management* by Richard Pascal and Anthony Athos reinforce conventional impressions that Japanese companies enjoy a culturally unique system and are privileged to do so because they are Japanese companies with Japanese workers. He asserts that these stereotypes persist due to a lack of well-balanced and reliable information about Japanese industrial relations and HRM practices.

Commenting on Ouchi's *Theory Z*, and related works Shimada (1986:46) stated:

> Professor Ouchi asserts that American firms do not lack capital or technology. What they lack is the human factor. He maintains that in successful business organizations, there exist trust, subtlety, and intimacy, elements typically observed in Japanese firms and in some uniquely successful American corporations. Ouchi proposes essentially a restatement of the classical stereotype of mystic Japanese industrial relations.

Shimada is referring to a number of misunderstandings that have spread due to lack of proper perspective. He claims that most foreigners studying Japanese management visited Japan after it had entered its stage of miraculous economic growth and ignored Japanese experiences in the difficult and painstaking period preceding the era of rapid economic growth. For example, labour-management relations up to the mid-1950s were far from peaceful or harmonious. Quite the contrary, they were hostile and adversarial and there were numerous strikes. In addition, Shimada also emphasizes that studying successful large corporations in Japan does not give an accurate picture of the general management practices in the majority of Japanese firms.

Considering the dual nature of the Japanese economy clarifies the above assertion. On the one hand, there are large strong competitive firms that actually do practice many of the often-idealized aspects of Japanese HRM. On the other hand, there are the majority of small and medium size enterprises (SMEs) where working conditions and HRM practices are quite different from those of the large successful firms. Employees of SMEs in Japan usually do not enjoy the same economic benefits as those of large corporations. Indeed, Sethi *et al.* (1984:47) claim that the benevolence of the Japanese management system is bestowed only on a minority of Japanese workers while the majority, who account for the greater part of the Japanese success, toil for substandard wages and work under unsafe conditions.

Many of the low cost, high quality goods sold by large Japanese MNCs are not necessarily an indication of productivity of neither Japanese managers nor even the blue-collar workers in these companies. SMEs employ the majority of Japanese workers and have been the backbone of Japanese manufacturing serving as cost-effective subcontractors and suppliers. Miyashita and Russell (1994) in their book, *Keiretsu*, clearly demonstrate from their research results that

SMEs in Japan are largely responsible for low cost high quality goods sold by large Japanese MNCs.

Another important point that requires clarification is that though Japanese blue-collar workers have achieved significant productivity gains during the post-war period, white-collar workers or managers in large Japanese MNCs are not necessarily very productive. Woronoff (1992:10/11) argues that praise for the 'soft' management at higher levels for white-collar employees in the Japanese firms is overblown. In fact, he insists that this is where the worst failings in Japanese-style management are to be found. A survey of section managers in Japanese firms reported in the *Nihon Keizai Shimbun* (15 March 1993), the Japanese equivalent of the Wall Street Journal, indicated that 43 per cent of the managers agreed that productivity of white-collar workers in the companies was low and had much room for improvement.

The long hours Japanese managers spend working at the office are not always an indication that they are accomplishing more than their counterparts of other nationalities. Managers in Japanese firms often have to stay at the office late at night just because a senior manager either must or desires to work late. It would be considered improper for a manager to leave before his (rarely her) manager leaves. Herbig and Palumbo (1994) also assert that in Japan an employee's presence is equal to productivity, and the time logged at one's desk or workstation is often a symbolic statement of submission to managerial power rather than a useful generator of work. They claim that the average Japanese employee puts in well over 225 hours a year more than the average American worker and is less productive.

If HCN managers at Japanese foreign subsidiaries expect that Japanese MNCs will create an environment conducive to high productivity based on Japanese-style management, they may be disappointed. Likewise, Japanese MNCs are likely to be disappointed if they expect the same unquestioning obedience from HCN managers in foreign subsidiaries that they expect from Japanese managers. It is doubtful that HCN managers would have the same feelings of dedication and obedience to the firm as Japanese PCNs do. As discussed in Chapter 2, the self-identity and self-worth of HCN managers will probably not be as closely tied to the Japanese subsidiary as they are in the case of Japanese PCNs and the parent firm. Therefore, HCN managers are not likely to submissively perform long hours of often marginally productive overtime. HCN managers are likely to have a rational and logical attitude towards their job and be frustrated by any pressure to spend unproductive overtime at the office. In addition, as demonstrated in Chapter 4, the career opportunities of HCN managers in most Japanese MNCs are severely limited so they do not have the same incentives as Japanese PCN managers have.

3.2 JAPANESE CULTURE AND SOCIAL TRAITS IN RELATION TO MANAGEMENT PRACTICES

It is beyond the scope of this book to offer a complete descriptive analysis of Japanese culture in terms of its similarities and differences with other cultures. However, it has been established that cultural traits cannot be ignored in any thorough analysis of the integration of HCN managers into the management process of Japanese subsidiaries, since dealing with HCN managers is essentially a cross-cultural management issue. Thus, the focus of this section is on key concepts of Japanese culture that manifest themselves in human relations and organizational behaviour in particular. Before examining individual aspects of Japanese culture, the first sub-section demonstrates how many Japanese believe that the Japanese culture is difficult for non-Japanese to comprehend due to its uniqueness. This belief is a significant barrier between Japanese and non-Japanese. Consequently, it negatively affects the relationship between Japanese PCN and HCN managers.

3.2.1 *Nihonjinron*, Stressing Japanese Uniqueness

Many Japanese are continuously stressing how they are culturally, socially, and racially unique. There is a large body of literature in Japan that stresses Japanese uniqueness and is collectively referred to as *nihonjinron* (discussions of the Japanese). The writers of *nihonjinron* in Japan include academics, journalists, critics and even business elites. The explanatory mode of *nihonjinron* is cultural determinism or cultural reductionism. Culture is seen as infrastructural, therefore, social, economic and political phenomena are often seen as manifestations of immanent culture.

The discussions of Japanese uniqueness in *nihonjinron* are understood in relation to other cultures and societies, or Japanese versus foreign. Japanese formulate an understanding of the foreign culture to affirm the differences between themselves and foreigners. Yoshino (1992:11) contends that China and the West have constituted the two 'significant others' from which Japanese have borrowed models and against which they have affirmed and reaffirmed their identity:

> For the Japanese, learning from China and the West has been experienced as acquiring the 'universal' civilization. The Japanese have thus had to stress their particularistic differences in order to differentiate themselves from the universal Chinese and Westerners. The *nihonjinron* or discussions of Japanese uniqueness are, therefore, discussions of 'particularistic' cultural differences of Japan from the 'universal' civilization.

The ideas concerning Japan and the West emphasized in *nihonjinron* may not necessarily represent empirical reality but they still function to reinforce Japanese identity. Regardless of whether or not these images or perceptions are grounded in a universal reality, it is important to understand the perspective of *nihonjinron* since perceptions shape the attitudes and behaviour of their beholders. In particular, the beliefs expressed in *nihonjinron* influence organizational behaviour in Japanese firms.

Examining *nihonjinron* enhances our understanding of the culturalist school of thought concerning the development of Japanese HRM practices and their transferability. Both *nihonjinron* and the culturalist school point to a strong link between traditional Japanese culture and modern day Japanese management. Though it may be asserted that proponents of both schools of thought are practising cultural determinism or cultural reductionism in explaining modern Japanese behaviour, there are valid points in their arguments that should not be ignored.

There is a strong interest among Japanese businessmen in *nihonjinron*. The social culture portrayed in *nihonjinron* is closely related to Japanese management and business practices. The company is regarded in *nihonjinron* as a typical social context in which the Japanese cultural ethos or underlying culture is externalized in the form of typical Japanese organizational behaviour. Yoshino (1992:105) argues that the experience of a Japanese person working in a Japanese company could significantly promote one's interest in Japanese uniqueness and encourage one's orientation to *nihonjinron* and to cultural nationalism.

Business elites are not only consumers of *nihonjinron*, they also produce it and disseminate it by writing popular works on Japanese culture and management. A number of the writers have been well-known leaders of major Japanese companies such as Akio Morita of

Sony who wrote *Made in Japan*. Large corporations also publish works in the form of textbooks or handbooks that describe aspects of Japanese culture and society and their manifestation in Japanese-style management (for example, Nippon Steel's *Nippon: The Land and Its People*). Such works are usually intended to prepare Japanese businessmen for intercultural discussions with non-Japanese. However, they also function to reinforce the idea that Japanese organizational behaviour, and consequently management policies and practices, are uniquely suited to Japanese society and culture.

Nihonjinron is also an important intellectual pillar of cultural nationalism in contemporary Japan. Economic nationalism characterized the Meiji period when Japan strove to catch up with the West and again during the period of reconstruction following the Second World War when the pursuit of economic growth became the highest national goal. Political nationalism was stressed during the war periods of this century. However, Japan's defeat and bitter war experience made the average Japanese an ardent pacifist and made political nationalism repugnant. Economic nationalism, rekindled during the post-war reconstruction, began to lose its appeal at the end of the 1960s when the signs of economic success were noticeable and people around the world began calling the Japanese 'economic animals.' Thereafter, cultural nationalism replaced GNP as a symbol of restored economic confidence and regained international status. There was a growing belief among the Japanese and many Westerners that Japan's economic success was mainly due to Japanese style management that was a product of traditional Japanese social culture.

The growth of cultural nationalism fed by the ever-increasing volume of *nihonjinron* theories and literary works produced both positive and negative outcomes. In the positive sense cultural nationalism preserves and strengthens a people's cultural identity. On the other hand, the negative effects of cultural nationalism in Japan include the overemphasis on differences and the ignoring of similarities between Japanese and other cultures as a way of defining Japanese identity. Such a form of cultural nationalism promotes a strong and problematic feeling of a 'unique us' versus a 'non-Japanese them.' As a result, many Japanese assume that Japanese thinking and behaviour are so unique that they cannot be fully understood by non-Japanese. As argued in Chapter 5, this attitude itself becomes a hindrance to communication and mutual understanding between Japanese and non-Japanese.

Nihonjinron rests upon the pillars of cultural relativism in the sense that it explains differences among peoples in terms of cultural conditioning and social milieu. Yoshino (1992:179) argues that the attempt of Japanese businessmen to improve cross-cultural understanding is made through the recognition and emphasis of cultural differences that exist, or are believed to exist, between Japan and other countries. He describes three propositions offered by Hatch (1983:9–11) concerning the cultural relativism behind this attempt. The first is historical relativism; that Japanese culture is unique and relative to Japanese history. The second is ethical relativism; Japanese judgments of right and wrong are relative to Japanese cultural and behaviour patterns and thus should be evaluated in their own light. The third is relativity of knowledge; that it is important for non-Japanese to recognize the uniqueness of the Japanese way of thinking and for the Japanese to point it out.

Nihonjinron has come under attack by both Japanese and foreigners who object to the extreme cultural reductionism in some *nihonjinron*-based arguments and seek a more balanced approach. An example of such a work is *The Myth of Japanese Uniqueness* by Dale (1986). The book is a critical review of the foundation on which *nihonjinron* rests as well as individual *nihonjinron*-based arguments. In the introduction to his book Dale states that in contrast to modern empirical research on Japan, *nihonjinron* is characterized by three major assumptions or analytical motivations:

> Firstly, they implicitly assume that the Japanese constitute a culturally and socially homogeneous racial entity, whose essence is virtually unchanged from prehistoric times down to the present day. Secondly, they presuppose that the Japanese differ radically from all other known peoples. Thirdly, they are consciously nationalistic, displaying a conceptual and procedural hostility to any mode of analysis that might seem to derive from external, non-Japanese sources. In a general sense then, the *nihonjinron* may be defined as works of cultural nationalism concerned with the ostensible 'uniqueness' of Japan in any aspect, and which are hostile to both individual experience and the notion of internal socio-historical diversity.

Though Dale makes some important valid points in his denunciation of the proponents of *nihonjinron*, the fact that there are many believers in the uniqueness of the Japanese culture and society remains. As argued above, such beliefs determine the attitude and behaviour of the beholders. Thus, for the purposes of this research, instead of attempting to prove the fallacies of such beliefs it is more productive to understand the beliefs themselves and how they determine attitudes and behaviour. The discussion of Japanese culture and society in relation to Japanese attitudes and management practices in this chapter employs such an approach. However, at the same time arguments that may question the validity of *nihonjinron* type beliefs are also presented. The following section deals with attribute/frame-based groups and the concept of *ie*.

3.2.2 Attribute/Frame-Based Groups and the Concept of *IE*

Before discussing the concept of *ie* (family, household), the notions of 'attribute' *(shikaku)* and 'frame' *(ba)* as understood by Nakane (1972a) are presented in order to set the stage for explaining the organizational behaviour aspects of *ie* in Japanese organizations. The primary prerequisite to the formation of a group is that the individuals concerned share a common attribute and/or are placed in a common frame. Attribute here refers to any specific quality of an individual in his social context. Examples include attributes inherent to the individual such as descent or hereditary status and acquired attributes such as academic background, social standing or occupation.

When the basis for forming a group is these types of qualitative criteria the group is considered to be based on attribute. On the other hand, the term frame is applied to groups that are formed by a set of individuals who, regardless of any difference in attributes, share a common situational position by belonging to a particular organization, for instance, accountant would refer to attribute, but a member of company X would be a frame. There may be cases where attribute and frame coincide in the formation of a group, but usually they overlap each other, with individuals belonging to different groups at the same time.

Nakane (1972a:8) suggests from her research that in some societies either attribute or frame takes preference over the other, while in others the two factors rank equally with each other. Furthermore, she states that the way in which these two factors are commonly weighted has a close relationship to the sense of values in the social consciousness of the people in the society. Nakane believes that Japan and India show the sharpest contrast. In the case of Japan, group consciousness depends heavily on frame while in the case of India the emphasis is on attribute (social group based on occupation and hereditary status).

The nature of firmly rooted latent group behaviour in Japanese society is expressed in the traditional and ubiquitous concept of *ie*. It extends beyond the household formed by family members, it may be considered to include social groups formed on the basis of an established frame of residence and/or managerial body. Human relations within this household group are considered to have priority over all other human relationships.

Fukutake (1982:28) explains how the traditional concept of the *ie* transcended the notion of a family as a simple group of living members. He asserts that *ie* was conceived as including the house and property, the resources for carrying on the family occupation, and the graves in which the ancestors were buried, as a unity stretching from the distant past to the present and occupying a certain position in the status system of the village or town. He maintains that the *ie* in that sense was far more important than the individuals who were at any one time living members of it, and it was seen as natural that the individual personalities of family members should be ignored and sacrificed if necessary for the good of the whole.

The modern-day corporation in Japan has an important social function in the form of *ie*. The company in Japan functions as a social group based on frame. As mentioned above frame tends to be more highly valued in Japan than attribute in the formation of groups. However, there are always attributes common to most or many of the members of Japanese companies and perhaps the most important attribute is that members are mainly ethnically Japanese.

Non-Japanese may not have the same attitude Japanese have towards the company due to differences in value systems concerning frame and attribute based groups. That is to say, the social functions associated with *ie* in Japanese companies may not be applicable to subsidiaries in non-Japanese cultural settings. Furthermore, since non-Japanese employees do not share the attribute of ethnicity they will probably not be fully accepted into the core in-groups within the company. This point is argued later in relation to Japanese attitudes towards non-Japanese.

Creating an atmosphere of rivalry toward similar but exterior groups is an effective method of fostering a sense of belonging to the same group among people with differing attributes. This method is an emotional approach and is commonly employed with group activities to strengthen the human relations among members of the same organization in Japan. The line between the company life and private life often becomes obscured as company related activities take up much time after normal working hours.

Some employees view these activities as an invasion of privacy while others find that it gives them a sense of belonging and security (Nakane, 1972a:13). The reaction is closely linked to cultural and social conditioning, however, in even the relatively homogeneous society of Japan the reactions of individuals varies. When similar methods of building a sense of unity and loyalty to the company in Japanese subsidiaries abroad are employed the reactions of HCNs also depend on cultural and social conditioning as well as individual preferences. In particular, the value orientation in regard to frame-based versus attribute-based groups strongly influences the effectiveness of these methods used to create a sense of belonging.

Stressing the unity of the group and calling for every member's emotional and total participation turns the group into a closed world and leads to a high degree of isolation. According to Nakane (1972a:20), this inevitably fosters family or company traditions that are emphasized as mottoes or devices to bolster the group's solidarity and sense of unity, and this contributes still further to the group's integration. These actions create a gulf between the group members and others with the same attributes outside the frame; however, they also simultaneously narrow the distance between people with different attributes within the frame.

The 'us versus them' or 'in-group' versus 'out-group' phenomenon is a quite noticeable aspect of the collectivist society in Japan. Japanese tend to operate in different modes of behaviour when dealing with 'out-group' versus 'in-group' members. Observing the rush hour in the Tokyo subway demonstrates that a people who strive to be extremely polite to those in their group may just as easily act uncaringly towards outsiders. Nakane (1972a) claims that groups formed on the basis of frame provide no scope for fostering sociability and produce a large number of people who go through life without experiencing the excitement or tension of coming to grips with people outside their circle of acquaintances.

Large enterprises in Japan clearly demonstrate the concept of *ie* and frame-based characteristics discussed here. Actually, the probability of heterogeneity of attributes increases with the size of a frame-based organization, and there exists a greater need to unite the members. As argued here, the Japanese way of dealing with heterogeneity is forced conformity to a given mould determined by the organizational culture. This discussion is indicative of cultural and social aspects of Japanese organizational behaviour that account for some of the difficulties Japanese MNCs face in dealing with HCN managers in their foreign subsidiaries. The following sub-section describes how *ie* has shaped Japanese HRM.

3.2.3 Familism/Paternalism Characterizes Many Aspects of Japanese HRM

Familism in Japanese organizations is believed by proponents of the culturalist school of thought to be an expression of *ie*. Whitehall (1991:52) maintains that Japanese familism *(kazokushugi)* is a basic value, which is reflected in many aspects of management such as the *shushinkoyo* (lifetime or long-term employment) system, emphasis upon length of service under the *nenko joretsu* system (merit of years of service or seniority system), and a generally paternalistic approach to human resources that is sometimes referred to as 'welfare capitalism.' Inohara (1990:40–1) refers to familism at Japanese companies as 'industrial familism.' He claims that the employees' present and future status in society and lifestyle as well as physical and mental development are largely, if not sometimes entirely, expected from the company. He therefore asserts that the company has a responsibility to take care of its employees in more circumstances than only the working situation here and now.

According to the familism perspective, Japanese companies are not mere economic entities, but more significantly are social organizations, which value social considerations in dealing with their *shain*. The term *shain* literally means company member and reflects the attitude that employees are members of a company 'family,' and the company serves the function of offering group identity to the individual, an important function in Japanese society. The fate of the family affects all the members and is shared by all. The individual's well-being is usually defined in the context of the family. The individual makes sacrifices for the good of the company and the company seeks to ensure that the individual's basic physical, psychological and emotional needs are met. This type of familism may exist in companies of all sizes in Japan, however it is more often found in the large stable companies that are usually more able than smaller companies to take care of the majority of their 'family members' during difficult economic times.

There are various accounts of the development of familism in Japanese enterprises. Abegglen (1958:99–100) takes the culturalist approach and suggests that these paternalistic labour practices in modern Japanese companies are a continuation of traditional employment methods. The culturalist view also holds that familism in the firm is a reflection of the pervasive familism characteristics of Japanese society. Other accounts lean more towards the structuralist approach, which, as previously stated, argues that the adaptation of familism in Japanese enterprises was an economically rational response of employers to severe shortages of desired types of labour.

Perhaps the most appropriate view of the development of familism should incorporate aspects of both the structuralist and culturalist approaches. Clark (1979:41) makes such an argument, stating that the idea of 'familism,' arose with apparent naturalness out of the circumstances of the time and was for that reason a powerfully persuasive doctrine. He claims that the metaphor of the family, besides harking back to Tokugawa tradition, was perfectly adapted to interpret employment practices forced on employers by the labour market. In addition, Clark believes that the notion of firm-as-family was also consistent with one of the central political concepts of the Meiji period, a concept widely supposed to have remote historical antecedents, but one which was in fact a new one in old threads: that the Japanese nation itself was a gigantic family with the emperor at its head.

In Clark's view of the development of 'familism' there are characteristics of a holistic view of society, which has been an important intellectual tradition in both academic and politicized theories of modern Japanese society. Yoshino (1992:88) introduced a new type of holism, which he termed 'reproductionism' or 'extensionism.' This perspective regards order in society as a reproduction or extension of order that is characteristic of Gemeinschaft or pre-industrial, communal society. The 'reproductionist' or 'extensionist' theories hold that familial and communal industrial society has been formed in the modernizing process of Japan.

In support of the holistic view of Japanese society it may be argued that familism or group orientation is also evident in the Japanese economy as a whole. The company may be thought of as the basic family unit to which each member (*shain* or employee) belongs. A company may in turn be vertically related to its suppliers and customers in a *sangyo keiretsu* (vertical *keiretsu*) or industrial grouping of supplier–customer relationships. Companies may also be affiliated to a larger family of companies horizontally related in a *kinyu keiretsu* (financial grouping) with a large bank and trading company at the hub. Thus, family type relationships not only exist at the micro-level between the employees and the company but also at the macro-level in the interlinking relationships between individual companies and groups of companies.

In modern-day Japan, the paternalistic aspect of Japanese industrial familism is revealed in the extent to which the company is involved in the lives of the employees. To begin with, large companies prefer to employ young attractive females who have prepared for marriage by studying the tea ceremony, flower arrangement, and other traditional Japanese arts. The object is to have a good selection of female employees who may marry the young male employees and 'retire' to raise a family. The advantage of this practice is that the male employees can spend long hours concentrating on their work and still find a suitable partner who also feels an emotional and psychological attachment to the company.

In order to promote a family-like atmosphere among employees and between superiors and subordinates, Japanese companies organize a variety of recreational activities that are, as stated in the previous section, a common way of building group unity in frame-based groups. These activities include *shain ryoko* (company outings or trips to places such as hot springs in the mountains) and *undo-kai* (a day for employees to participate in athletic events together, similar to a traditional company picnic in the US). Employees of large firms often live in *shataku* or company housing. Thus the private life of the employee is closely tied to the company and its other members (employees,) just like one big family. Since maintaining *wa* or harmony is paramount, Japanese families who live in *shataku* must always be careful in their relationships with the other residents who are also fellow members of the same company. At times such situations can become very stressful since it becomes impossible to separate one's private life from that of the company.

Even if employees do not live in company housing, they rarely escape company affairs when they leave the office. After-hours socializing among co-workers including superiors and subordinates is also a very important part of the management process. As is discussed in the section on communication and decision-making in Chapter 5, a lot of frank and open exchange of opinions takes place over a meal and drinks. These types of social activities are important for building relationships. If a manager is unable to build close relationships with other managers in the company his influence and effectiveness will be weak.

Some researchers are skeptical of the attributes attributed to the family concept in Japanese firms. For instance, Yoshimura and Anderson (1997) argue that the motivation of the employees of the company to conform does not necessarily originate from family-like attitudes towards the firm. Furthermore, they also question whether foreign employees can really become family members of a Japanese firm and question the extent to which trust among employees extends throughout the firm (Yoshimura and Anderson, 1997:101–2):

> The *gaijin* (foreign) employees of Matsushita and Fujitsu discovered that even membership is not guaranteed in many contexts. Those who expect the Japanese firm to be a warm fuzzy place are in for a rude awakening. Relationships in the *kaisha* can superficially resemble those in families, because employees feel pressure to adhere to group norms and to get along with others whose approval they need in order to maintain group membership. When the group pressures do not apply, however, conflict erupts just as it would in the West. Within the firm, trust holds together only very small groups, and loyalty is created principally by the context that the junior–senior relationships supply.

The transferability of HRM policies and practices associated with familism to foreign subsidiaries for the most part would depend on the attitude of the HCN employees towards the particular practices and policies as well as the general labour market conditions. From a cultural standpoint, some of the policies and practices may not be appropriate, particularly if frame-based groups are not emphasized in the host country culture. Even if HCN managers come from a strong collectivist society it does not mean that they will necessarily be receptive to familism based policies and practices since the firm may not normally be considered a significant in-group in that society. In addition, from a structuralist viewpoint, the mobility in the labour market may be such that HCN employees readily change jobs in search of greater monetary rewards and/or managerial responsibility and the appeal of some of the family-based HRM policies and practices may not be strong enough to retain them.

In the following sub-section the focus shifts to the importance of a particular superior–subordinate relationship found in Japanese organizations, which is the product of the vertical structure of Japanese society.

3.2.4 The Vertical Structure of Japanese Society

Human relations may be viewed in terms of vertical and horizontal relationships. The superior–subordinate represents the former while the colleague relationship is an example of the latter. The relative importance of or emphasis placed on the relationships differs amongst societies. Vertical relationships are considered more important than horizontal relationships in Japanese society and the *oyabun-kobun* or superior–subordinate relationship is an expression of the vertical structure of Japanese society.

Oyabun-kobun (*oya*, father; *ko*, child) is the basic single-unit interpersonal relationship between two Japanese persons in Japan's vertical system. Members in a work-related group, or in any Japanese organization are tied together by this kind of relationship. According to Nakane (1972a), while the *oyabun* may have several *kobuns*, the *kobuns* can have but one *oyabun* and within the *oyabun-kobun* group, each member is tied into the one-to-one dyadic relation according to the order and time of his entry into the group. These dyadic relations themselves form the system of the organization. Therefore, the relative order of individuals is not changeable. Even the *oyabun* cannot change the order. It is a very static system in which no one can creep in between the vertically related individuals. The essential requirement of the *oyabun* is that he treat his *kobuns* with equal fairness according to their status within the group, otherwise he would lose his *kobun* because of unfair treatment.

The *oyabun-kobun* relationship is developed not only through social norms, but also through time-consuming group-centred activities. Rohlen (1975:197) describes the *oyabun-kobun* relationship in corporate life as having the following five characteristics:

1. The senior manager is older than his junior, has worked longer for the company, and is in a position of relative power and security. This position enables the senior to assist the junior.
2. The senior is beneficially disposed toward the junior and befriends him.
3. The junior accepts the friendship and assistance from the senior.
4. These acts and related feelings are the basis for the relationship. There is no explicit agreement.

5. Ideally, the junior feels gratitude toward the senior for his beneficence, and this feeling is accompanied by a desire on the part of the senior to become a good older friend for the younger.

The powers of the *oyabun* (superiors) are restricted in very many respects when compared to leaders in many other societies. Due to the vertical structure in which the *oyabun* maintains direct close contact with a few *kobun* (subordinates) who in turn deal with their own *kobun*, leaders exert power over most of the members indirectly, through immediate subordinates. As a consequence, the leader's immediate subordinates acquire an extremely preponderant voice in matters so that the leader is liable to be placed in a position resembling that of a consultant to two or more of such members. Considerable tension can arise in the distribution of power among the leader's immediate subordinates since each of them is representing the interests of the members under his control.

Nakane (1972a:67–9) points out that this sort of mechanism frequently subjects the leader to criticisms and demands, and the leader is compelled to devote a good deal of energy to the adjustment of the balance of power. Furthermore, personal relationships between the *oyabun* and *kobun* and the distribution of the power among the latter often affect decisions concerning managerial actions. The emotional considerations extended by a leader toward subordinates, *onjo-shugi* or paternalism, move leaders to accept the views of subordinates and to comply with their wishes. The lack of directorial capacity on the part of leaders is a major cause of sectionalism and factionalism.

The etiquette of communication and social interaction is also dominated by rank consciousness. It is also difficult for Japanese to interact with one another without first establishing each other's relative rank. The exchange of name cards is an important ritual that provides time to establish relative rank and adjust to the situation. The traditional arrangement of a Japanese room is a decisive factor in relating seating practices with rank. When speaking with anyone, Japanese must observe the subtleties governing the use of honorific expressions, the order of precedence or the time allowed each speaker according to his rank.

The question arises whether or not the *oyabun-kobun* type relationship can be found in the environment of the Japanese overseas subsidiary between PCNs and HCNs. There are obvious parallels to the *oyabun-kobun* relationship, for example the mentor relationship often found in Western-style organizations. However, the mentor relationship is not exactly the same. Japanese PCN managers' experience being in *oyabun-kobun* relationships may not necessarily prepare them for creating a mentor style relationship with HCN managers at overseas subsidiaries.

Another consideration is the fact that the *oyabun-kobun* relationship is a product of the strong value in Japanese society placed on vertical relationships. If similar cultural and social conditions do not exist at a foreign subsidiary the *oyabun-kobun* relationship will probably not develop. Furthermore, the *oyabun-kobun* relationship carries with it the expectation that the individuals in the relationship develop the ability to implicitly understand the needs and desires of each other. This is a very difficult task when there are language and cultural barriers inhibiting the development of such ability. In addition, the relationship requires a great deal of submission on the part of the *kobun* to which few HCN managers are likely to yield. Thus, it may be conjectured that the *oyabun-kobun* relationship rarely develops between PCN and HCN managers to the extent it normally does between Japanese in the domestic Japanese environment.

3.2.5 The Importance of Harmony and Teamwork

In a comparative study (Baba, 1984:79–80) of Japanese and American managerial attitudes, more Japanese managers than American managers considered harmony important. Inohara (1990:27) states that the organizational principles of the Japanese company are market orientation, continuous innovation, and emphasis on relationships. The first principle expresses that Japanese companies seek to respond to the needs of the market and are customer-focused. The second principle refers to the importance of technological and managerial innovation. Finally, the third refers to the importance of relationships in doing business and Japanese companies tend to put greater emphasis on relationships than on functions. The primary relationships are those relationships the company has with its employees, customers and suppliers. Relationships among employees are the arena where the importance of harmony and teamwork is stressed the most.

Western management tends to be more functionally oriented leading to specialization, while the relationship orientation of Japanese management usually results in generalization of management skills over specialization. Japanese organizations are based more on relationships than functions. Thus in a Japanese organization, managers prefer to develop general knowledge rather than specialization. The individual must be flexible and versatile in order to function well within the group. The physical layout of a Japanese office promotes teamwork and makes it difficult for an individual to separate from the group. Usually managers and subordinates work together in a large room with desks facing one another in long rows with the desks of the *kacho* (section chief) and/or *bucho* (department chief) facing the rows of subordinates.

Maintaining *wa* or harmony and promoting good human relations between all employees, suppliers and customers is considered by most Japanese to be essential for human resource development and the overall success of the company. Thus, one of the central responsibilities of a Japanese manager is to ensure there is harmony and co-operation among the subordinates and between sections and departments (Rohlen, 1974). Relationships form the glue that holds the company together. Employees are constantly transferred to various sections and departments during their career and the relationships formed over the years are important channels of communication among the various functional departments. Knowing the needs and desires of other departments and how decisions and actions will affect them is essential in order to maintain harmony among departments.

Japanese collectivism is strongly expressed in the manner in which work is carried out as group effort in the majority of Japanese companies. There is no detailed job description *(shokumu kijutsu-sho)* for individual employees. Employees given new assignments or promotions receive a *jirei* (assignment notice), which indicates only limited information such as the title of the new position and the date of commencement. The content of an individual's work depends on the task at hand and the needs of the unit to which one is assigned. The focus is on the group and not the individual. The Japanese manager is expected to lead the group not by exercising authoritarian control but rather through direct participation in the group process offering support and assistance to subordinates.

Inohara (1990:33) points out that group management and supervision are incorporated in the Japanese organizational structure. He maintains that leadership does not necessarily require the highest technical competence in the group; rather what is required is competence in human relations so that a harmonious and co-operative atmosphere prevails. It is interesting to note that a study carried out by Baba, Perloff *et al.* (Baba, 1984:24) revealed a difference in the concept of teamwork among employees of Japanese in American firms. From the results of their analysis they concluded that Americans saw teamwork as being concerned with relations with co-workers in their own work teams. On the other hand, Japanese employees included relations with their superiors in their view of teamwork.

The importance of teamwork is often reflected by the methods of employee evaluation at Japanese companies. The evaluation of work performance is made more on the basis of contribution to teamwork and corporate productivity than on an individual's efficiency. Important evaluation items are work attitude, regular and punctual attendance, co-operation with co-workers, in addition to efforts made for attaining targets, oftentimes more than actual results. Furthermore, evaluation of an individual is made in balance with that of other employees. In essence, no employee is evaluated as outstanding (far above the rest of the group), or as very poor (far below the average level of the group) (Inohara, 1990:39).

Even though harmony and teamwork are important in Japanese organizations, it should not be understood that there is no conflict in Japanese organizations and that trust prevails among all the employees. On the surface the appearance of harmony in teamwork is considered mandatory. However, there definitely exists the possibility of conflict and the lack of trust between individuals and/or groups of individuals in Japanese organizations. The maintaining of the appearance of harmony is a product of the highly valued trait of *gaman* (endurance, or acceptance even though one does not agree with a plan or decision approved by the majority or significant individuals).

Yoshimura and Anderson (1997:82–3) argue that those who believe that trust and consensus make Japanese companies work, mistake an effect for a cause. Their argument is based on the strong pressure for conformity in Japanese organizations. That is to say that once a particular interpretation of the context is accepted everyone falls into line and deviant behaviour is severely punished in a system that depends on avoiding social embarrassment. Thus, the apparent harmony is actually just a result of unexpressed dissension. They maintain that beneath the surface of Japanese organizations, hidden from outsiders, trust gives way to interdepartmental conflict that is at least as bitter as that found in Western organizations.

Yoshimura and Anderson's assertion has a lot of credibility considering, as discussed in Chapter 2, Japan has a tight culture where conformity is expected and deviant behaviour is not easily accepted. HCN managers who come from cultures and societies where differences of opinion are more openly expressed and discussed may have difficulties in dealing with Japanese PCN managers who believe that open expression of differences in opinion is contentious if not handled very carefully. Potential difficulties between Japanese PCN managers and HCN managers are not due to Japanese PCN managers ignoring the possible conflicts in their organizations, rather the difficulties arise in how conflict is allowed to be expressed and how it is handled. The following section discusses salient dyadic concepts in Japanese society and culture that are related to the strong distinction between insiders and outsiders in Japan.

3.2.6 *Omote-Ura, Soto-Uchi, Tatemae-Honne*

Omote-ura, soto-uchi, and *tatemae-honne* are paired opposing dyadic concepts, two sides of the same coin, which cannot be separated and the existence of one defines the existence of the other. These concepts have universal characteristics and to a certain extent may be used in describing human relations in all cultures. However, there is a particular awareness among Japanese of these dyadic relationships and any simple direct translation into English is misleading. Doi (1985 and 1973) offered the most extensive analysis of these concepts in his works *Amae no Kozo* (The Anatomy of Dependence) and *Omote to Ura* (The Anatomy of Self). Doi explored the universality of these concepts in his works, but at the same time he stressed that the Japanese people seem to have a particularly strong awareness of the concepts in their dealings with fellow Japanese. The following discussion of these concepts is largely based on an understanding gained from reading Doi's works.

Some of the modern Japanese meanings of *omote* may be translated as the front-side, surface or exterior while in this context *ura* would be rendered as the backside or interior. Simply stated, the *omote* is the part that can be easily observed while the *ura* is concealed. In classical Japanese *omote* means *kao* (face) and *ura* means *kokoro* (mind, heart, soul). The face expresses the mind. Here the face is not limited to the expression and appearance of the actual face itself; rather it refers to the whole of a person's appearance including voice, tone, body language, etc. The face is what we can observe using our senses.

The words *omote* and *ura* are used in combination with other words in opposing concepts. *Omote-muki* refers to that which is public, open, official; *ura-muki* suggests something private, closed, personal. The mind is never completely revealed in the face even if a person intends it to be. The ability to read the mind expressed on the face is augmented by familiarization with the individual in question and the culture that has helped shaped that individual's mind. The homogeneity of Japanese society relative to that of America has created significant differences in the way the mind is expected to be revealed in the face. This concept is related to the high-context communication mode of Japan and the low context communication mode of America discussed in detail in Chapter 5.

Soto and *uchi* constitute a dyadic pair that is close to 'outside–inside' in English. This is clear in the contrast made in human relations between *soto no hito* (outsiders) and *uchi no hito* (insiders) (Doi, 1985:33). The *omote* is what is presented to *soto* while *ura* is not presented to *soto* and only revealed to *uchi*. That is to say, people put on a particular face for those who do not belong to a defined intimate circle or in-group while members of the in-group are privy to more intimate knowledge not revealed in the face. The general use of the word *soto* connotes outside in the sense of the outside part of an object or outside of a building, and in particular outside the home. On the other hand, *uchi* not only connotes inside, it is also the word which, depending on the context, corresponds to such words and phrases in English as home, our house, our place, in our case, our company, our family, etc.

In Japan there is a clear and sharp distinction made between *uchi no hito* (insiders) and *soto no hito* (outsiders) and there is sometimes an 'us versus them' connotation. This dichotomy may be found in all cultures but the relative importance of the concept in human relations often depends on the degree of individualism and collectivism in the society. Though I have not found any studies confirming a positive correlation between the degree of collectivism and the importance of the distinction between *uchi* and *soto*, many years of experience in numerous diverse cultures leads me to conclude that such a relationship should exist.

There is no simple way to express the *tatemae-honne* dyadic concept in English. *Tatemae* is often thought of as the façade that a person puts on when dealing with *soto no hito* (outsiders) or those people who do not belong to a particular in-group such as the in-group composed of family members. The *honne* is that which is not revealed. Doi (1985) points out that Japanese have begun using the dyadic concepts of *tatemae* and *honne* quite frequently, often with the implication that *tatemae* is directed solely at *omote* and therefore is false, and that *honne* is the real truth. However, he points out that this has not always been the case. An understanding of the concepts should not be shackled with this value judgment which appears to be the result of greater Western influence during the post-war period and the concurrent increase in individualism.

According to dictionary definitions, *tatemae* can be a set of principles or rules that have been established as natural and proper. Doi (1985:36–7) suggests that *tatemae* also refers to conventions created by people on the basis of consensus. Thus, *tatemae* always implies the existence of a group of people in its background who assent to the *tatemae*. In contrast to this, *honne* refers to the fact that there are individuals who belong to the group, even while they consent to the *tatemae*, each have their own motives and opinions that are distinct from it, and they hold these in the background.

Tobin (1991) discusses the concepts of *uchi-soto*, *omote-ura* and *tatemae-honne* in relation to the development of the Japanese personality. He stresses that Japanese must learn more than just distinguishing *omote* from *ura* and describes how pervasively these concepts affect Japanese behaviour (Tobin 1991:18):

> To have a proper, two-tiered Japanese sense of self, one must learn to step back and forth across the gap dividing *omote* from *ura* in the course of a conversation, or indeed, even in the midst of a single phrase. A slight wink of an eye or a change in the level of politeness of a verb ending suddenly signals a slight but crucial warming up or cooling down of relations. As Doi suggests, *omote* and *ura* are complementary rather than opposing. There is *omote*, inevitably, in *ura* and *ura* in *omote*. In even the most formal, public transactions *(tatemae)* there is the potential for experiencing real human feeling *(honne)*. In even the closest of relationships there is always a hint of *omote*, an unspoken awareness of the chasm that separates all human beings and that makes a degree of restraint necessary even among family members.

The important question for this section is how these dyadic pairs, which describe important aspects of Japanese society and culture, affect the HCN integration. The most significant effect on HCN integration is the extent to which HCN managers remain outsiders who are not privy to information to the same degree PCNs tend to be. Only the insiders in the corporation have access to important information. It should be understood that there are often many different in-groups in a Japanese MNC and the flow of information to individuals depends on acceptance into these in-groups. It is argued in Chapter 2 as well as in this chapter (particularly the following section) that non-Japanese often experience barriers to being accepted into certain in-groups and this affects their participation in decision-making (see Chapter 5).

Yoshimura and Anderson (1997:77–9) claim that regardless of what the organization chart says, junior Japanese salarymen assigned overseas are part of the decision-making circle, whereas their normally senior American colleagues are outside of it. They maintain that it is extremely difficult for a *gaijin* (foreigner) to become a true insider, even though members of his section may regard him as one for limited purposes in pursuit of a common goal. The logic is that Japanese fear that no one from a different background without similar experiences inside the firm can have or meet the uniform expectations that the reference groups impose. Consequently, Yoshihara and Anderson report that many HCNs conclude that real decisions in a Japanese firm are made after five o'clock in closed meetings where only Japanese is spoken. The next section deals specifically with the characteristics of Japanese society that directly obstruct the acceptance of non-Japanese into the various in-groups that are found in Japanese organizations.

3.2.7 Racism, Ethnocentrism, and Xenophobia

Except for a brief period in the sixteenth and seventeenth centuries, Japan was an isolated, closed society until the 1850s. During this long isolation, Japanese religious tenets and various leaders installed a sense of superiority in the nation's people. It is not clear to what extent these historical factors still shape the Japanese collective mentality; however, it is certain that the Japanese have developed a very strong us-versus-them mentality between themselves and non-Japanese (Fernandez and Barr, 1993:37). This mentality is evident in the clear line Japanese draw between what they feel is Japanese and what is foreign.

Things both tangible and intangible are borrowed from the West but they are almost always modified to fit the 'Japanese' way. Distinctions between Japanese and non-Japanese things are easily expressed in the Japanese language. For example, the prefix *'wa'* is used to indicate things Japanese *(wa-shoku*: Japanese food; *wa-shitsu*: a Japanese style room), while the prefix *'yo'* is used to refer to foreign, usually Western, objects *(yo-fuku*: Western-style clothing, *yo-ma*: a Western-style room). However, what makes Japan a closed society is not just the strong us-versus-them mentality and the strong distinctions between things Japanese and foreign, it is also the attitude of the Japanese people towards foreigners.

Among the terms in Japanese referring to foreigners, *gaijin* is probably the most commonly used. The word *gaijin* is actually a shortened version of the word *gaikokujin*. The three Chinese characters that make up this word mean 'outside country person.' When the middle character is removed the term is rendered *gaijin* or 'outside person.' This is perhaps the most appropriate interpretation of the word because it most closely reflects the attitudes of the majority of Japanese towards non-Japanese. Foreigners in Japan are foreigners no matter how many generations they live there. In the case of non-Asians who speak Japanese and do things in a Japanese way, they are called *henna gaijin*, or 'strange outside person.' It is ironic because as foreigners make efforts to lower the boundaries separating them from the Japanese by learning the language and adopting Japanese customs the Japanese people draw an even sharper psychological dividing line.

Even Asians cannot become Japanese no matter how hard they try. The Koreans forcibly brought to Japan as labourers during the occupation of Korea in the earlier part of this century are still considered foreigners and not granted Japanese citizenship unless they change, give up their original name and adopt a Japanese one. Therefore, there are thousands of Koreans born in Japan who no longer speak Korean but are still denied the rights of Japanese citizenship. It is very common that before someone gets married the parents hire a detective to make sure the potential marriage partner is not a Korean, Chinese (who have adopted Japanese names) or some other 'undesirable' person.

There is a strong connection between race, ethnicity and culture in Japanese society. All the respondents (businessmen and educators in a typical Japanese city) in Yoshino's study of cultural nationalism in Japan considered it impossible for foreigners to behave and think like the Japanese (Yoshino, 1992:116). Most Japanese perceive themselves as a 'racially' distinct and homogeneous people even though there is no biological foundation for this claim. Actually, Japanese are a product of a long period of mixture with peoples from northeastern Asia. However, the belief in a distinct Japanese race plays an important role in Japanese identity as illustrated by the following comment by Yoshino (1992:24):

> Belief in the immutable quality of Japanese people is just as important as, if not more important than, belief in distinctive Japanese

culture in Japanese perceptions of their national identity, as is typically shown in the statement, 'You have to be born a Japanese to understand Japanese mentality.' A Japanese expresses the immutable or natural aspect of Japanese identity through the imagined concept of 'Japanese blood.'

Yoshino (1992:28) also notes that the relationship between racial and cultural differences is closely related and may be divided analytically into two separate propositions. The first is that genetically transmitted traits determine (or condition) cultural traits (genetic determinism), while the second is that particular cultural traits should belong to, or are the exclusive property of, a particular group with particular phenotypic and genotypic traits (racially exclusive possession of a particular culture). It may be argued that Japanese believe in genetic determinism because they are strongly aware of their racial and cultural distinctiveness from other peoples and because they closely associate race and culture. Furthermore, in the case of the Japanese the second proposition, 'racially exclusive possession of a particular culture,' predominates over the first, genetic determinism. Therefore, the attitude that non-Japanese (racially) cannot become culturally Japanese is a form of racism commonly found among Japanese people. This type of racism manifests itself in the form of the 'us-versus-them' attitude that non-Japanese often perceive in Japanese people.

Mannari and Befu (1991:34) also discuss the issue of Japanese identity based on unfounded perceptions. They present a day in the life of a hypothetical salaryman who appears to indulge in a very Western-style life and then comment:

What is it that makes him so sure that he is 100 per cent Japanese and no less? It is indeed because the question of being Japanese excludes any middle ground. You either are or are not. The identity of the Japanese resides in an absolute exclusion of foreigners and in a total identification as one race and one culture. Scientific reasoning aside, the conviction of racial unity and cultural homogeneity is unshakeable, leading to an ultimate belief that the unique essence of Japanese culture is transmitted genetically. Because, as the belief goes, the Japanese are one race, they are also of one culture. Any infusions of Chinese and Western culture detract not at all from the essential core of Japanese culture, even though they may have penetrated beneath the surface.

As previously mentioned, Japanese racial attitudes are manifest in their IHRM practices and are clearly apparent in their FDI patterns. Japanese managers appear to view certain races such as African Americans as inferior employees and thus have sought to avoid, when possible, hiring them. Since any overt discriminatory practices would be noticed and lead to legal, political and social problems in such countries as the United States, Japanese firms seek to stealthily implement discriminatory hiring by locating their facilities in the United States in regions where there are few African Americans and other minorities (Cole *et al.*, 1988). Nevertheless, a number of Japanese firms have been sued for discrimination (discussed in Chapter 4). In addition, according to a study by Ichimura (1981), Japanese managers tend to have a low opinion of the managerial talent of the HCN managers at their Asian subsidiaries. It may be inferred that Japanese attitudes towards foreigners discussed in this section have a definite influence on the opinions of the Japanese PCNs towards the Asian HCN managers.

Now that an overview of Japanese cultural characteristics has been presented, the focus shifts to describing the main attributes of the Japanese HRM system. First, the role of the personnel department is examined in the next section.

3.3 THE *JINJI-BU* OR PERSONNEL DEPARTMENT

Inohara (1990) explains that there are two departments that neither in function or structure have a true counterpart in Western organizations. One is the *somu-bu* (the so-called General Affairs Department) that administers legal matters, shareholders relations, corporate documentation, internal regulations, maintenance, external relations, and so on. The other one is the *jinji-bu* or personnel department that is an offspring of the *somu-bu* when the company grows to a certain size. Inohara (1990:40–1) maintains that the *jinji-bu* is more than just one of several functional sections or departments in a Japanese business organization; it is special because it embodies the corporate philosophy of industrial familism. He asserts that the *jinji-bu* functions as the central agency in all personnel matters and, with fair treatment being the rule, there is little room left for an individual manager's factions in the field of personnel management. He concludes that such personnel matters are administered company-wide by the *jinji-bu*, through a complex and detailed set of regulations and procedures, whereby it makes its own indispensable contribution to harmony, and fulfils its function in the corporate group.

Japanese employees are not usually hired for a specific position but rather a type of position. Depending on their education and the type of company, an employee may be hired for a blue-collar job or a white-collar job even though Japanese companies prefer not to clearly distinguish between white-collar and blue-collar. In the case of white-collar employees in large firms, they expect to be transferred numerous times among various sections and departments. Each time employees work in a different section or department they form new relationships and group loyalties.

The *jinji-bu* handles the transfer of employees and thus in one sense the employee is constantly under the control of the *jinji-bu* and in this way it is at the centre of the company in terms of strategy and control. The superiors in each section or department evaluate employees. The evaluations from the various departments are collected at the *jinji-bu* and there they monitor the employees' development. Given its important function within the firm, the *jinji-bu* is usually under the control of the most senior and most respected managing director (Vogel, 1985:151–2).

When Japanese managers are transferred to foreign subsidiaries they usually continue to be under the care of the human resource department of the parent company. As discussed in Chapter 4, being transferred abroad had been considered as a risk in the career development of a manager since while abroad the manager is away from the power base of the company. However, this attitude towards working in foreign subsidiaries is changing in some companies as the importance of international experience is being recognized. As for HCN managers, as pointed out in Chapter 4, they are rarely considered global human resources and the *jinji-bu* at the parent company does not usually closely track their development.

3.4 RECRUITMENT PRACTICES IN JAPANESE COMPANIES

The ideal for the Japanese company in recruiting its regular workforce is the employment of new school graduates who would stay with the company until they reach the company specified retirement age limit. New recruits are employed as new members of the working family. The focus is not on individualized technical merits, but rather on their potential. The criteria for screening applicants are more social than economic in nature (Inohara, 1990:55). Unlike in most Western companies, detailed job descriptions rarely exist. The company seeks to determine if the prospective employee has the type of personality that fits in well with the atmosphere at the company. New recruits are not usually selected for a certain position within the company rather they are considered to be more like blank sheets of paper ready to be trained for various functions within the organization. These recruitment practices are an integral part of the development of an internal labour market in Japanese firms.

The attitude of new school graduates corresponds to this situation. Students in Japan rarely hold any part-time jobs until they reach university level and thus have very little work experience when they begin looking for career-oriented employment. They are not so much looking for a particular job; rather they are looking for a particular type of company in terms of size, philosophy, and the type of business (for example manufacturer, retailer). Most graduates prefer large, stable and growing companies that are more likely to be able to offer the type of employment practices that are so often idealized in Japan and abroad such as long-term employment. Traditionally, those graduates who are unable to find positions in well-known large corporations must settle for jobs with medium or small size companies.

Since large stable firms receive many more applicants than small and medium size firms, they are able to be more selective. The greater the prestige of a firm the more likely the firm will concentrate on recruiting from the most prestigious universities in Japan. Very large firms establish a designated school system (*shiteiko seido* or *tokuteiko seido*) and recruit exclusively from a selected number of elite universities. The seven old traditional imperial universities, with *Todai* (Tokyo University) at the top of the list, are among the most prestigious universities along with a few well-known private universities such as Keio and Waseda. Students at universities in Japan tend to view the four years of study as a time to enjoy themselves before they enter the workforce.

The quality of education a student receives at one of the prestigious universities does not differ much from that of many lesser-known universities in Japan. However, the students who have successfully entered prestigious universities have had to endure and prevail in extremely difficult and competitive entrance exams and are therefore considered to be the brightest or most diligent. Unless companies are looking for particular technical knowledge or skills they are not overly concerned about what a student has learned at the university or the marks they receive. Students are more often questioned about their extra-curricular activities to determine if they are group players. Involvement in sports is usually considered positive since such activities tend to build character and teach teamwork. Large companies in particular prefer to educate new recruits in their way of doing things, thus previous work experience and the content and quality of university education are often not important factors.

Large corporations rarely hire mid-career employees who have left other firms. They depend on their own in-house bred employees to fill the management positions open due to employee promotion or expansion of activities (the development of an internal labour market). Mid-career employment is practised mostly by small enterprises, looking for some specific skills as well as unskilled workers, to meet immediate needs (Inohara, 1990:10). Managers are rarely recruited from the outside. The exception is when older managers sent from affiliated firms fill high-level managerial positions. In such cases, the firm sending the managers has a great deal of leverage over the company receiving the managers. The sending firm may be a main customer or a main bank with either a vertical industrial or horizontal *keiretsu* relationship with the receiving company. A manager may be sent to an outside firm to offer expertise or because the sending firm simply wants to get rid of him.

When a Japanese company undertakes large-scale expansion of overseas activities and must recruit experienced HCNs to fill newly created management positions they are faced with problems that rarely occur domestically. There is usually not enough time when starting up operations overseas for a firm to recruit graduates from the host country and develop them into managers in the same way as in the domestic environment. Japanese firms may experience difficulties integrating experienced HCNs into the management process of their subsidiaries since such people usually have developed work attitudes and habits that may differ from those desired by the Japanese firm. Furthermore, even when recruiting graduates Japanese companies must compete with firms of other nationalities in foreign countries and may not be able to attract good talent as easily as they do in Japan.

The recruiting practices of Japanese auto manufacturers for their plants in the US demonstrate how Japanese firms often deal with these issues. Most of the Japanese auto manufacturers preferred recruits who had no prior experience in order to avoid what they considered inappropriate work habits and attitudes. Though implementing this approach in recruiting blue-collar workers appears to be quite feasible, it is not so easily achieved in the case of managerial recruits. The candidates for managerial positions are usually older with more experience and have developed ideas and attitudes concerning the role of managers.

Before concluding this section and moving onto further discussion of traditional characteristics of Japanese management, it should be noted that new economic realities of the past decade have brought about fairly rapid changes in the behaviour and attitudes of Japanese in general and companies in particular. Japan is suffering from the Heisei recession, which is the economic malaise that set in after the economic bubble burst at the onset of the 1990s and chronologically corresponds with the era of the new emperor. Though the essence of the practices described in this section remains intact, it is not business as usual. For example, large companies are not as attractive as they used to be since they have also proved to be vulnerable to economic distress. On the other hand, Japanese companies are beginning to expect more from their new recruits in terms of what knowledge and skill they have attained during their education. The next section also describes how the new economic reality is affecting so-called pillars of Japanese management.

3.5 *SHUSHINKOYO* (LIFETIME OR LONG-TERM EMPLOYMENT)

In this section the following questions concerning *shushinkoyo* are addressed:

1. What is *shushinkoyo* and how extensively is it actually practised in Japan?
2. How did the practice develop?
3. What are its merits and demerits?
4. What is the future of *shushinkoyo* in Japan?
5. How does it really differ from practices in other developed economies such as the United States?
6. Is the practice transferable to non-Japanese employees in Japanese subsidiaries abroad?

3.5.1 What Is *Shushinkoyo* and How Widely Is it Practised in Japan?

Among Japanese and non-Japanese observers alike, there are many misconceptions about the practice of *shushinkoyo* (lifetime or long-term employment) in Japan. Perhaps it is best to state what it is not. The most literal translation of the term would be lifetime employment since the characters used to write the word in Japanese mean 'end-body' and 'employment,' however, with mandatory retirement at ages as young as 55 among a population with a life expectancy of over 70, the expression long-term employment is a more appropriate translation (nevertheless, I use the terms interchangeably along with the original Japanese term).

It is never a legal binding contract between employer and employee; as a matter of fact the Labour Standards Law prohibits an employment contract for more than one year. Thus, the basis for this practice is implicit mutual understanding and trust. The employer trusts that the employee will stay and perform well during his or her most productive years and the employee trusts that the company will do everything possible to retain the employee even during difficult times. Of course it is impossible to retain employees when a company is financially unable to do so or goes bankrupt. Bankruptcy is common among small companies in Japan and the majority of the working population is employed in medium and small businesses; as discussed later this is one of the reasons that the majority of Japanese do not receive the benefits of *shushinkoyo*.

Nevertheless, a number of scholars both Japanese and non-Japanese have praised *shushinkoyo* and have attributed the success of Japanese enterprises to its practice. For instance, Hasegawa (1986:11) remarks that lifetime employment is often cited as a key factor behind Japan's startling industrial successes and the majority of Japanese firmly consider it the very backbone of Japanese management. Sasaki (1981:2) views the lifetime employment system as the major factor contributing to the creation of character in the Japanese firms as a system and claims that under the lifetime employment system loyalty is strengthened as one's position rises within an organization. Sasaki also points out that the seniority system (*nenko joretsu*) supports *shushinkoyo* from inside. The resulting system almost completely eliminates the possibility of labour mobility among firms, making it extremely difficult to find a job in other firms with similar, let alone improved, terms and conditions.

One of the distinguishing features of *shushinkoyo* that has earned it praise is that layoffs are always the last resort in dealing with difficulties. According to Hasegawa (1986:14–15) a company in distress will exhaust every alternative before resorting to layoffs. First, management will make large-scale reductions in the pay of top executives, followed by cuts in the salaries of managerial staff. Next, dividends to shareholders will be slashed, then and only then will management begin to discharge workers. Employees are kept abreast of developments at every step. In the late 1970s and early 1980s Mitsubishi Heavy Industries, due to the oil crisis and the crisis in the Japanese shipbuilding industry, was forced to release a vast number of employees in order to avert bankruptcy, in effect violating the principle of long term employment it had steadfastly maintained since 1921. However, before such drastic action was taken salaries and dividends were cut and some of the excess personnel were relocated to subsidiaries.

On the other hand, a number of researchers argue that *shushinkoyo* is little more than a myth and that it is sheer folly to believe that it is a bastion of Japanese management (for example: Watanabe, 1993; Hamada, 1991; Plath, 1983). According to data presented by Tachibanaki (1984:82), most Japanese workers change jobs at least once in their career. His data showed that among male university graduates working for large corporations, only about a third (34.1 per cent) of those in their early fifties (50–54), more than a third (39.1 per cent) of those in their late forties (45–49), and slightly more than half (52.1 per cent) of those in their early forties (40–44) had worked for only one company. The often-quoted estimate of the working population employed at companies where *shushinkoyo* is actually practised is only 30 per cent (Shimada, 1986:47).

Thus, it is best to think of the practice of *shushinkoyo* as an attitude, an ideal, or a goal that may not always be realizable. Indeed, in spite of his positive comments, Hasegawa (1986:2) still maintains that *shushinkoyo* is no more than a general guiding principle and that it is by no means a guarantee of long-term employment. He also believes that the idea that everyone in Japan is assured a job for life is pure myth since, in actuality it is only the large companies that can afford to assure employment.

However, even among the employees at large stable corporations not all employees receive the benefits of *shushinkoyo*. Japanese companies distinguish between regular or formal employees *(seishain)* and non-regular employees that may be temporary employees *(rinji-shain)* or day labourers *(hi-yatoi)*. Non-regular employees may in some cases perform the same or similar work to that of regular employees but do not receive the same benefits. Non-regular employees offer a buffer stock of labour that can be increased or decreased in order to meet economic and market fluctuation in demand. A decrease in the use of non-regular employees is not considered to be the same as laying off workers in Japan. Thus, discussing the occurrence of layoffs in Japan and the US is to a certain extent like comparing apples and oranges.

The use of subcontractors by larger manufacturing firms is another way in which large corporations avoid laying off their core group of regular employees. Many manufacturers, especially automotive and electronics, outsource a significant portion of their manufacturing to suppliers and their subcontractors. For example: suppliers and subcontractors do as much as 70 per cent of Toyota's total manufacturing work. The manufacturer–supplier chain resembles a pyramid with the large manufacturer on top controlling a key group of first tier suppliers.

These suppliers are usually large corporations themselves, like Nippon Denso, Toyota's main automotive air-conditioning and electronics supplier. First tier suppliers control a group of key suppliers and subcontractors. The manufacturer–supplier chain continues in the same fashion with each tier containing a larger group of suppliers and subcontractors. At the very bottom are family-run operations with few employees who are not immediate family members. Large suppliers tend to maintain human resource management practices similar to those of the main large manufacturers, such as long-term employment. The higher a company is in the pyramid the more likely that it will be able to practice long-term employment. The reason is that the larger companies higher up in the pyramid adjust to the demand of the customers above them by decreasing the demand to their suppliers and subcontractors below them. In other words, when a firm is squeezed from above it squeezes those firms below.

In addition, the practice of *shushinkoyo* is largely restricted to men. Though it is now illegal for Japanese employees to discriminate on the basis of gender, in practice, women are not expected to stay with the company during all their working years. Women in large companies are often expected to marry male employees in the same company, quit, raise children and then later perhaps return to work for the company on a part-time basis without benefits. Women usually receive clerical positions that do not lead to any significant managerial responsibility. Munchus (1993:11) states that there is a simple explanation as to how Japan keeps its unemployment figures at only two per cent; the full-time, lifetime employees are all men. However, even with these practices the cconomic malaise in Japan has caused unemployment to hover around five per cent by the end of the century.

One common misconception is that there is hardly any mobility in the Japanese labour market due to the practice of *shushinkoyo*. Though it is true that the core employees of large corporations tend to remain till retirement, there is notable mobility in small enterprises. Inohara (1990:3–6) analysed statistics from the Ministry of Labour and concluded that employees generally do not move horizontally between large companies and they do not move in an upward direction either, going from a small enterprise to a large company. However, Inohara pointed out that a downward mobility takes place and mobility between small enterprises is rather frequent and younger employees are more mobile than older ones. Furthermore, Shimada (1986:47–48) demonstrated that between 1965 and 1980 10 to 20 per cent of all employees left their firms each year. Turnover rates were higher for females than for males and higher for small firms than for large ones. Roughly half of newly hired people had an occupational experience somewhere else and recent school graduates accounted for only a quarter to a third of total recruits.

3.5.2 How Did the Practice of *Shushinkoyo* Develop in Japan?

There can be many arguments made concerning the cultural tradition behind the practice of *shushinkoyo*. Most arguments would be based on the collectivist nature of Japanese society stemming from the group orientation of rice cultivation that formed the economic and social structure of Japan for many years during her long recorded history. For example, according to Hayashi (1989:87–92), common features of rice cultivation are repetition, teamwork and patience. The philosophy of many white-collar employees in large companies or organizations in Japan is based on a rural metaphor: if you patiently stay in one place, the crop will ripen and the harvest will be ample. Thus, Hayashi concludes that Japanese employees prefer long-term employment with one organization and regular promotion through seniority, in contrast to their counterparts in the US.

Another cultural-based argument in support of the practice of *shushinkoyo* in Japan is the strong collectivist nature of Japanese society. In Japan there is a strong tendency to define one's existence (self-concept) by the group to which one belongs. This is related to the concept of *ie* discussed earlier. According to Hayashi (1989:68), the term *ie* is associated with the rise of the samurai class and the struggle of military families to survive in medieval Japan. Samurai organized around a leader, formed an *ie* which became a stronghold, and defended their land. They extended their land holdings and were led by feudal lords, or daimyo. All samurai rallied to the defense of their leader and were willing to give their life.

Today the term *ie* may refer to a person's primary organization which is often the company where they work. If a company faces a serious crisis, for example, no matter what the personal cost or inconvenience, all employees must defend the *ie* group. Thus, there is an important psychological or emotional element in the practice of long-term employment. The company offers employees a group or *ie* to which they can belong and achieve their sense of group identity and at the same time the company benefits from the employees' loyalty and commitment. This type of loyalty and commitment would weaken considerably if the company withdrew the promise of long-term employment.

In spite of the cultural arguments for the development and practice of *shushinkoyo*, some scholars believe the system developed its present form during the post-war period. For example, Woronoff (1992:78) argues that the present arrangements of the system did not exist in Tokugawa Japan, in Meiji Japan, nor in pre-war Japan. However, Shirai (1992) argues that the system originates with government employees and those of high-ranking personnel in state-run enterprises and concerns in the late part of the Meiji Period. He claims that it spread to male white-collar workers in big enterprises during the period from the early part of the 1890s to the end of the First World War and then later to male blue-collar workers in the process of rationalization after the Showa depression and in the transition to a war-time economy.

In addition, Okada (1984:18) claims that Japanese enterprises were already practising long-term employment for their white-collar employees before the First World War, but this did not extend to blue-collar workers. After that war, in the 1920s, Japanese companies finding themselves faced with a severe shortage of skilled labour, began showing greater concern for employees. They began to provide more training and to take other actions to boost employee loyalty and to retain their services permanently. Given further impetus by legislation restricting labour mobility during the Second World War, lifetime employment was preserved after the war by the labour unions' fight for job stability.

Shushinkoyo is also supported by the nature of Japanese human relationships. The relative strength of an individual in the group tends to be proportional to the length and intensity of actual contacts with other group members. Thus, the length and intensity of contact with group members becomes, in itself, the private capital of the individual. Since this capital is not transferable to any other group, a move from one group to another group would result in a heavy loss. Managers must work hard to gain the confidence and support of subordinates and fit in well with colleagues (Nakane, 1972a:24–25).

3.5.3 What Are the Merits and Demerits of *Shushinkoyo*?

Although long-term employment is by no means universal, many Japanese strongly proclaim its merits. It fosters a sense of stability, a strong feeling of belonging and commitment. It cuts down on worker restlessness and insecurity and creates an atmosphere of co-operation and harmony. From the corporate viewpoint, long-term employment provides a rationale for training new employees. Costs associated with recruitment, training and unemployment compensation are reduced. New employees believe that if they work hard and diligently, their wages will gradually increase, and in due course they will become eligible for promotion.

Indeed, with few exceptions, managerial staff and company executives are promoted within the company, not hired from the outside. *Shushinkoyo* facilitates job reassignment and introduction of new technology. One such example is Honda's experience in introducing welding robots. The workers at Honda did not resist the introduction of the robots since they felt secure in their jobs and they welcomed the chance to be relieved of the difficult welding tasks and receive new training for reassignment to other jobs (Hasegawa, 1986).

Non-Japanese scholars around the world have sung the praises of *shushinkoyo*. Such authors usually buy into the stereotypic image of *shushinkoyo* and recommend that non-Japanese companies should adopt the system. For example, in his book *Japan As Number One, Lessons for America* (1985:137) Vogel states that the company's interest in the long term is also related to the system of permanent employment whereby an ordinary employee remains in the firm from the time he first enters after leaving school until he retires:

> The firm is committed to the employee and provides a sense of belonging, personal support, welfare and retirement benefits, an increased salary and rank with age. Barring a serious long-term depression, the employee expects that he will never be laid off, and even if the company were to disband or be absorbed by another company, he expects that a new job elsewhere will be arranged.

Ouchi's *Theory Z* claims that the needs of employees and the corporation are integrated in companies that practice *shushinkoyo*. Under long-term employment, employees' present performance contributions are exchanged for deferred rewards offered by the company throughout the career development process. Employees' trust in this exchange leads to high integration through high involvement and productivity. However, Takagi (1984:2) claims that his preliminary study indicates that many executives in large Japanese companies believe that lifetime employment does not always generate the high involvement among employees as predicted in *Theory Z*:

> In their firms, there are actually a substantial number of employees who use their loyalty to the company to ensure job security while giving only a minimal commitment to their jobs. In fact, this passivity that is often observed under conditions of lifetime employment is commonly referred to in Japan as the 'Large Company Disease.'

Yoshino (1968) also supports the view that *shushinkoyo* does not achieve the positive results that some people expect. He states that observant senior executives in a number of firms candidly admitted that many highly capable and motivated young men lost their initial enthusiasm as they became affected by what one executive described as the tepid environment (1968:226). Yoshino claims that the long-term employment system and the seniority-based reward system breed a feeling of complacency among employees.

Another one of the demerits of *shushinkoyo* is the resulting decrease in labour mobility in Japan that impedes an individual firm's ability to adapt to changes in the market place and the economy as a whole. Corporations may also experience difficulty in assimilating and developing new ideas and technology with only in-house trained employees. Due to the closed nature of the system in large corporations, it is rare that a company can hire outside experts on demand. Shortages of managerial and/or technical talent often occur in growing areas of the economy while firms in declining industries often suffer the burden of underemployed personnel. Large corporations frequently have too many managers doing too much busywork or employees with little or no productive tasks to perform. Such managers are so common in Japan that they have even been dubbed *mado-giwa zoku* (window tribe) since such managers have little more to do than look out of the window.

Schlender (1994:98) comments that Japan has the world's most efficient manufacturing plants and some of the most inefficient offices anywhere. He maintains that the efficient factories are the legacy of the late W. Edwards Deming while the bloated company bureaucracies are the result of long-term employment, consensus decision-making, and hierarchical organizations based on seniority. Schlender goes as far as to claim that lifetime employment is at the root of most of today's management problems in Japan.

3.5.4 What Is the Future for *Shushinkoyo* in Japan?

There are various opinions concerning the continued viability of *shushinkoyo* among large Japanese firms. Kobayashi of Aoyama Gakuin University believes that the previously mentioned three foundations of Japanese human resource management *shushinkoyo, nenko joretsu*, and *kigyo-betsu rodokumiai* (long-term employment, seniority system, and enterprise-based unions) are crumbling and that there are major changes ahead (quoted in Kilburn, 1994:45). Kobayashi points out that while major corporations can still maintain much of the substance of long-term employment by off-loading excess employees to subsidiaries or affiliates, few now see this as more than a stopgap solution. Noguchi of Hitotsubashi University states that white-collar employees need to get used to the idea that they can lose their jobs (quoted in do Rosario, 1993:22). Noguchi believes that it is a long-term trend that will not go away when the economy picks up.

It is not just employers who are having second thoughts about *shushinkoyo*. More and more employees themselves have a desire to seek new opportunities outside their present company. In Japan a term borrowed from English 'u-turn' refers to the phenomenon of leaving big city jobs to go to smaller towns in order to enjoy a better life-style or freedom from the constraints of working in a large company. The number of employees opting for the 'u-turn' saw a significant increase from the mid 1980s.

There is also evidence of lack of job satisfaction among Japanese managers. In a survey conducted by Sumitomo Bank of 500 men in their forties and fifties, only 4.6 per cent said they would choose their present jobs again if given another chance, and only 12.4 per cent said they were satisfied with their current jobs. Many of those surveyed cited dissatisfaction with low pay, limited holidays, and extensive overtime. It is clear that when companies of all sizes are considered, labour mobility has been on the increase since the mid 1980s, when the high yen forced corporate Japan to embark on industrial restructuring. According to Japan's Ministry of Labour, in 1989 almost three million people switched jobs and a study of 10,000 Tokyo men between the ages of 20 and 39 found that nearly 40 per cent were thinking of changing jobs (Frankel and Takayama, 1993:51).

Furthermore, in December of 1994 the Asahi Bank conducted a questionnaire survey on 304 clients of the bank (Japan 21st, 1995:21), the results of which indicate that the breakdown of the personnel management system in Japan is progressing at an enormous pace with the simultaneous revision of the wage system. As to *shushinkoyo*, 27 per cent of all enterprises surveyed felt that this system is already breaking down, while 64 per cent predicted that it would have to be revised in the future. Smaller companies were less likely to voice support for *shushinkoyo*. Of the companies capitalized at less than one billion yen, 30.2 per cent felt that the system had already collapsed, while only 5.3 per cent thought that the system should be maintained hereafter. As to new employment, only 17.1 per cent of companies employed exclusively new university graduates, while 87.1 per cent did not care if their employees had worked elsewhere previously. They are no longer insisting on new graduates, which had served as the basis of long-term employment.

An important point in the analysis of the future prospects of *shushinkoyo* in Japan is that the system depends on continuing rapid economic growth for ease of implementation. Economic crises have always caused Japanese management to weigh the benefits versus the costs. Japanese firms are subject to the same economic forces that cause companies to cut costs in order to survive. The economic difficulties Japan faces in the 1990s after the bursting of the bubble economy of the latter half of the 1980s are more severe and complex than those experienced previously during the post-war period. There are strong indications that the present economic difficulties are structural in nature as well as cyclical.

Export markets can no longer offer the same opportunities to stimulate the Japanese economy. Many countries already complain about their present trade imbalance with Japan. In response, Japanese companies have moved a significant portion of their production abroad. Furthermore, there is greater competition from other industrializing nations in industries such as electronics. Japanese companies will no longer be able to avoid dealing with the problem of excess employees. Pioneer Electronic Corp. received much publicity in 1993 when it threatened to dismiss 35 managers if they did not 'voluntarily' retire (Watanabe, 1993). Other companies have also taken steps to trim their payrolls of excess clerical and management personnel.

It is clear that, for the Japanese enterprise system as a whole, *shushinkoyo* is an ideal rather than a reality. One is not forced to give up one's beliefs in ideals even when they cannot be realized. From this perspective, executives from top Japanese corporations can truthfully say they will seek to maintain the policy of lifetime employment in the face of economic hard times, even though they may simultaneously seek to reduce the number of full-time employees through decreased hiring, early retirements, relocations to subsidiaries, and so on. In their hearts the executives may wish to continue the family style relationship between employees and the company. Thus, they rationalize their actions that contradict their desire to maintain lifetime employment.

3.5.5 Is the Practice of *Shushinkoyo* Really Unique to Japan?

The myth that all workers in Japan are guaranteed employment for a lifetime at one company is as erroneous as the myth that workers in the US constantly change jobs and companies brutally cut their workforce at the first sign of an economic downturn. There are many large successful companies in the United States where a substantial number of employees spend most if not all their working years. Furthermore, the mandatory retirement age in the US tends to be higher than that of Japan. In fact, a comparative study of Japanese and American managerial practices and attitudes, found that the proportion of Americans wishing to stay with the same company until retirement is, as in Japan, high (Baba, 1984:133). The major difference between the US and Japanese firms is that at US firms layoffs have tended to be much more common. Furthermore, in the US there is not the same degree of stigma as in Japan associated with changing companies so there has been greater labour mobility. Therefore, *shushinkoyo* is unique to Japan only in the sense of the particular role it has played as part of the Japanese human resource management system, but not in terms of employees simply working all or most of their life at one firm.

3.5.6 Is *Shushinkoyo* Transferable to Japanese Subsidiaries Abroad?

Hasegawa (1986) claims that when Japanese companies move overseas, they take with them the valuable principle of long-term employment and that it has been largely successful. He states that the morale of the American workforce at Japanese subsidiaries has been high and the rate of absenteeism at Sony USA is a striking 0.1 per cent. However, it is not always true that Japanese companies practice *shushinkoyo* with non-Japanese employees even when they profess to do so. For example, when Kyocera purchased a company in the US they continued to promise employees that if they worked hard they would always have a job with Kyocera and that they were part of a family. However, Kyocera later suddenly laid off many workers who thereafter filed a class-action suit against the company.

Furthermore, even when a Japanese firm truly aims to implement *shushinkoyo* at overseas subsidiaries, local labour market conditions and other external environmental factors may prevent them from doing so. Logically it is more difficult to implement such employment policies in areas where there is high labour mobility and high demand for managerial talent. In a study of Japanese subsidiaries in the US carried out by Beechler and Yang (1994) local labour market characteristics, industry features and economic conditions had a strong negative impact on the firms' abilities to transfer Japanese HRM practices. The highly competitive labour market conditions, the high annual employee turnover rates in the city, and the values and ambitions of American white-collar employees and professionals hired by Japanese companies, all discouraged Japanese service companies from practising *shushinkoyo* along with other Japanese-style HRM practices. After the 1987 stock crash, subsidiaries of Japanese financial firms in the US were laying off people as much as American firms (Beechler and Yang, 1994:479).

In addition, Ichimura (1981) surveyed Japanese subsidiaries in Southeast Asia and concluded that *shushinkoyo* does not seem to be of great significance in the region. He claims the mentality of the Southeast Asians is different from that of the Japanese concerning loyalty. However, it is not because they cannot demonstrate loyalty to the company where they work, rather it is because the Japanese subsidiaries do not have the long history of local firms and thus do not command the same degree of respect as well-known local firms. As many as 42 per cent of the Japanese managers who responded to Ichimura's questionnaire recommended giving up expecting loyalty to the company on the part of HCN employees.

Finally, in trying to answer the question about the transferability of *shushinkoyo* to Japanese foreign subsidiaries it is important to keep in mind the context in which *shushinkoyo* is practised in Japan. First of all, the practice of *shushinkoyo* at large successful Japanese firms is part of a total HRM system of recruitment practices discussed above and *nenko joretsu* (seniority system) as discussed below. When a Japanese firm establishes foreign subsidiaries it is not often possible to follow the same recruitment, pay and promotion practices that support the practice of *shushinkoyo*. HCN managers may not feel the same loyalty and be willing to make the same sacrifices that Japanese managers often do for the sake of job security.

3.6 *NENKO JORETSU* (SENIORITY SYSTEM)

In this section the following questions concerning *nenko joretsu* are addressed:

1. What is *nenko joretsu* and how extensively is it actually practised in Japan?
2. How did the practice develop?
3. What are its merits and demerits?
4. What is the future of *nenko joretsu* in Japan?
5. How does it really differ from practices in other developed economies such as the United States?
6. Is the practice transferable to non-Japanese employees in Japanese subsidiaries abroad?

3.6.1 What Is *Nenko Joretsu*?

Another major characteristic of Japanese human resource management is the *nenko joretsu* or seniority system. Though nenko is most often translated as 'seniority,' this translation often leads to misunderstandings among Westerners. In the West, when layoffs occur seniority tends to protect workers while in Japan it tends to work the other way. Though layoffs in large Japanese firms have historically been less common during the post-war period, when they do occur the older employees with more years of service are encouraged to leave the company since their pay is higher than younger employees with fewer years of service. Furthermore, middle managers tend to be less productive than their subordinates due to Japan's bottom-up consensus system, and the job of many managers is simply to approve or disapprove proposals by junior staff. The layoffs of older managers are often disguised as early retirements.

In general, a Japanese worker's wages are increased and he is promoted in accordance with the length of his service in one company. In practice this system, like long-term employment, is a general principle, a kind of rule of thumb. It is not guaranteed and is not always strictly adhered to (Hasegawa, 1986:17). The *nenko* system is often contrasted with the so-called merit system but it is not a simple clear-cut contrast. Japanese companies do not determine salaries and promote employees strictly on the basis of the number of years of service to the company. Rather, as Inohara (1990:24) pointed out, *nenko* recognizes that a man grows and matures humanly and technically as his working-life experience increases, and this recognition is reflected in salary and promotion. *Nenko* refers to all the merits that an employee has accumulated over the years in co-operation with his colleagues, and includes both technical and social ability. The longer an employee is with the company, the better he is in terms of multiple job experience and human relations inside and outside the company (Inohara, 1990:85).

The combination of merit evaluation and seniority contrasts sharply with the situation in pre-war Japan. At that time power was in the hands of a small group of *zaibatsu*. When the Americans broke up the *zaibatsu*, top management was purged for their participation in the war effort and middle management took over. People began to be promoted from within the company. Employees were gradually promoted according to seniority until they finally assumed positions as management executives. Then it became clear that length of service could not be depended on to provide material for a first-rate managerial staff. At this critical juncture, the notion of combining the seniority system with the merit system was conceived (Hasegawa, 1986:23).

However, Nakane (1972a) argues that in traditional Japanese society a method of judgment suitable for the implementation of the merit system never existed as a system of employment and Japanese people are far less inclined to pay attention to differences in ability than is customary in other societies. She wrote that (1972a:34) traditionally the Japanese give attention to differences in effort between individuals, for instance 'hard worker' and 'idler,' but hold an extremely deep-rooted belief in an equality of ability in the sense that anyone can succeed if he tries. Okada (1984:18) believes that the seniority-based system did not finally become established in large Japanese corporations until after the Second World War. He states that most of these corporations had previously paid wages on personalized schedules that emphasized age, academic record, and years of service and that the efforts to adopt the Western practice of paying wages according to position and ability were opposed by the enterprise unions organized at most large firms after the war.

Under the present *nenko joretsu* system, pay increases continue to accumulate according to length of service with only minor adjustments to reflect employee performance. For young employees who have been with a company only a few years, the merit adjustment is very small. Until a worker's colleagues acknowledge an employee's achievements and reach an unspoken consensus on his role, morale is best served by treating everyone in as equal a manner as possible. This attitude continues to pervade company policy at all levels. Fairness towards the group to which an employee belongs is important in maintaining harmony. Therefore, the promotion of an individual employee cannot be considered in isolation, but in relation to fairness to the others in the same group. Quick promotions are usually considered to result from favouritism towards certain individuals and discrimination against others.

As mentioned before, in most Japanese firms in which the spirit if not the letter of the *nenko joretsu* system is practised, personnel appraisal is characterized by its group orientation and regardless of performance, care is taken not to promote an employee too quickly or too slowly. Promotions take place at a slow pace since the focus is on the long-term. Demotions are very rare and only occur as a severe form of punishment. Delayed promotion is considered to be more effective from a motivational point of view. Furthermore, delayed promotion allows time for further education of the employee before assuming positions of greater responsibility.

3.6.2 What Are the Merits and Demerits of *Nenko Joretsu*?

One apparent merit of *nenko joretsu* as practised in large Japanese corporations is the fact that it goes hand in hand with the practice of *shushinkoyo*. It helps in maintaining a workforce that is in balance between older employees, with much accumulated experience and higher pay, and younger employees learning all about the company and its business while receiving substantially lower pay. Newly hired employees are considered no more than trainees and their pay is relatively low. They are expected to work hard to receive slow but steady promotions and increases in salary. *Nenko joretsu* encourages workers to stay at one company by assuring regular pay raises and promotions. Unless exceptionally attractive conditions are offered, workers will normally decide to stay where they are. Thus the employee receives a sense of security and the company maintains a dedicated work force.

After the Second World War, many Japanese companies endeavoured to introduce the American-style merit system. These attempts ended in failure since no objective standards to evaluate merit could be found, at least none that could be adapted for use in Japanese corporations where group effort is more important than individual effort. If no clear-cut objective reason can be found for promoting one employee over another and the selection were made on the personal preferences of management, there is a good chance that resentment will grow and that morale will be undermined (Hasegawa, 1986:21). Thus, during the post-war period *nenko joretsu* has proved to be more suitable to the working environment of Japanese corporations where *shushinkoyo* has been practised.

However, increasingly there are shifts in the attitudes of employers and employees towards *nenko joretsu* as changes in the economic environment in Japan have illuminated some inherent demerits of the system. *Nenko joretsu* has recently been criticized for holding back the growth rate and competitiveness of Japanese companies. These criticisms are based on the judgment that new values and attitudes are forming among employees and employers concerning individual reward. *Nenko joretsu* is now seen by some as a hindrance to promoting and rewarding talented workers. Many of Japan's 5.3 million males born in the post-war 'baby-boom' period from 1947–51 are now in mid-level and senior management positions. The 'baby boomers' have turned the companies' pyramid-shaped power structures into inverted ones overladen with managerial layers (do Rosario, 1993:22).

The cost of the *nenko joretsu* system has also become a burden during this period of economic difficulties in Japan. *Nenko joretsu* depends on continuing rapid economic growth for ease of implementation in the same way as *shushinkoyo*. The same arguments against the continued practice of *shushinkoyo* may be applied to argue against the continuation of *nenko joretsu*. In particular, there are too many overpaid managers who do not have sufficient productive and meaningful work to perform and not enough young new recruits at low pay coming into the company to maintain a balance in salary expenditures. A survey conducted by the Research and Survey Group regarding excess employment indicates that the highest redundancies exist among managers and clerical staff aged 45 years and older (Sato, 1994:6).

Another problem with the *nenko joretsu* system is the eventual promotion of less competent but older managers over more competent younger ones. Though the promotion of a manager may be delayed as a form of punishment or as a sign that the manager in question has not performed adequately to advance along with others in the same age group, eventually the manager will move up the ladder so as not to fall farther behind. In this way, an employee who is not as capable will gain promotion ahead of younger more talented employees.

3.6.3 What Is the Future of *Nenko Joretsu*?

According to the 1994 Asahi Bank survey (Japan 21st, 1995), the breakdown of the *nenko joretsu* is proceeding at a still higher pace than *shushinkoyo*. Of the companies surveyed, 48.7 per cent replied that they would revise the system in the future, while 45.7 per cent replied that the system had already broken down. *Nenko joretsu* needs to be modified by adjusting salaries according to merit in order to control the wage expenses and to motivate employees to work harder.

Margerison (1993) argues that a number of large Japanese firms are turning away from *nenko joretsu* and adopting systems with a greater emphasis on merit. Honda, Ryobi, and Chugai Pharmaceutical are examples of Japanese companies that have developed and begun to implement merit-based systems in determining promotion and pay. Margerison claims the advantages to Japanese companies of the merit-based system over the *nenko joretsu* are: (1) ability to attract talented new recruits; (2) ability to promote talented workers to managerial positions without co-workers feeling disgruntled; (3) ability to position highly specialized workers in an area which suits their expertise, rather than placing them into a managerial post, without them feeling they have been overlooked for promotion; (5) increased work productivity; and (6) improved control over staff performance levels. Though the general concept of merit-based systems for pay and promotion tend to run against the trend of Japanese society's accepted system, improved employee satisfaction has been reported upon the adoption of such new systems.

Honda is an interesting example of a large Japanese firm reforming the appraisal and promotion system. The company has scrapped its old system of monthly salaries based on *nenko joretsu* and replaced it with a merit-based annual salary. Honda has set five to seven performance model types for each level of management. Employees are assessed once a year, according to the year's criteria and salary figures are determined accordingly. Promotion is an integral part of Honda's new system with the definite possibility that poor performing managers may be demoted in favour of more results-oriented managers. It is now also possible for successful managers to jump over several levels of the organizational structure at a time. Honda adopted this new system for its 4500 managers hoping that the new system would destroy the complacent atmosphere prevailing in the firm (Margerison, 1993).

Mroczkowski and Hanaoka (1989) suggest that the seniority system has been slowly declining since the late 1970s with the weighting of seniority pay in determining wage increases declining by 12 per cent over the period from 1978 to the late 1980s. Thus the present revisions to the *nenko joretsu* system may be just more dramatic manifestations of a revision process that has been under way for more than a decade. For example, according to Sato (1994:8), Nissan is introducing a new system for promotion and appraisal under which the present weighting of age and service will be reduced from 40 per cent to 15 per cent. In addition, it can be discerned from increases in articles in the popular press and documentary television programmes at the end of the century that both *shushinkoyo* and *nenkojoretsu* are quickly fading into history.

3.6.4 Is the Practice of *Nenko Joretsu* Really Unique to Japan?

Shimada (1986:49) argues that wages that increase with length of service or experience are not unique to Japanese industries. In Western industrial countries wage rates increase with promotion. In Japan wage rates that increase with age or experience are also accompanied by increases in the level of skills or status. Furthermore, Shimada analysed age–wage profiles for blue- and white-collar workers with different educational levels for both the United States and Japan. He demonstrated that the Japanese age–wage profiles are quite similar to those of the US workers except for the younger groups. The relative differences between white- and blue-collar workers are remarkably similar between the two countries, suggesting that age–wage profiles are affected significantly by technological and organizational factors regardless of national differences. However, there are important differences such as the great deal of consideration given to the effect a promotion or wage increase has on the group as a whole. This difference can be explained by the relatively greater collective orientation of Japanese society and the relatively greater desire to maintain harmony amongst fellow employees.

3.6.5 Is *Nenko Joretsu* Transferable to Japanese Subsidiaries Abroad?

There are a number of conditions that impede the implementation of *nenko joretsu* in Japanese foreign subsidiaries. First of all, when a Japanese firm establishes a large operation in a foreign country there is an immediate need for HCN managers who already have experience and expertise in various fields. In order to recruit such HCN managers from other local or other foreign firms it is necessary to offer competitive salaries that reflect the demand for such personnel. Thus, in the first stages of developing a foreign subsidiary, Japanese firms tend to introduce a number of HCN managers at various salary levels. *Nenko joretsu* entails the hiring of new school graduates at low salaries with the promise of long-term employment and gradual increase in salaries as their experience and abilities increase. Depending on the labour market and local customs this practice may be possible. Certainly, the practice of *nenko joretsu* is not apparent during the initial developmental stage of the foreign subsidiary.

There have been clear cases of discrimination against HCNs in favour of Japanese PCNs in terms of employment opportunity, managerial responsibility, promotion and pay at Japanese foreign subsidiaries. It is true that most expatriates or PCNs of foreign subsidiaries receive special benefits and compensation when stationed at foreign subsidiaries; however, the nature and extent of the practice at Japanese subsidiaries seems to have received much more criticism than that of non-Japanese foreign subsidiaries. Court cases were brought against Sumitomo and C. Itoh in the US for such discrimination (Sethi *et al.*, 1984).

3.7 *KIGYO-BETSU RODOKUMIAI* (ENTERPRISE-BASED TRADE UNIONS)

Co-operation between management and enterprise-based unions *(kigyo-betsu rodokumiai)* comprising exclusively employees of the respective companies is often cited as one of the factors, which has led to Japan's economic success. Together with *shushinkoyo* and *nenko joretsu*, these three practices are often called the 'Three Sacred

Treasures' (Shimada, 1986:44). Before discussing the contribution of *kigyo-betsu rodokumiai* to the development of the Japanese economy a brief overview of Japanese industrial relations is presented here. The labour movement in Japan is structured at three levels: national, industrial, and enterprise-based.

3.7.1 What Is the Structure of Organized Labour at the National Level?

At the national level, four national labour centres represented organized labour until 1987. These centres were: Sohyo (General Council of Labour Unions of Japan) with 4.1 million members; Domei (Japan Confederation of Labour) with 2.1 million members; Churitsu-Ronen (Federation of Independent Unions) with 1.6 million members; and Shin-Sambetsu (National Federation of Industrial Organizations) with 66,000 members. The two largest, Sohyo and Domei, were rivals as the former supported the Japan Socialist Party and the latter was associated with the Democratic Socialist Party.

In 1982, Zen-Min-Rokyo (All-Japan Council of Labour Unions in the Private Sector) was organized as an attempt to prepare the unification of all organized labour under one national centre. It started by grouping private sector unions affiliated with different national labour centres and claimed about 4.8 million members. In 1987, it officially became a federated body, Rengo (All-Japan Federation of Private Labour Unions), with 5.5 million members: other national centres dissolved, except Sohyo, which decided to dissolve in November 1989. The new centre, Shin-Rengo (Japanese Trade Union Confederation), is the result of a kind of merger of Rengo and Sohyo affiliated public sector unions. Shin-Rengo is expected to be the only national centre, covering all unions in both the private and public sectors. The total number of members is estimated to be about 8 million (Inohara, 1990:124–5). There are other national organizations in addition to Shin-Rengo, which are mostly councils such as Kinzoku Rokyo (International Metalworkers Federation).

Shin-Rengo is expected to strengthen the role of the former national labour centres that represented organized labour in some advisory capacity at various governmental deliberation and private industrial councils. Shin-Rengo must function with an agenda formed by the highest common denominator of the various labour interests it represents. Thus, the function is much more general than that of industrial unions or enterprise-based unions. The national labour centres protect labour's interests though the legislative process. It does not get involved in collective bargaining at the enterprise level.

3.7.2 What Is the Structure of Organized Labour at the Industrial Level?

Industrial federations *(tansan)* are mostly a federated body of enterprise unions by industry. In principle, they are the sole affiliates of national labour centres; in some nationwide enterprise unions are treated as industrial federations and qualify to directly affiliate with a national centre. Examples of such exceptions are Zen-Dentsu (National Union of Telecommunication Workers of Nippon Telegraph and Telephone Company) with 268,000 members. As in the case of the national centre, the industrial federations are not expected to participate in collective bargaining at the enterprise level. Similar to the national centre, industrial federations represent workers in their respective industries, for example, at industrial trade councils such as in the textile, steel and chemical industries (Inohara, 1990:127).

3.7.3 What Is the Structure of Organized Labour at the Enterprise Level?

Of the total number of labour unions in Japan, 94.2 per cent are in-house enterprise-based unions that comprise exclusively the employees of the respective companies; of the remaining, 2.6 per cent are industrial unions, 1.0 per cent are craft unions, and the remaining are miscellaneous types including general unions. In the case of a company that has branch offices or local plants, the registration is made by each such establishment where workers join the union, and the union of all the employees of the company takes the form of these office and plant unions. There are two distinct forms of labour unions. One is the *tan-i kumiai* (unit union) to which workers are affiliated individually and directly, but the organization does not have any subunits. A typical example is a union organized in a small enterprise that does not have any branch. The other type is the *tan-itsu kumiai* (single union), to which individual members affiliate directly, but the organization has branches that function similarly to a unit union. A typical example is an enterprise union organized in a large company that has a number of branch offices and local plants (Inohara, 1990:128).

Enterprise-based unions tend to support long-term co-operation with management in an effort to ensure the steady growth and survival of the company to which all the members of the union belong. All the members are in-house, that is only regular employees of the respective enterprise are allowed to join the unions under the post-war tradition of 'one company, one union.' Such an arrangement allows the union to focus its attention on the interests of the employees and the company. Employees of Japanese firms identify more strongly with the company they work for than with the type of work that they do. That is to say, an electrical engineer at Nippon Denso views himself as a member of the Nippon Denso corporate family first and as an electrical engineer second.

Furthermore, the greater importance of enterprise-based unions over industrial or national unions in Japan may also be understood in terms of Nakane's (1972a:44–5) theory of organizations based on frame and attribute. There is little solidarity fostered among workers doing the same job but working in different companies. Such craft-based unions flourish in societies that value association based on attribute, type of occupation, greater than association based on frame, employees of the same organization. Enterprise-based unions are formed first, and then industrial unions emerge as collective bodies of such unions.

The general assembly, executive committee, secretariat, and various committees govern enterprise-based unions. Some enterprise unions have full-time officers who keep their employee's status *(zaiseki senjyu-sha)* although their salaries are paid by the union; their period of union office is counted as service years for the company. The experience gained through union activities is much appreciated by management and will be taken into consideration for future promotion to managerial positions. However, if a union official leaves his enterprise-union to work full-time for the industrial federation or the national centre to which his union is affiliated, he usually terminates his employment relationship with the company. Thus, there is a clear distinction between the 'in-house' *(uchi)* nature of the enterprise-based union and the 'outside' *(soto)* nature of other labour organizations (Inohara, 1990:131–2).

Collective bargaining at the enterprise level takes place between the director in charge of personnel, assisted by personnel managers, and the union president, assisted by officers. Thus, in the collective bargaining process all the participants are insiders *(uchi)* and officers from the industrial federation or the national centre are not allowed to participate. No other outsider *(soto)* such as a lawyer or government official participates either. These outsiders may be consulted informally but do not directly take part in the formal collective bargaining process. Where a grievance machinery and a joint consultation system are established, collective bargaining tends to be a formality to confirm what has already been agreed upon through other means, in particular, joint consultation (Inohara, 1990:134).

These practices reflect the *kazokushugi* (familism) nature of the relationships inside most Japanese corporations. Any antagonism or dispute between management and workers is a household problem. However, according to Nakane (1972a:45) a union that is formed within the household or company has a great weakness on account of the internal structure that thwarts the antagonism between parties in conflict. She argues that the household is an *ichizoku-roto* (one family and its retainers) type of group and its members share a common destiny, a dispute goes on in conditions involving emotional and economic ties, which while illogical remain indissoluble, a situation that resembles a state of confrontation between father and son at home.

Labour-management joint consultation *(ro-shi kyogi-sei)* was promoted in the 1960s almost simultaneously with the productivity movement. Unlike the grievance procedure *(kujo-shori)*, which was an import from the United States that did not take root in Japan (today it is maintained only by 34 per cent of Japanese companies), the joint consultation system is 'active' in more than 72 per cent of Japanese companies (87.9 per cent of unionized and 40.7 per cent of non-unionized companies). 'Active' was defined as at least nine formal sessions were held each year (Ministry of Labour, 1985:10–16). Shimada (1986:51) maintains that joint consultation is the unique aspect of Japanese industrial relations. Joint consultation usually involves discussion between management and worker representatives on various matters relating to management policies, production plans, working conditions, fringe benefits, and the like.

Returning to the question posed earlier – how great is the contribution enterprise-based unions have made to the development of the post-war Japanese economy? Inohara (1990:252) points out that today less than 28 per cent of the qualified employees are unionized; they are mostly employees of large corporations and in the private sector. Therefore, unionism does not affect labour-management relations in Japan much except for the involvement of employees in the nationwide spring wage offensive *(shunto)*. Instead, formal and informal joint labour consultation *(ro-shi kyogi-sei)*, small-group activities *(sho-shudan katsudo)*, and other communication means seem to function as effective substitutes. That is to say, an effective system of communication between labour and management and harmonization of labour-management interests has developed during the post-war period in many Japanese enterprises, and enterprise-based unions are just a part of this system.

In order to present a true picture of organized labour in Japan it is necessary to consider those workers who do not seemingly benefit from organized labour organizations. As mentioned above the majority of workers are not unionized and the use of part-time or temporary labour is widespread among Japanese corporations of all sizes. Van Wolferen states (1992:68–9) that in the post-war system a large segment of low-cost labour is supplied by a pool of non-unionized 'temporary' workers, who are often in fact permanent but at a lower level of the economic hierarchy. He notes that enterprise unions shut out workers formally classified as temporary, even though they may have worked for the firm for many years, for the very reason that they are not in the lifetime-employment category. He adds that in the smaller companies, whose existence as low-cost sources of subcontracted work is a decisive factor in the competitiveness of many large firms, unions are very rare and no attempt is made by the national federations to establish them.

3.7.4 Organized Labour and Japanese Overseas Subsidiaries

Though the focus is on HCN managers rather than HCN workers, understanding Japanese industrial relations domestically and internationally is part of gaining an overall view of Japanese IHRM policies and practices. From the discussion of Japanese organized labour above it is clear that, like most firms of any nationality, Japanese firms prefer a compliant and obedient workforce. Enterprise unionism may be viewed as a method employed by large Japanese firms to preempt strong national-based or industry-based unions from interfering with the control they exert over their blue-collar employees. The compliance of enterprise-based unions to the wishes of the firm is based on the close relationship between management and the unions. Indeed, union leaders themselves will often join management at a later stage, similarly commanding the obedience from their underlings in the union.

In light of this attitude of the majority of Japanese firms towards organized labour it is not surprising that there have been numerous reports of Japanese MNCs seeking to avoid unionism in their overseas subsidiaries by selecting areas where there is minimal union activity. Japanese firms often find it difficult to implement their flexible work rules and other practices, which have been attributed to their success in gaining high productivity, when they have had to deal with existing local unions in their overseas operations (Beechler and Yang, 1994). However, it is true that NUMMI, the joint venture between Toyota and GM in California, successfully implemented Toyota's well-known labour management practices with employees belonging to the United Auto Workers Union. However, this should be viewed more as the exception than the rule according to the complaints of various organized labour groups in the US.

3.8 TRAINING AND DEVELOPMENT IN JAPANESE CORPORATIONS

Training and development in large Japanese firms should be viewed in the context of the Japanese education system and the various HRM practices discussed above. Unlike some countries in Europe where vocational training is an important part of the education system, in Japan elementary and secondary education emphasizes the general studies of science and the humanities. Thus companies must provide their own occupational training for new school graduates. Since employees are expected to stay with the company, training is continuous and long-term mainly through on-the-job training through job rotation. Older employees function as mentors to younger employees. Constant job rotation offers general knowledge of many aspects of the companies' operations. The goal is to develop generalists who become adept at human relations and teamwork.

A study of the Japan Productivity Centre found differences in the attitudes towards training in Japanese and American firms (Baba, 1984:61–7). Though respondents in both countries recognized the effectiveness of training in improving performance appraisal, the Americans gave a stronger positive response towards its effectiveness. On the other hand, Japanese managers appear to be more prepared to give training opportunities to their subordinates when it is requested and tend to have better established training programmes. In the case of American respondents, they are more apt to check the necessity of the training first before granting the request. This may be due to less labour mobility in the Japanese companies compared to the American companies in the survey. However, when questioned concerning job rotation, an important aspect of training in Japanese companies, American superiors more often considered the needs of the employee more important than those of the organization than was the case with Japanese managers. One of the main considerations in examining the application of this approach at Japanese foreign subsidiaries is the degree of labour mobility among HCN managers. Japanese firms will obviously be reluctant to train and develop HCN managers if they feel that the managers are not likely to stay with the company for a long time.

3.9 TRANSFERABILITY OF JAPANESE MANAGEMENT PRACTICES

Examining the transferability of Japanese management practices to Japanese overseas subsidiaries is an important aspect of the research undertaken here. Though the subject is addressed throughout this chapter, this section offers a theoretical overview. In addition, the results of some existing research on the transfer of Japanese management to subsidiaries in various parts of the world are presented. By examining the results of research on this subject in greatly differing regions it is possible to demonstrate commonalities of issues among the regions.

There is a wide range of opinions concerning the transferability of Japanese management practices. For instance, on the one hand, Bartlett and Yoshihara (1988) maintain that many of the HRM strategies employed by Japanese firms in the domestic environment, that have been credited for making the firms so successful, are difficult to implement in their overseas subsidiaries. They argue that practices appropriate to the domestic labour force and widely accepted in Japan may not be flexible enough for application to international operations. On the other hand, Ouchi (1981) claims that some form of the essential characteristics of Japanese companies must be transferable.

Beechler and Yang (1994:469) describe three major streams in the literature that deal with the issue of Japanese HRM practices overseas. The first school, known as the culturalist school, is discussed in relation to the development of Japanese management policies and practices in Section 3.1.1. As argued in Chapter 2, it is perilous to ignore the influence of culture when considering the transfer of HRM practices developed in one culture to a different cultural environment.

On the other hand, it is not very fruitful to seek solely cultural-based explanations for the success or failure of transferring HRM practices to overseas subsidiaries.

The second school of thought is the rationalistic school (or structuralist school) also presented in Section 3.1.1. This school argues that Japanese HRM practices were formulated as rational responses to industrial development, competitive pressure, and production. Therefore, when appropriate conditions exist these practices can be successfully implemented. For example, Koike (1981) insists that the three pillars of Japanese management are not unique to Japan and he found similar phenomena in Western countries. The culturalist and rationalistic schools may complement one another or contradict one another, depending on whether one takes an eclectic approach recognizing the explanatory merits of both approaches, or whether one solely advocates the logic of one to the extent that it denies the significance of the other. The third school of thought is the technology–HRM fit school. According to Beechler and Yang (1994:470) writers in this school use a contingency perspective and focus on the rationality of the production technologies and product control processes in Japan and how these 'hardware' systems organically integrate with 'software' systems, that is to say HRM practices.

Beechler and Yang (1994:471) argued that all three schools fail to link HRM practices explicitly to Japanese MNCs' domestic and global strategies and the reasons why Japanese firms should want to transfer their HRM systems overseas. Thus, they sought to integrate aspects from strategic human resource management into the analysis and outlined a contingency theoretical model that specifies the factors that are hypothesized to impact the transfer of Japanese-style HRM practices to overseas subsidiaries. Though their findings are limited to five Japanese service firms in New York and five Japanese manufacturing firms in Tennessee, some of their hypotheses and findings offer interesting insights into the issue of dealing with HCN managers in Japanese subsidiaries. These key contingency factors include the parent firm's administrative heritage, host-country economic, social and cultural conditions and the cultural distance between the home- and host-country environments (1994:468). Out of these factors, the data they collected demonstrated the importance of administrative heritage and top management beliefs in the transfer of Japanese HRM practices overseas.

Difficulties in transferring Japanese human resource strategies may be linked to the resource accumulation orientation of Japanese firms.

Pucik and Hatvany (1983) summarize Japanese HRM strategies as: (1) the development of an internal labour market, (2) company philosophies that stress strong ties between the company and employees and (3) an intensive socialization process that emphasizes co-operation and teamwork. The first strategy, the development of an internal labour market, entails the practice of *shushinkoyo*. As previously explained, the Japanese firm recruits fresh graduates with the intent of employing them during the major portion of their productive lives. The second strategy is implemented by taking advantage of collectivist tendencies and creating a strong bond between the employee and the company through socialization and the way benefits are structured. The third strategy is achieved by the promotion of a group-oriented mentality.

In Japanese foreign subsidiaries there are many barriers to the implementation of the above-mentioned strategies. First of all, it is difficult for Japanese subsidiaries in many labour markets outside of Japan to recruit fresh graduates who are willing to stay with the firm most of their careers. As described in this study there are many factors limiting the careers of HCN in Japanese firms such as the domination of top management positions by Japanese PCNs. Furthermore, the HCN employees are usually not considered employees of the Japanese MNC; rather they are simply employees of the foreign subsidiaries. Thus, as argued in Chapters 2 and 4, HCN managers do not enjoy the same benefits and opportunities as PCN do and are unlikely to develop the degree of loyalty and sense of belonging to the firm, which is an essential to the implementation of Japanese human resource strategies.

It appears that some Japanese firms attempt wholesale transfer of their management and production practices to overseas subsidiaries. For example, through extensive interaction with managers at hundreds of Japanese 'transplants' in the US I observed that many Japanese manufacturers seek to ensure achievement of production quality and standards at their foreign subsidiaries by duplicating their Japanese operations overseas. They establish a sister-plant relationship between the newly established manufacturing plant overseas and the Japanese manufacturing plant after which it is modelled. Managers, supervisors and even workers from the Japanese plant assist in the start-up of the foreign plant. This system seems to be effective in replicating manufacturing processes and transferring knowledge. However, problems usually occur after start-up as the many Japanese managers or advisers (sometimes called 'shadow managers' by HCNs) remain to control the decision-making at the subsidiary. HCN managers often become frustrated by their lack of participation in decision-making. Likewise, Thome and McAuley (1992:87) reported comments from Singaporean HCN managers reflecting such problems:

> Headquarters always controls the overseas offices and sends out management teams to make sure they duplicate what would have been done in Tokyo. Japanese companies have relocated their production facilities and operational offices overseas but have never become truly multinational in their thinking. There is still the tendency to keep the Japanese way and expect all to be done in the Japanese tradition. Head office remains supreme and maintains control; procedures at home are expected to be replicated at overseas offices.

Insight into the difficulties in transferring Japanese management policies and practices may also be discerned from the literature examining problem areas between Japanese PCN and HCN managers. For example, Tsurumi (1978) outlines seven areas where Japanese and American managers frequently disagree and where troubles in their relations are likely to surface: (1) mismatch of expected leadership style; (2) views on formal and informal organization; (3) verbal vs. written communication; (4) lifetime vs. mercenary employment; (5) avoidance of confrontation; (6) management and rank-and-file dichotomy; and (7) size, accommodation, and conflict. In addition, reviewing the performance of Japanese subsidiaries in the US, Johnson (1977) pinpoints four general areas where success or failure was likely to be determined. The first is the speed of 'Americanization;' the second is headquarters–subsidiary relations; the third is Japanese–American communications; and the fourth is staff selection policies. Johnson also maintains that persistent difficulties encountered by Japanese subsidiaries were caused by the painstaking struggles to weld American HCNs and Japanese PCNs into a team, group or section in terms of organizational cohesiveness and harmony.

There have also been a few studies focusing on the transfer of Japanese management to foreign subsidiaries in other Asian countries. For instance, Lim (1991:116) studying Japanese subsidiaries in Singapore concludes that Japanese subsidiaries appear to be less attractive to Singaporean employees compared to Singapore government institutions, public enterprises, and Western MNCs. He also states that the Japanese-style managerial system without modifications and rectifications is not suitable for such heterogeneous societies strongly influenced by Western cultures such as Singapore. Furthermore, Lim argues that Japanese-style management must be internationalized and localized if it is to make greater positive contributions towards Singapore's rapid economic development.

Sammapan (1995) studied the transferability of Japanese practices to their subsidiaries in Thailand using a sample of 34 firms. He found that the following practices appeared to have been successfully transferred: (1) avoiding lay-offs of employees; (2) emphasis given to on-the-job training; (3) promotion from within the organization; and (4) promotion and salary based on seniority. On the other hand, Sammapan concluded that the practices that were not successfully transferred included: (1) lifetime employment; (2) job rotation; (3) non-specialized career paths; (4) retirement benefits; (5) large bonuses; and (6) harmonious union–management relations. It appears that Japanese firms are not developing HCNs for top management positions by fostering the development of generalists as is usually done in Japan.

3.10 JAPANESE HRM AND EMPLOYEE COMMITMENT

The relationship between Japanese HRM practices and the supposedly strong employee commitment is of great interest to many scholars and people in business alike. There are a number of scholars who claim Japanese companies enjoy a greater degree of employee commitment than other developed industrial nations such as the US. They believe that Japanese corporations offer a model for the rest of the world. Among the most well-known proponents of this argument are Lincoln and Kalleberg (1990:1) who wrote:

> From industrial psychologists to organizational sociologists to Marxist labour process theorists, a focus on the efforts by companies to foster dependence, loyalty and identification in a workforce has superseded older scholarly concerns with industrial attitudes, performance, and conflict. There is a wide variety in the labels given by diverse writers to the organizational form that has evolved around an imperative of maximizing workforce commitment, but the pattern they describe is very much the same. For Ronald Dore (1973), it is 'welfare corporatism,' a set of workplace institutions that has reached its highest development in Japan but is fast replacing

the 'market individualism' of early industrialization in the Western countries as well.

Lincoln and Kalleberg (1990:3) also remarked that many scholars believe Japan to be in the vanguard of a movement spreading fundamental change throughout the economic institutions of the capitalist world. The earmarks of that movement are:

1. The abolition of destructive Western-style industrial relations and its replacement by a new harmonious order in which labour and unions collabourate with management in advancing the fortunes of the firms.
2. The creation of organizational and job structures that increase workers' control over the production process and make work more meaningful and rewarding.
3. The provision of job security, welfare services, and training programmes which integrate employees in an inclusive and ongoing enterprise community providing broadly for its members and demanding loyalty and commitment in return.

These types of praises may be found in the literature of other apologists of Japanese management (for example: Shimizu, 1989; Lu, 1987; Abegglen and Stalk, 1985a; Vogel, 1985; Ouchi, 1981; Pascale and Athos, 1981). However, not all researchers agree with the conclusions of Lincoln and Kalleberg that Japanese employees demonstrate greater employee commitment than employees of other industrialized nations.

For example, a study by Hodgetts and Luthans (1989:42) analysed a representative sample of employees from widely diverse organizations in the United States, Japan and Korea. According to the data, Japanese and Korean employees showed no difference in levels of commitment. Furthermore, both the Japanese and Korean employees were less committed to their organizations than US employees were. Hodgetts and Luthans (1989:43) claim that these and other research findings show that Japanese HRM approaches are not synonymous with higher worker satisfaction and commitment. They state that especially when telling their true feelings on an anonymous questionnaire, Japanese workers might be considerably less satisfied and committed in comparison with their American counterparts. Yoshimura and Anderson (1997:82) also maintain that a substantial body of research casts doubts upon the claim that Japanese employees tend to be more committed to their companies than employees in other nations:

> Polls frequently show that Japanese workers are less committed to their companies and less satisfied with their jobs than American workers are. One survey in the late 1980s, for instance, reported that 15 per cent of Japanese employees described themselves as satisfied with their current employment situation, compared to 52 per cent of American employees. A good deal of academic research finds that the workplace commitment is lower in Japan than it is in the United States.

One explanation for the results of the survey quoted above is that there is much less labour mobility in Japan among manager-level employees. Therefore, while a manager experiencing dissatisfaction with a job may seek a new position in a different company it is much harder for Japanese managers to find a position in a different firm in Japan. However, it should also be noted that some scholars (for example, Takashita, 1989) believe that Japan is experiencing changes in the national work ethic and increased labour mobility among managers that may lead to less commitment to the company. This trend has definitely become more pronounced during the Heisei depression (the 1990s). As previously noted, new economic realities of this prolonged period of low or even negative economic growth are weakening the ties between employees and their companies.

Perhaps the greatest challenge to Lincoln and Kalleberg's findings comes from Besser (1993). Besser points out that even though the results of Lincoln and Kalleberg's studies indicate that there is greater commitment among US employees than among Japanese employees, they seek to explain away the results and maintain that the commitment is greater among Japanese employees. In relation to this point Besser states (1993:878):

> Despite the rhetoric and interpretations to the contrary, research consistently demonstrates that American workers express higher levels of commitment toward their employing organizations than do Japanese workers. However, the behaviour of Japanese workers suggests higher commitment – Japanese have lower rates of absenteeism, turnover, tardiness, and militancy than do American workers. I argue that the incongruity of these two statements is more apparent than real. First, various aspects of the political and social

contexts make turnover and militancy less likely in Japan than in the United States, regardless of workers' attitudes. Turnover may not be a valid measure of commitment in comparisons between the US and Japan.

It is beyond the scope of this book to seek a final resolution to this ongoing debate concerning the relative commitment of Japanese and US workers. The debate is mentioned here because there are important points in the arguments made by the researchers that have a direct relationship with the research problem, the integration of HCN managers into the management process of Japanese foreign subsidiaries. Most significantly, the researchers in this debate seek to account for the committed behaviours of the Japanese workforce by offering various explanatory factors. Besser (1993:879) contrasts factors such as pressures of the work group, family, and community with strong attitudes of commitment to the organization. She is stressing that strong attitudes of commitment to the organization do not necessarily exist among Japanese employees even though they may demonstrate committed behaviours such as low rates of absenteeism, turnover, and tardiness.

I offer the following classification of the factors accounting for committed work behaviours: (1) factors external to the organization (social and culture pressures concerning accepted or proper behaviour, attitudes towards group membership), (2) factors internal to the organizations (such as HRM policies and practices which seek to enhance the employees' involvement and identification with the organization), and (3) personal factors (such as preferences for certain types of work environments and responsibilities). Most of the researchers participating in this debate would probably acknowledge that factors from all three categories work together to generate committed work behaviours. However, they would most likely disagree on the degree of influence of the various factors.

Nevertheless, most researchers would concede that many of the HRM practices discussed in this chapter such as a focus on recruitment of new school graduates, *shushinkoyo*, *nenko joretsu*, *kigyo-betsu rodokumiai*, on-the-job training through job rotation, and the general atmosphere of corporate familism may be viewed as a system designed to maximize employee dependence, commitment and loyalty. However, it may also be argued that there are important social and cultural factors that enhance the acceptance and effectiveness of these HRM policies and practices. Japanese companies are channelling the collectivist tendencies of their employees towards forming an in-group bond with the company. Thus, it is possible to assert that the sense of belonging to the in-group, in this case the company, may be more important in generating committed work behaviour than an attitude of commitment that stems from job satisfaction or identification with a certain profession. This view is supported by Cole (1979:231), who concluded from his research and that of others that Japanese employees have unusually strong identification with the company, but not necessarily high job satisfaction or strong commitment to the performance of specific job tasks.

The above argument is also supported by other research results. For instance, Baba (1984:24) carried out a comparative study in 1983 of management in Japan and the US. The results of this study indicate that in the US commitment stemmed mainly from employees' interest and satisfaction in their own work. On the other hand, they conclude that Japanese employees entrust their lives to the organization in a kind of parent–child relationship, and commitment stems from a feeling that theirs and the organization's fate are one. Their statement is basically a reaffirmation that commitment to the firm in Japan is based on familism and the concept of *ie*. Their conclusions also confirm that the characteristics and basis for employee control and commitment should vary between national cultures. Consequently, the Japanese domestic HRM policies and practices may not yield the same desired employee control and commitment in foreign subsidiaries. Most importantly, if Japanese fail to provide engaging and stimulating jobs to their HCN managerial staff they are likely to fail in developing strong loyalty and commitment amongst them.

4 International Human Resource Management

Chapter 4 focuses on the variable IHRM in the Conceptual Model of Factors Affecting HCN Integration. First, an explanation of how the timing and characteristics of the development of Japanese MNCs have shaped their organizational structures is offered. Then the IHRM of Japanese MNCs is described in terms of Perlmutter's (1969) ethnocentric, polycentric, regiocentric, and geocentric paradigm. The section thereafter deals with the centralization/decentralization dichotomy and subsidiary autonomy. In this regard, an analysis of the control systems employed by Japanese and other MNCs as well as subsidiary autonomy indicates that there is a high degree of centralized control in Japanese MNCs. The next section demonstrates how the staffing of foreign subsidiary management positions with Japanese PCNs is an important method of subsidiary control employed by Japanese MNCs. The consequences of these ethnocentric staffing policies are also examined.

Chapter 4 also covers selection and training of PCN managers for overseas assignments and related issues. This establishes the background for interpreting the data that measure the impressions of PCN competence in cross-cultural management positions. In addition the social/cultural environment of Southeast Asia and Australia as well as Japan's overall relationship with these countries is covered. This discussion provides a view of the social, cultural and economic environment in which the Japanese firms covered in my study are operating. The final section discusses reference group theory and its effect on HCN integration.

4.1 PATTERNS OF MNC ORGANIZATIONAL DEVELOPMENT AND IHRM

This section discusses the relationship between patterns of organizational development and patterns of IHRM with a focus on Japanese MNCs. The evolution from a purely domestic to a truly global organization generally involves numerous stages. However, companies do not always develop in the same way or at the same speed, nor do they all go through the same stages.

Most firms begin with an export department, and then when international sales increase they may establish a sales subsidiary. Foreign production often follows the establishment of a sales subsidiary. As the size of FDI increases the organization structure evolves to include an international division. The international division is in charge of all international activities and managed by a senior executive at corporate headquarters. Most organizations at this stage of internationalization place great emphasis on control mechanisms and staff foreign subsidiaries with PCNs (Dowling and Schuler, 1990:23). The subsequent stages of development, depending on the industry, are often going towards becoming geocentric as described later.

4.1.1 Characteristics of the Development of Japanese MNCs and Their FDI

There are a number of factors that have limited the scope of Japanese FDI. First, Japanese MNCs developed later than their European and American counterparts. Japan followed a policy of isolation until 1853 when confronted in Tokyo Bay by the black ships from America led by Commodore Perry. This effort on the part of the US to open Japan for trade contributed to the movement which led to the Meiji era and subsequently Japan's efforts in the later part of the 19th century to emulate the industrialization occurring at that time in Europe and America. It was at this relatively late point in modern world history that Japan embarked on its road to modernization and large Japanese firms began to develop.

Second, most Japanese businessmen suffered from a general lack of experience in dealing with non-Japanese and the inability to communicate effectively enough in a foreign language to carry out international business. Thus, trading companies, or *sogo-shosha*, developed to perform the role importing raw materials, technology, and capital from abroad while exporting Japan's manufactured goods. Sasaki (1981:123-4) argued that while trading companies promoted the manufacturers' internationalization in the short run by providing them with export information and expedient entry into the export market, this process hindered the development of IHRM practices. He concludes that though many Japanese manufacturers seem to have been internationalized in the sense that their products are sold worldwide, they do not have a mechanism to produce the international management resources necessary to integrate their business with the local climate, cultures and management systems.

Third, all overseas investments had to be approved by Japan's Ministry of Finance (MOF) due to exchange controls. Until the late 1960s MOF gave preference to upstream natural resource projects and downstream trade-related operations rather than offshore manufacturing investments. As a result of these factors among others, Japanese manufacturers were slow to expand their international operations beyond the scope of sending a few sales and technical personnel abroad to support exports from their domestic manufacturing facilities.

The timing of the international expansion of MNCs in relation to the evolution of trade liberalization also greatly influenced the pattern of their FDI and their organizational structure. On the one hand, when there were numerous restrictions on the flow of goods and services across borders, many US and European MNCs were obliged to establish manufacturing operations in each national market. Though in the initial stages of development centralization and ethnocentric policies were apparent, over time decentralization and rationalization were the resulting trends in organizational structure among US and European multinationals.

On the other hand, the international expansion of Japanese firms occurred later during the post-war period as trade restrictions were relaxed. Japanese firms were able to centralize production in Japan and penetrate international markets through exports. Thus, Japanese MNCs were able to expand their international business without the same degree of pressure that was applied to US and European firms to engage in FDI in the form of manufacturing facilities in the markets they served. Bartlett and Goshal (1989) offer a similar analysis of the relationship between the characteristics of MNCs and the timing of their development in regard to the liberalization and expansion of international trade.

It was not until the pressure of the strong yen (*endaka* in Japanese) as a result of the Plaza Accord and the protectionist pressures against imports from Japan that Japanese MNCs began in earnest to expand FDI. 'At 180 yen to the dollar, corporations are going to have to reconsider where they want to base production,' explained a manager of Japan's giant Sumitomo Corporation in early 1986, noting that in most cases the choice was only of sink or swim (*Asian Wall Street Journal*, 3 April 1986). Thanks to *endaka*, Japanese capital poured into Asia in ever increasing quantities: 1.6 million US dollars in 1987, 3.6 billion US dollars in 1987 and over five billion US dollars in 1988.

By 1990 the stream had turned into a torrent reaching eight billion US dollars and making Japan the largest foreign investor in Southeast Asia, a position traditionally held by the US and Europe. Despite the massive exodus, by 1990 Japan had only shifted eight per cent of it's manufacturing capacity overseas. This is a small amount compared with the US (17 per cent) and Germany (20 per cent) (Bartu, 1993:47).

The observation that Japanese MNCs were still in the early stages of developing IHRM policies and practices when this surge in FDI began is supported by the research results of various scholars. For example, Kobayashi (1985) studied the patterns of management style developing in Japanese MNCs in the early 1980s and found that many Japanese firms were at the early stages of internationalization that focused on trade with an export department at the home office managing overseas sales of products produced in the home country. Kobayashi concluded that there were many areas in which the multinationalization of Japanese firms lagged behind that of the major MNCs based in the United States and Europe.

Hanada (1989) described five phases in the development of IHRM through which Japanese firms pass as they become increasingly involved in global activities. In phase one the firm's international activities are limited to export of its products and its IHRM function is mainly concentrated in an export department. Entering phase two, a firm establishes foreign assembly or limited production facilities. The increase in human resource requirements is usually handled by creating an overseas operations department. The establishment of an overseas human resource department characterizes phase three, and the structure of the firm is substantially modified to reflect the increasing interaction between domestic and foreign operations. In phase four the firm yields greater control of its international operations to an overseas operations department, allowing for increased decentralization of decision-making. Hanada refers to the fifth and final phase as the 'globalization stage.' When a firm reaches this phase the firm is thoroughly internationalized and there is no distinction between foreign and Japanese employees with the international division.

If non-differentiation between PCN and HCN managers is a criterion of the 'globalization stage' then very few if any Japanese MNCs have even come close to a global approach to human resources. This assertion is supported by Bird and Mukada (1989:438) who found at the time of their study of Japanese IHRM practices that no Japanese MNCs had reached phase five. Furthermore, they stated that during the 1980s as FDI by Japanese firms in the form of overseas production facilities increased dramatically, the firms tried to move quickly from phases one and two through to phase four. However, they maintain that by the end of 1989, it had become apparent that many lacked the necessary manpower to manage their foreign subsidiaries well. This view is confirmed by the results of many other researches as well as the research carried out in this study.

4.1.2 Ethnocentric, Polycentric, Regiocentric and Geocentric IHRM

The evolution of IHRM policies and practices as well as the relationship between the headquarters of an MNC and its subsidiaries have often been discussed using four types of orientation: ethnocentric, polycentric, regiocentric and geocentric. Perlmutter (1969) first introduced these categories and later elaborated on them in co-operation with Heenan (1974 and 1979). The definitions of these categories given below are based on their use by Perlmutter and Heenan (1979:17–21) as well as Dowling and Schuler (1990:35–40 and 48–51).

1. Ethnocentric: The home-country culture and practices are considered to be the most appropriate in managing the foreign subsidiary. The organization of the MNC is highly centralized and there is little decision-making autonomy granted to HCN managers in the subsidiary. PCN managers tend to dominate the key management positions in the foreign subsidiaries. There is a lot of communication between the parent company and the subsidiaries.

The ethnocentric approach tends to coincide with the first stages in the process of the development of MNCs. During these stages the organization tends to be complex in the home country and relatively simple in the overseas subsidiaries. When companies first begin to expand their international operations they usually prefer to rely on management practices with which they are familiar and utilize PCN managers until appropriate HCN managers are found or developed. Perlmutter and Heenan (1979:17) claim that ethnocentrism is often not attributable to prejudice so much as to inexperience. However, in the case of Japanese MNCs, others argue (Fernandez and Barr, 1993; Sethi *et al.*, 1984) that ethnocentrism as a style of IHRM in Japanese organizations is significantly related to the strong ethnocentric attitudes, racism and xenophobia in Japanese culture and society.

The use of PCNs facilitates communication between the parent company and the subsidiary. The parent company can maintain a high degree of control over the operations of the subsidiaries since decision-making authority is in the hands of PCNs who dominate the key management positions. There is usually a lot of advice or directives from the parent company. PCNs bring essential knowledge and experience concerning the company's products and services, company culture, and the actual functioning of the organization in the home country. Thus, PCNs can play an important role in transferring knowledge to the foreign subsidiary and instilling the corporate culture of the parent company.

However, there are substantial problems with the ethnocentric approach. Zeira (1976) revealed that MNCs practising ethnocentric IHRM policies suffered numerous problems such as low productivity, friction between HCN and PCN managers, and high turnover of HCNs. Since PCNs dominate the key management positions the promotion opportunities for HCNs are limited. The ambitious HCN managers wishing to develop their career are often frustrated by the lack of opportunity. As a result their motivation dwindles and they often leave the firm in search of better opportunities. Thus, MNCs practising ethnocentric IHRM policies often suffer high turnover among HCN managers and find it difficult to attract highly qualified HCN candidates to fill managerial positions at their subsidiaries.

There are also problems and costs associated with PCNs themselves. They often suffer from problems related to the adaptation process to the overseas environment. During the adaptation period PCN managers may not be as effective in their job as they were in the home country environment. In addition, PCNs usually receive much higher incomes and more benefits than HCNs. This gap in compensation often leads to friction between the HCNs and the PCNs. Furthermore, the high costs of maintaining PCN managers at foreign subsidiaries are a strain on the profitability of the operations. Finally, there is often a lack of continuity when HCN managers rotate in and out of key management positions.

2. Polycentric: HCNs are considered to be the most suitable candidates for managerial positions at the subsidiary due to their knowledge of local conditions. Thus, the subsidiary is mainly managed by HCN managers and they are granted significant decision-making autonomy. As long as the HCN managers are successful in the management of the subsidiary there is little interference from

the parent company. The MNC treats each subsidiary as a distinct national entity and does not seek to create synergy among them. The organization of the MNC is decentralized. HCN managers are rarely promoted to positions at headquarters.

The advantages of the polycentric approach are that they overcome many of the disadvantages of the ethnocentric approach to IHRM. First, HCN managers have ample opportunity to participate in the management of the subsidiary. Since PCN managers do not dominate key management positions in the polycentric firm there are more career opportunities for HCN managers. Second, the adjustment problems suffered by PCNs are eliminated. Third, HCN managers are more likely than PCN managers to have better knowledge of the host country language, culture, business environment, and government regulations. Finally, there is greater continuity in the management of the subsidiary since the PCN managers do not rotate in and out of the key management positions.

Perhaps the most important disadvantages of the polycentric approach are associated with the development of the headquarters–subsidiary relationship. In polycentric organizations there are few PCN managers at the subsidiaries to help overcome any language and cultural barriers that may occur. The organizational culture of the subsidiaries may also develop differently from that of the parent company. An organizational culture of the local subsidiary in tune with the local environment has advantages, however, if essential positive elements of the parent corporate culture are not incorporated into the corporate cultures of the subsidiaries it may be difficult to share common goals and values throughout the MNC.

Another problem of the polycentric approach is related to HCN and PCN career development. In the case of HCN managers, though they may have more opportunities for career development than is the case when the ethnocentric approach to IHRM is employed, their opportunities are still confined to the local subsidiary. As for PCN managers, their opportunities to gain experience outside the parent company are limited. Lack of international experience among the PCN managers in the parent company makes it more difficult to carry out strategic planning on a global basis and to be sensitive to the needs of foreign subsidiaries.

3. Regiocentric: The organization of the multinational is structured on a regional basis. HCN managers from each region are

considered the best candidates for managerial positions within the region. Like, the geocentric approach, it utilizes a wider pool of managers. However, the managers tend to move within the region but are usually not promoted to managerial positions at headquarters. Each region enjoys a degree of decision-making autonomy.

The regiocentric approach may also be viewed as an expansion of the polycentric approach by considering the units to be regions instead of individual countries. However, unlike the polycentric approach TCNs play an important role in the staffing of management positions in the subsidiaries within each region. PCNs may also be used to a greater extent than they would be in the polycentric approach depending on the type of experience and expertise required. The use of the regiocentric approach to IHRM corresponds with the MNC organizational structure in which co-ordination and control are facilitated by regional offices.

Such a structure and IHRM approach are usually employed when the markets have strong regional characteristics and subsidiaries are highly interdependent on a regional basis. The decision-making authority tends to be concentrated in the regional office and/or there is a high degree of collaboration among subsidiaries in the region. The regiocentric approach incorporates some of the advantages of the polycentric and geocentric approaches. It offers more opportunities for HCNs than both the polycentric and ethnocentric approaches. The disadvantages of the structure are associated with the possible limited interaction between subsidiaries of different regions and between individual subsidiaries and the parent company.

4. Geocentric: Selection of managers is based on ability rather than nationality. The best person for the job no matter where he or she comes from is selected. Geocentric firms seek to co-ordinate decision-making among the subsidiaries and headquarters. The organization is balanced between centralized and decentralized in order to effectively and efficiently employ all types of resources on a global basis. It is common to have TCN managers in geocentric firms.

The geocentric approach has several major advantages. First, this approach to IHRM allows the MNC to develop a group of executives who understand the international operations of the company and use their experience and expertise wherever necessary. Second, it offers the most opportunities for all managerial employees to develop their careers regardless of their nationality. Third, it helps develop a global organizational culture and helps avoid parochialism and the development of limited vision and loyalty. Managers given the opportunity to work throughout the MNCs global network will tend to think in terms of the good of the company as a whole rather than just the good of a certain subsidiary. A global culture facilitates the process of developing and implementing strategic plans for the optimal use of resources on a global scale.

Though the benefits of the geocentric approach in global industries can be substantial, the actual implementation of geocentric IHRM policies is problematic. Most host countries have policies and corresponding regulations restricting the employment of PCNs and TCNs in the local subsidiary in order to promote the employment of HCNs. Thus, even though the HCN managers at the local subsidiaries may benefit greatly in terms of increased career opportunities from a geocentric IHRM approach, host country governments' policies often create stumbling blocks in the way of its implementation. Another problem with geocentric orientation is the cost associated with such practices. There are often extra costs stemming from increased management training, relocation, and a higher overall standardized compensation system for all managers.

Few MNCs probably fit neatly into any single one of these four types and most MNCs will most likely exhibit characteristics from a combination of each of these types of organizations. In the case of ethnocentric organizations management is mainly in the hands of the PCN managers while in the other three types HCN play a greater role. It would appear that ethnocentric firms are at the bottom of the evolutionary ladder while geocentric firms are at the top. However, in some cases forms other than the geocentric form of organization may be appropriate in order to achieve maximum competitive advantage. For example, in multidomestic industries such as distribution and insurance, the competition takes place in each individual country and is essentially independent of competition in other countries. At the other end of the continuum are global industries such as semiconductors and consumer electronics. Porter (1986:18) insists that in a global industry, a firm must in some way integrate its activities on a world-wide basis to capture linkages among countries.

Though twenty to thirty years ago the majority of US and European MNCs had ethnocentric management styles, the IHRM problems they encountered encouraged them to adopt other approaches in recent years. By now, most American and European MNCs have shifted to polycentric, regiocentric, or geocentric forms of organization. On the other hand, Japanese MNCs seem to follow an ethnocentric approach or a compromise somewhere between a pure ethnocentric approach and a pure polycentric approach. Only a few of the most progressive Japanese MNCs have adopted or come close to adopting a truly polycentric, regiocentric, or geocentric approach (Kopp, 1994b:39).

Kopp (1994a) reported the results of a survey comparing IHRM policies and practices in Japanese, European and United States multinational companies. The survey focused on the use of PCNs over HCNs in overseas management positions, adoption of ethnocentric policies, and incidence of IHRM problems. These problems included the inability of the MNC to fully utilize the talents of non-PCNs, re-entry problems for PCNs returning home, general discontent among HCN managers, HCN dissatisfaction with communication and decision-making, HCN frustration with limited promotion opportunities, and high turnover of local employees. Kopp demonstrated an empirical link between ethnocentric policies and practices and the occurrence of IHRM problems. Regression analysis on the entire sample indicated that ethnocentric staffing and policies are associated with higher incidence of IHRM problems. Furthermore, the results revealed that the IHRM policies and practices of Japanese MNCs are more ethnocentric than those of US and European MNCs. Consequently, Japanese MNCs experience more IHRM problems than do American and European MNCs.

Schenk (1988) studied the relative geocentricism of Japanese and US multinationals. Simply stated, he defines geocentric management as taking a global view of people, markets and resources, using these resources without regard to the source of those resources. He compared the FDI of Japanese and US MNCs in developing countries on the basis of industry codes and host country economic status. He concludes that US are more geocentric than Japanese MNCs. This conclusion is drawn from the literature as well as the results from his research, which demonstrated that US MNCs are in more developing countries and have more affiliates in those countries than Japanese MNCs do. Furthermore, Schenk concluded that Japanese FDI was often in response to protectionist measures taken by foreign countries rather than part of a strategy for developing a global network.

4.1.3 IHRM Development During Times of Rapid International Expansion

Whenever a firm experiences rapid development of its international operations, regardless of its national origin, the firm can expect to confront difficulties in keeping pace with the corresponding human resource needs. However, the difficulties may be more acute in the case of Japanese firms compared to American firms. The logic to support this contention is found in contrasting the different approaches of Japanese firms and American firms to the acquisition and development of human resources.

Historically, Japanese firms have been characterized as resource accumulators rather than resource deployers (Kagono et al., 1985). As discussed in detail in Chapter 3, Japanese firms in the domestic environment, large firms in particular, prefer to hire new employees directly out of school without any previous experience. These practices are often accompanied by the practice of long-term employment and job-rotation for the development of generalists. That is to say, Japanese firms tend to accumulate human resources by developing and retaining them in-house (the same concept as the development of an internal labour market).

It is engaging in exaggerated stereotyping to say the American firms are merely deployers of human resources rather than accumulators, since there are obviously HR development programmes at US companies. However, it is true that American companies are more apt than Japanese companies to hire personnel with experience for their expertise to fill a specific need. Thus, the difference in the way Japanese and American MNCs confront greater requirements for human resources in times of rapid economic expansion stems from the Japanese preference to develop such resources and the American willingness to hire skilled white-collar employees from the open job market. Obviously, the latter approach allows for greater flexibility.

4.2 CENTRALIZATION VS DECENTRALIZATION

Centralization/decentralization has been conceptualized in various ways. However, the most widely used definition is the level of the organizational hierarchy at which similar decisions are made (Takamiya, 1985). This is the concept adopted here for the discussion of the degree of centralization in Japanese firms. First centralization is discussed by examining the characteristics of the typical control systems used in Japanese firms. Thereafter, centralization is discussed in terms of subsidiary autonomy.

4.2.1 Control Systems

The control structure of Japanese companies has a significant impact on their ability to integrate HCN managers into the management process of their foreign subsidiaries. This point may be illustrated by contrasting what may be considered as typical control systems in the majority of Japanese and US multinationals. There are two major control systems: output-oriented control and culture-oriented control systems (Dowling and Schuler, 1990:30).

An output-oriented control system focuses on objective, measurable data such as financial results and profitability indices. The managers' actions are controlled by the fact that they must act in such a way that their output matches the performance goals expected of them. In contrast, culture-oriented control systems are less clear-cut, being based on socialization of employees so that they understand the company's culture and goals. The managers' actions are controlled by training that leads them to act in accordance with accepted standards of behaviour within the company (Kopp, 1994b). Lebas and Weigenstein (1986) claim that an organization has shifted towards culture along the continuum of approaches to control when objectives, rules and procedures, and roles become internalized.

There are no MNCs that rely completely on one system, and actual control systems employed combine both output-oriented and culture-oriented elements (Ray, 1986). Nevertheless, control systems may be classified as dominated either by output-oriented or culture-oriented elements. In the case of US MNCs output-oriented elements tend to dominate while in the case of Japanese MNCs culture-oriented elements tend to dominate. The US control system has developed in a labour market where there is substantial mobility among white-collar workers. Thus, even though US firms may understand the value of a strong corporate culture and commitment, the structure of the firms in terms of role definition and job responsibility is usually well-defined and correspondingly there are usually clear output-oriented measurements to monitor and encourage good performance.

On the other hand, the Japanese control systems have developed along with the practice of *shushinkoyo* (lifetime or long-term employment).

Job responsibilities and measurements tend to be vague since the emphasis is on teamwork rather than individual effort. Japanese MNCs seek to develop generalists who are strongly indoctrinated in the company culture. Managers are frequently rotated to offer them experience in various departments and divisions as well as in order to promote co-ordination and teamwork in the firm. During this rotation process the managers also have the opportunity to develop the all-important *jin-myaku* or human network throughout the corporation in order to facilitate decision-making. Lebas and Weigenstein (1986) also discussed the difference in control systems based on national culture. They asserted that the collectivist tradition, dominant in Japan, finds culture a natural control approach, while US national culture is strongly individualistic and culture's importance and efficacy are accordingly underplayed.

Another way to view the reasons for the differences in the control systems employed by US and Japanese MNCs is to examine the role versus person dichotomy. US MNCs may be viewed more as a set of roles than a set of people, while Japanese MNCs are more a set of people than roles. That is not to say that the quality of the people performing the roles is not considered important in US MNCs. On the contrary, US MNCs seek to employ the best possible people to perform the roles. Thus, there are usually clear measurements to determine how well a person performs a particular role. If there is a mismatch between the person and the role, alternative roles may be sought for the person if the person is considered valuable to the organization, otherwise the person may be fired.

On the other hand, Japanese MNCs put less emphasis on the role and seek to develop people who can work together to accomplish the tasks which are not very clearly assigned to any particular roles and individual measurements are not well-defined. The output-oriented controls allow MNCs to delegate more authority to HCNs in their foreign subsidiaries. Since the well-defined roles are relatively easy to communicate, MNCs can seek the best HCN manager to perform a given role. In contrast, the greater reliance on culture-oriented controls in Japanese MNCs inhibits the entrusting of employees with managerial authority. PCN employees at Japanese MNCs absorb the company culture over many years and it is not possible to achieve the same level of cultural inculcation with HCN managers in foreign subsidiaries. Furthermore, due to the fact that corporate culture in Japan is firmly embedded in Japanese culture it is difficult to transmit to non-Japanese employees.

4.2.2 Subsidiary Autonomy

From 1976, the Institute of International Business at the Stockholm School of Economics carried out a major research project with a focus on managing relations between headquarters and foreign operations. The project involved researchers and MNCs from multiple countries. Though this research is dated, it offers an interesting insight into how misunderstandings concerning Japanese management occur. In a summary of the findings, Otterbeck (1981) discusses the degree of influence subsidiary management have over a set of decisions.

This set includes decisions on such items as production schedules, pricing, cash flow, borrowing funds from local banks, and choice of advertising agency. The data were collected from a sample of 158 subsidiaries of 39 MNCs originating from the US, Japan, Germany, Sweden and the UK. Otterbeck argues that there is a very strong indication of the existence of one world-wide norm for managing MNCs, accepted and used by all MNCs but with strong national bias (Otterbeck, 1981:340–41). Otterbeck also maintains that the same data demonstrate that Sweden and Japan are the two countries that give their subsidiaries the highest autonomy.

However, in the analysis of their data Otterbeck and his fellow researchers did not consider the real nature of decision-making autonomy in Japanese subsidiaries. The data did not indicate who at the Japanese subsidiaries made the decisions and how they were made. That is to say, were the managers in positions of decision-making authority in the subsidiaries mainly Japanese PCNs or HCNs, and to what extent did the parent company influence or control the decision-making? Failing to address these issues yielded the conclusion that Sweden and Japan were the two countries that give their subsidiaries the highest autonomy.

My research as well as research carried out by numerous other researchers (discussed below) indicate that management positions in Japanese subsidiaries are filled by PCNs to a much greater extent than is the case with US and European subsidiaries. Furthermore, the nature of Japanese decision-making is such that the PCN managers maintain close contact with the management at headquarters and they rarely make any significant decision without the knowledge and approval of headquarters. There is considerable evidence supporting this contention not only from my research but from that of many others as well. For example, Thome and McAuley (1992:87) report that control from the head office is intense and there is a great deal of consultation between the PCNs at the subsidiaries and the parent company concerning almost all decisions.

In my study of decision-making at Japanese foreign subsidiaries (Keeley and Doi, 1995 and 1996), I sought to ascertain who (PCN or HCN) had the most influence in the decision-making process concerning numerous items that include those investigated by Otterbeck. A true comparative understanding of decision-making autonomy of foreign subsidiaries cannot be attained without considering the PCN/HCN dichotomy and the nature of the decision-making process of the MNCs. A conclusion that Japanese subsidiaries enjoy a high degree of autonomy can lead to the hypothesis that HCN managers in Japanese foreign subsidiaries may have a substantial degree of decision-making autonomy. The data I present in this book in Chapter 6 clearly shows this is not usually the case.

4.3 STAFFING OF FOREIGN SUBSIDIARY MANAGEMENT POSITIONS

This section focuses on the issues concerned with the staffing of management positions in overseas subsidiaries. First of all, there is additional discussion of the positive and negative aspects of staffing management positions with PCN, HCN and TCNs. Thereafter, the assertion that the top management positions of Japanese foreign subsidiaries are dominated by PCNs is examined by reviewing the results of other researchers. Finally, the phenomenon of HCNs as expatriates in their own country is discussed.

4.3.1 Positive and Negative Aspects of PCN, HCN and TCN Staffing

There is evidence indicating that PCN domination of management positions in foreign subsidiaries negatively affects performance. Yoshihara (1996:7–9) claims there is a possible cause–effect relationship between the comparatively low profitability of Japanese subsidiaries and lack of management localization. This assertion is supported by data gathered by Pucik *et al.* (1989:36–7). They found that in many decision-making areas, as well as in the aggregate, the size of the localization gap was negatively correlated with most performance measures:

Firms where executives perceived a smaller localization gap performed better. Specifically, the overall performance and employee morale are affected the most. Product development, pricing decisions and reward systems for executives are the three areas where the perceived localization gap may have the most impact on the performance of the subsidiary.

In addition, Yoshihara (1996) identifies three other general problems. First, since basically Japanese foreign subsidiaries are managed by Japanese PCNs it is difficult to meet the expectations of HCN managers for promotions. Furthermore, since HCN managers are not involved in making important decisions they do not often experience a will to participate or sense of achievement, and frustration is common. Secondly, superior managers have a strong desire to be promoted and receive delegation of authority. It is difficult for Japanese subsidiaries to meet the expectations of superior HCN managers and they usually end up quitting. Thirdly, there are problems and high costs associated with having to send so many PCNs from Japan to manage overseas subsidiaries. Japanese managers are often reluctant to leave the parent company to work in a foreign subsidiary. They sometimes suffer from lack of motivation and desire to return to the parent company.

Furthermore, Amago (1992:133–4) found in his studies of overseas Japanese subsidiaries an inverse relationship between the number of Japanese PCN managers and the level of satisfaction of HCN managers. Amago claims that the source of dissatisfaction is not related to prejudices of the HCN managers. Instead, he offers the following four reasons for the dissatisfaction (my translation from Japanese):

1. A large number of Japanese PCNs lowers the overall average managerial ability.
2. HCN subordinates believe that Japanese PCNs have a poor understanding of local society, culture and people.
3. HCN subordinates feel that the company is not becoming localized and there is a colonial-type control.
4. Japanese PCN managers experience difficulties in absorbing accurate information from their HCN subordinates making it problematic to develop highly reliable plans.

There are numerous advantages to be gained by employing HCN managers, most of which are presented in Chapter 1 and the previous discussion of the ethnocentric–geocentric IHRM continuum. Due to these advantages, other researchers have indicated that there is a trend towards increasing HCN staffing. For example, Pucik points out that most global firms have moved forward to implement major programmes aimed at increasing the participation of HCNs in the management of foreign subsidiaries (1992:69):

> Tapping into the potential of local managers is in line with the focus on global human resources. One of the driving forces behind this development is the sound belief that hiring local nationals may be a good strategy to limit the resentment of foreign managerial dominance in the subsidiary. The focus on developing a strong local management team may help satisfy the rising ambitions and expectations of many local employees and also cuts immediate staffing costs by eliminating transfer-related expenses and adjustments.

On the other hand, Kobrin (1988) argues that the reduction in the use of expatriates by American MNCs has gone too far and has resulted in costs in terms of identification with the global strategy and organizational control, and the internationalization of managers. However, Kobrin is not advocating that US firms return to an ethnocentric approach and staff all the key managerial positions at US foreign subsidiaries with PCN managers. On the contrary, his argument actually calls for a more global approach to IHRM. He simply bemoans the fact that fewer American PCN managers are gaining experience abroad. Kobrin believes that the solution is to carry out managerial selection on the basis of qualifications regardless of nationality; that any individual joining the company in any country in the world would have the same chance of becoming CEO. However, he argues that unless the expertise from overseas assignments is gained in other ways, Americans may simply become unqualified for top management roles in the future. Thus he advocates short-term expatriate assignments whose purpose is avowedly development for both the individual and the organization.

As previously stated, a firm that follows a geocentric IHRM strategy seeks to choose the best individuals regardless of nationality. Thus, in a global firm one would expect to find TCN managers as well as HCN and PCN managers. Phillips is a good example of a firm with a global IHRM strategy. Phillips considers it very important to develop interdisciplinary skills and an international perspective. The candidates considered having the most potential for tomorrow's top management positions are usually sent abroad for at least three to four years. Phillips considers on-the-job training, coupled with multicultural experience to be the best development tool they can provide. It is Phillips' goal to internationalize management. The performance and appraisal systems allow them to identify the best people in different countries, placing them in jobs where they are most needed. Van Houten (1989:110), a member of the management board at Phillips comments:

> The job rotation practice leads to a rich exchange of perspective. When you send a Norwegian to Brazil, a Pakistani to Singapore, or an American to the Netherlands, the cultural influences that are traded are bound to result in an international point of view in the company as a whole. There are problems in managing such international exchanges. These range from salary levels in different countries to the cultural shocks of adjusting to different standards of living.

4.3.2 Japanese Foreign Subsidiaries Dominated by PCN Managers

A number of researchers have carried out studies over the past 20 to 30 years comparing the staffing of Japanese overseas subsidiaries with America and European foreign subsidiaries. For illustrative purposes a number of these studies are examined in this section. The gist of the results indicates a dominance of management positions of authority by Japanese PCN managers in their subsidiaries around the world. This problem has received significant attention by government authorities not only in the host countries but in Japan as well. For instance, the Japanese Ministry of Trade and Industry (MITI) aware of the problem of overstaffing subsidiaries with Japanese nationals, issued a guidance that the Japanese–local employee ratio should be at least 1:30 (Sethi *et al.*, 1984:172–3). It is remarkable that studies carried out in the 1970s appear to yield almost the same results as recent studies carried out in the 1990s.

First, studies carried out in the 1970s by Tsurumi (1976a:190–3 and 260–1) of Japanese overseas operations in Asia indicated that Japanese affiliates had three to four times as many PCN managers and engineers than comparable American or European enterprises. Compared with their occidental counterparts, PCNs in Japanese affiliates even occupied very low-level management positions in the organizational hierarchy. Furthermore, while American and European companies hired TCNs, Japanese did not.

Negandhi (1980) also compared the human resource practices of American, European, and Japanese MNCs in their foreign subsidiaries by interviewing the top executives of 124 MNCs as well as many other individuals in the host countries where the MNCs are located. He claims that the IHRM policies of American MNCs have been acclaimed as the most advanced and sophisticated; a fact acknowledged not only by host government officials, educators, and union leaders, but also by executives of the European and Japanese multinationals themselves. The reasons given are (Negandhi, 1980:152):

American MNCs have been regarded as fair and equitable in dealing with their employees in terms of providing attractive wages and salaries, fringe benefits, training, and promotion opportunities. Because of such enlightened personnel policies, other industrial and commercial enterprises, including European and Japanese MNCs, have experienced difficulties in attracting and retaining a high-level workforce in the developing countries. American MNCs were also the first to deal with the demand of the developing countries to localize management of foreign subsidiaries.

Negandhi (1980) found that the majority of the top-level executive positions in the US subsidiaries were filled with HCNs while Japanese multinationals (78.9 per cent) did not employ even one single HCN in the top-level management ranks. His study also indicates that Japanese multinationals are likely to employ Japanese personnel, even down the organizational ladder, despite the availability of skilled and competent personnel in the host country. He states that it was not uncommon in Japanese multinationals to find that their first-line supervisors were Japanese nationals and that such practices contributed quite significantly to the operational-level problems with which the Japanese multinationals were plagued.

Later, Tung (1984a) obtained data from 80 US MNCs and 35 Japanese MNCs concerning their staffing policies of overseas subsidiaries. Though in her book in which this data is presented Tung makes a case for Japanese MNCs providing superior training of PCNs for overseas assignments, the data she gathered may be applied to the analysis at hand. Her data for Japanese subsidiaries in the US clearly show that at the time of her study Japanese PCN managers dominated the senior level (83 per cent) and middle level (73 per cent) management positions. Furthermore, Japanese PCNs even occupied 40 per cent of the lower level positions.

In addition, there is a marked contrast between Japanese firms and US firms in all the eight regions studied by Tung. Japanese MNCs employed considerably more PCNs in their overseas operations at all levels, particularly at the senior and middle levels. In the case of US MNCs, PCN managers held 33 per cent of the senior level, five per cent of the middle level, and none of the lower level managerial positions. On the other hand, Japanese PCN managers occupied 77 per cent of the senior level, 43 per cent of the middle level, and 23 per cent of the lower level managerial positions. Furthermore, in Tung's data set TCNs were rarely employed by Japanese MNCs, they only appeared in seven per cent of the senior level management positions in Africa where only 29 per cent of the Japanese firms responding had subsidiaries. On the other hand, TCN managers were employed at various management levels in all the regions in the case of US MNCs.

Tung (1984a:7–8) also asked the respondents to identify the reasons for staffing overseas operations with PCNs, HCNs and TCNs. For the US sample, the most important reasons mentioned for staffing with PCNs and the relative frequencies with which the reasons were cited were: (1) foreign enterprise is just being established (70 per cent) and (2) technical expertise (68 per cent). The most important reasons for staffing with HCNs and the relative frequencies with which the reasons were cited were: (1) familiarity with culture (83 per cent); (2) knowledge of language (79 per cent); (3) reduced costs (61 per cent); and (4) good public relations (58 per cent). The most important reasons for staffing with TCNs and the relative frequencies with which the reasons cited were: (1) technical expertise (55 per cent) and (2) TCN is the best man for the job, all things considered (53 per cent).

For the Japanese sample, the most important reason for staffing with PCNs and the relative frequency with which the reason cited was, PCN is the best man for the job, all things considered (55 per cent). All the other reasons were considered relative unimportant. Japanese MNCs gave the same response pattern for why they selected HCNs as managers. Since Japanese firms rarely used TCNs as managers no reason was given for their selection.

There are some interesting points that should be made concerning this data. First of all, the response is 'the best man for the job, all things considered' was cited by the US as one of the most important reasons only in the case of TCNs. On the other hand, it is the only reason considered important by the Japanese firms in all cases. In the case of US firms this response seems very appropriate given the difficulties associated with employing TCN managers in overseas subsidiaries such as visas. A firm would be willing to deal with these extra difficulties only if the person were truly the 'best man for the job, all things considered.' On the other hand, Japanese firms are obviously using this response as a *tatemae* or response for public consumption, and not revealing their *honne* or real reasons why PCN managers are employed to such a great extent at all managerial levels in overseas subsidiaries.

Kobayashi (1985) carried out a study using the hiring and promotion of locally recruited employees (HCNs) for managerial positions as a measure of a firm's multinationalization (globalization). For this purpose he developed the following scale: one point to firms with no HCNs having ever been promoted to managerial positions in their overseas subsidiaries, two points to firms with some HCNs in managerial positions, three points to firms that encourage the exchange of HCN managers among their overseas subsidiaries, four points to firms which employ HCNs in higher management levels of their organizations, and five points to firms which treat HCNs equally with PCNs. He applied this instrument to 89 Japanese firms and nine major European and US firms. The average score of the Japanese firms sampled was only 1.6, in contrast to the US and European firms' score of 5.0.

Shiraki (1995:8) presented data on Japanese PCN managers in Japanese foreign subsidiaries in Korea, Taiwan, Hong Kong, Singapore, and Thailand. The data were based on a survey of 255 Japanese subsidiaries in these countries carried out by *Shakai Keizai Kokumin Kaigi*, a Japanese research organization, in 1989. There were significant differences between subsidiaries wholly owned by the parent company and joint ventures as well as differences between subsidiaries located in different countries. In the case of joint ventures it was more common to have an HCN as president. However, in almost 98 per cent of wholly owned subsidiaries the president was a Japanese PCN.

The Ministry of International Trade and Industry (MITI) surveyed 1043 Japanese corporations and their overseas subsidiaries in comparison with 1052 foreign companies operating in Japan for the fiscal year 1986 (1 April, 1986–31 March, 1987). The results (MITI, 1987) also show that Japanese companies are far more likely to staff management positions in their foreign subsidiaries with PCNs than foreign companies operating in Japan. Similar data resulted from MITI's (1991) *Dai Yon Kai Kaigai Jigyo Katudo Kohon Chosa*, (the Fourth Study of the Activities of Firms Overseas).

According to this MITI study, the position of highest managerial responsibility *(saiko keiei sekininsha)* is occupied by a Japanese PCN in 82 per cent of Japanese subsidiaries in North America, 73.1 per cent of Japanese subsidiaries in Europe, and 63.9 per cent of Japanese subsidiaries in Asia. The MITI study also gives figures for the percentage of departments that are headed by Japanese managers. In North America these figures are 51.8 per cent for the human resources department, 66.1 per cent for the accounting department, 51 per cent for the sales department, 53.8 per cent for the research and development department, and 58.2 per cent for the planning department. The figures given for Japanese subsidiaries in Europe and Asia are similar, Japanese managers occupy approximately half of the top positions in these departments.

An example of a more recent study is that carried out by Kopp (1994a). She reported results from a survey of Japanese, European and US subsidiaries concerning staffing. The survey results indicated that there is a 'glass ceiling' for HCNs at MNCs of all three nationalities included in the survey. However, this 'glass ceiling' is substantially lower in Japanese MNCs since the percentage of PCNs in the top positions at Japanese overseas subsidiaries (74 per cent, $n = 26$) is greater than those at American (31 per cent, $n = 20$) and European (48 per cent, $n = 21$) overseas subsidiaries. In addition, while a TCN held the top position in some of the US (18 per cent) and European (eight per cent) firms included in the sample, no TCN was in the top position in the Japanese firms. Furthermore, the percentage of HCNs in all managerial positions in Japanese overseas subsidiaries (48 per cent, $n = 27$) was substantially lower than in US (88 per cent, $n = 22$) and European (82 per cent, $n = 17$) subsidiaries.

In addition, Yoshihara (1996:1–6) compared the data from MITI's 1991 study with the data he obtained from US and European subsidiaries in Japan and found a sharp contrast. In the European and US subsidiaries in Japan surveyed by Yoshihara, a Japanese HCN held the position of highest managerial responsibility *(saiko keiei sekininsha)* in 63 per cent of the cases. His data also indicate that Japanese HCNs ran most of the departments; 92 per cent of the general affairs departments, 92 per cent of the human resource departments, 84 per cent of the accounting departments, 83 per cent for the sales departments, 87 per cent for the production departments, and 81 per cent for the research and development departments.

Japanese MNCs will not make significant progress in localization of the management of their foreign subsidiaries until they implement organizational and operational practices to create and environment that will attract and retain HCN managers. An indication of the problems that must be addressed may be understood by considering a comment made by Pucik *et al.* (1989:88):

> For the large majority of the American managers and executives with whom we met, a long-term career with a Japanese company was seriously considered. However, the perceived exclusion from decision-making and strategic planning, the absence of training and management development programmes, and the apparent lack of career opportunities discouraged even the most loyal and determined individuals from long-term commitment to the company. Strengthening the human resource management system is necessary to enhance the recruitment, motivation and retention of capable American executives; this in turn will improve the effectiveness of the top management team.

4.3.3 HCN as Expatriates in Their Own Country

Bird and Mukada (1989) reported on Japanese MNCs hiring foreign students in Japan upon graduation and later sending them to their own country to work in the management of the MNCs' foreign subsidiary in that country. Kurata (1990) also reported on the phenomenon in his research on HCNs in Japanese companies. He interviewed 33 foreign employees at seven Japanese companies. There appeared to be two main benefits of hiring foreigners first to work in Japan and then back in their home country. First of all, these HCNs can gain a good understanding of the parent company and act as a link between the Japanese headquarters and the foreign subsidiary. Secondly, by assigning foreign nationals to various sections and departments in the company as generalists, the company expects them to have a positive impact on their Japanese co-workers in the sense of helping them think more internationally.

4.4 ISSUES CONCERNING STAFFING WITH PCNs

As discussed above there are both advantages and disadvantages in employing PCN and HCN managers. Certainly each subsidiary operates in a unique environment; thus, no single staffing policy can

International Human Resource Management 121

hope to meet the needs of different subsidiaries (Boyacigiller, 1990 and 1986). However, given that there are always cases in which it is decided to send PCN managers to foreign subsidiaries, this section focuses on their selection and the training they receive for overseas assignments as well as other related issues such as repatriation. The effectiveness of PCN managers directly affects the integration of HCN managers into the management process.

4.4.1 Selection Criteria and Cross-Cultural Adaptation/ Management Skills

It is essential to select PCNs who have a high probability of success in a management position at a foreign subsidiary. The costs of expatriate assignment failure are heavy. In the case of US MNCs, Caudron (1992) cites an estimate between 250,000 and one million US dollars, depending on the employee's salary, location and whether the family was involved. Sohn (1994) points out that possessing and developing social knowledge, cross-cultural management skills, and cultural–linguistic communication abilities are essential to the success of PCN managers at foreign subsidiaries.

According to a survey of human resource and other executives conducted by Beamish and Calof (1989), communication skills were ranked as the most important skills for positions of international responsibility. When the HCN manager does not speak the native language of the parent company, foreign language ability is one of the cross-cultural communication skills that the PCN manager should posses. Certainly, in all cases, PCN managers should have a good understanding of the local culture as well as of their own culture.

The topic of PCN adjustment to the environment of the foreign subsidiary has received considerable scholarly attention (for example: Mendenhall and Wiley, 1994; Black *et al.*, 1991; Tung, 1988, 1987, 1984a, 1982, 1981; Mendenhall and Oddou, 1986, 1985). In a number of such studies the importance of the family adjustment is also treated. For example, Briody and Chrisman (1991) indicate that in the case of US subsidiaries, adaptation problems experienced by the spouses of PCN managers are one of the main causes of poor PCN manager performance or failure. In the case of Japanese PCN managers this tends to be less of a factor. One of the reasons is that many Japanese PCN managers will work at a foreign subsidiary and leave the family in Japan *(tanshin funin)* for reasons such as continuity in the children's education. Or another reason is that when the family accompanies the PCN manager, the wife will be much less likely to complain about any problems with adjusting to the local culture and general environment, she will endure it in silence *(gaman)*.

4.4.2 PCN Training and Factors Affecting Performance

Effective training in MNCs is considered to be an essential element of IHRM. Cross-cultural management training aims at achieving three related outcomes. Black and Mendenhall (1990) state that the training teaches: about the other culture; how to adjust to the other culture; and factors relating to job-performance within the other culture. Mendenhall and Oddou (1986:73) argue that the PCN acculturation process has not been understood well enough and that the research in expatriate acculturation has tended to address the phenomenon in a one-dimensional approach, often ignoring other variables that may affect acculturation. Variation in individual behaviour patterns plays an important role in determining subsequent acculturation, productivity and failure of PCNs. Thus, they developed a taxonomy of PCN acculturation profiles employing three factors (self-orientation, others-orientation, and perceptual orientation).

Though no specific research data applying these profiles to Japanese PCN managers appears to be available, assertions may be made based on observations of Japanese PCN behaviour patterns. The others-orientation factor refers to the degree to which PCN managers are concerned about HCN co-workers and desires to affiliate with them. It also includes relationship development and the willingness to communicate. Though there will always be notable exceptions among Japanese PCN managers, there is substantial evidence that the majority of Japanese PCN managers appear not to develop strong relationships with HCN managers and that there are substantial communication difficulties between the two groups (for example: Keeley and Doi, 1995 and 1996; Oyama, 1994; Bartu, 1993; Nishida, 1991 and 1985).

Kobayashi (1985:238) measured the ways in which corporations train and supervise the PCNs they send abroad in order to evaluate the degree of multinationalization (globalization). For this purpose he developed the following scale: five points to a firm whose training and supervision are fully integrated into its corporation-wide operations as a long- or medium-term project; four points to firms in which such activities are restricted to the overseas project department alone; three points to firms which have no systematic programme but are careful in rotating managers between the home office and overseas operating units; two points if the firm depends on employees recruited from other firms in its overseas operations; and one point to firms which give no special consideration to any programme.

He applied this instrument to 89 Japanese firms and nine major European and US firms. The average score for the Japanese firms was 3.7 while that of the European and US firms was 5.0. All of the United States and European firms studied incorporated training and supervision for employees sent abroad into their regular, long-term career development programmes. More than a third (38 per cent) of the Japanese firms surveyed employ a similar system, while nearly half (49 per cent) take the special demands of work overseas into account in rotating personnel between the home office and branches abroad, though there is no systematic programme.

4.4.3 Repatriation Adjustment of PCNs

The other side of PCN adjustment to the environment of the foreign subsidiary is repatriation adjustment. PCN managers returning to Japan often experience a type of quarantine, which is an effort to rid the PCN managers of the foreign cultural and psychological contamination. The term for this foreign contamination in Japanese is *nanpo boke*, which literally means tropical amnesia. This quarantine includes practices such as keeping recently returned PCNs at the same level for a while without any promotions. During this decontamination period the PCN managers are scrutinized to see if they are still Japanese.

Another factor making repatriation adjustment difficult for some Japanese managers is the differences in housing and general living conditions between Japan and the country where the overseas subsidiary is located. Japanese managers interviewed in White's (1988) study indicated that housing was a serious repatriation problem. This is particularly true if the PCN manager works in crowded areas of Japan such as Tokyo or Osaka and is returning from a subsidiary where much more spacious housing is affordable such as certain areas of the US or even in many developing countries. The standard of living is Japan is very negatively affected by crowding in urban areas where the headquarters of many Japanese MNCs are located. Therefore, the general living conditions at overseas subsidiaries are often better. The returning Japanese manager may also find it difficult to adjust to the expectation of working late hours at the home office.

Black (1994) indicated that age was a positively related to Japanese managers' ability to readjust. The older PCNs had a much easier time readjusting than the younger PCNs. Black postulates that younger PCN managers are more open to the conditioning of the foreign environment and are less willing to conform once again to the norms of Japan than the older PCN managers. Furthermore, older PCN managers have more connections at the parent company, which allow them to stay informed and thereby facilitate their re-entry.

4.5 SOCIAL CULTURAL ENVIRONMENT IN SOUTHEAST ASIA AND AUSTRALIA

I gathered data from Japanese subsidiaries in four countries: Australia, Malaysia, Singapore and Thailand. Thus, it is important to include a discussion of the general business and cultural environment in each of these countries. Furthermore, the relationship between the Japanese and the peoples of Asia and Australia is also considered in this section.

4.5.1 Application of Hofstede's Dimensions

The literature on cross-cultural management and work-related value systems contains many examples of the application of Hofstede's dimensions. Thus, it is appropriate to apply these dimensions in an analysis of Japan and the four countries where the Japanese subsidiaries included in this research are located. First, a short review of Hofstede's work in this area is given. Hofstede used data from a survey of IBM employees at the companies various subsidiaries around the globe to compare national work-related value systems. On the basis of the data from respondents in forty countries, he identified four value dimensions, which together explain about 50 per cent of the differences among work-related value patterns (Hofstede 1980).

The set of countries was later expanded to fifty plus three multi-country regions. The four dimensions were named (Hofstede, 1985:347):

1. Power Distance, which is the extent to which the members of a society accept that power in institutions and organizations is distributed unequally.

2. Uncertainty Avoidance, which is the degree to which the members of a society feel uncomfortable with uncertainty and ambiguity, and which leads them to support beliefs promising certainty and to maintain institutions protecting conformity.
3. Individualism, which stands for a preference for a loosely knit social framework in a society in which individuals are supposed to take care of themselves and their families only; as opposed to Collectivism, which stands for a preference for a tightly knit social framework in which individuals can expect their relatives, clan, or other in-group to look after them, in exchange for unquestioning loyalty.
4. Masculinity, which stands for a preference for achievement, heroism, assertiveness, and material success; as opposed to Femininity, which stands for a preference for relationships, modesty, caring for the weak, and the quality of life. In a masculine society, even the women prefer assertiveness (at least in men); in a feminine society, even men prefer modesty.

As discussed in Chapter 2, national culture (national values) shapes organizational culture (organizational values) along with other factors such as the values of the founder of the organization as well as its present leaders. However, even though the founders of organizations are unique individuals, they are also children of a national culture, so the founders' national values appear to be reflected in the values of their organizations, even if the organizations spread internationally (Hofstede, 1985:349). As argued in Chapter 2, in spite of variations in organizational culture among Japanese MNCs, the similarities are greater than the differences. Thus, it is possible to predict, on a very general level, the fit between the work-related values of Japanese overseas subsidiaries and the work-related values of the HCN managers applying Hofstede's dimensions.

Hofstede asserts that the dimensions of Power Distance and Uncertainty Avoidance affect the structuring and functioning of organizations (Hofstede, 1985:352):

> The two central problems in any organizing act are, after all, how to distribute power (who should decide about what?) and how to control uncertainty (in members' behaviour, in the quality of output, and for assuring continuity). The organizing act itself consists in the manipulation of symbols, which should induce in members the intended behaviour. But this presupposes that members are

culturally conditioned to attach the intended meaning to these symbols, such as job titles, written instructions, reward and punishments.

Hofstede (1980:320) states that large Power Distance plus strong Uncertainty Avoidance leads to people viewing an organization as a 'pyramid of people,' that is a hierarchical bureaucracy. Small Power Distance plus strong Uncertainty Avoidance leads to viewing it as a 'well-oiled machine,' that is an impersonal bureaucracy. Small Power Distance plus weak Uncertainty Avoidance leads to viewing it as a 'village market,' that is an ad-hocracy. Large Power Distance plus weak Uncertainty Avoidance leads to viewing it as a 'family.' Referring to Hofstede's data (1985:351) where 50 countries are plotted on a matrix of small to large Power Distance index (x-axis) and small to large Uncertainty Avoidance index (y-axis), classifications can be obtained for the countries involved in this research.

Japan is in the large Power Distance plus strong Uncertainty Avoidance quadrant. However, its position is just barely inside the large Power Distance side while very clearly in the strong Uncertainty Avoidance side. Thus, according to Hofstede's definition, Japanese tend to view organizations as a 'pyramid of people.' Thailand is also in the same quadrant as Japan but not part of the same cluster drawn by Hofstede. Thailand's position indicates that the degree of strength of its Power Distance is slightly greater than that of Japan, while the size of its Uncertainty Avoidance is much smaller than that of Japan. Therefore, according to Hofstede's classification, while the Thai people also tend to view organizations as a 'pyramid of people' there is also a slight tendency towards viewing it as a family.

Malaysia is in the large Power Distance plus weak Uncertainty Avoidance quadrant. Thus, according to Hofstede's definition, Malaysians tend to view organizations as a 'family.' It should be noted that Malaysia has the largest Power Distance index of all the 50 countries plotted on Hofstede's matrix. Singapore is also in the large Power Distance plus weak Uncertainty Avoidance quadrant. Thus, according to Hofstede's definition, Singaporeans also tend to view organizations as a 'family.' It should be noted that Singapore has the weakest Uncertainty Avoidance index of all the 50 countries plotted on Hofstede's matrix. Australia is in the small Power Distance plus weak Uncertainty Avoidance quadrant. Thus, according to Hofstede's definition, Australians also tend to view organizations as a 'village market.'

The countries may also be classified using Hofstede's other two dimensions (Masculinity/Femininity index and Individualism/Collectivism index). Japan is collectivist and masculine. The masculinity index was the strongest out of all 50 countries. The collectivism index was not as strong as those of Singapore, Malaysia and Thailand. Malaysia, Singapore and Thailand were all very similar in these two dimensions and were in the same cluster as drawn by Hofstede (collectivist and feminine). The three countries all exhibited very strong collectivism, as a matter of fact all three countries were much higher on the collectivist scale than Japan. Thailand was the most feminine of the three. Australia was very strongly individualist and somewhat masculine but to a much lesser degree than Japan. However, the individualist index, for Australia was the strongest of all 50 countries.

4.5.2 Japan's Relationship with Asia

At times Japan's relationship with Asia has been characterized by such negative feelings as fear, loathing, and hate as well as such positive feelings as admiration and respect. As Japan became a modern industrialized nation there was a tendency among the Japanese to identify with the modern Western nations since there were as yet no other examples of modern industrialized nations in Asia. Thus, the Japanese have developed an almost schizophrenic Asian/Western identity. Toba (1981) noted that Japanese society has long been marked by a venerable struggle between the forces advocating a Japanese retreat from Asia *(datsu A)* and those calling for a reintegration into Asia *(fuku A)*. The Hong Kong-based correspondent George Hicks (*Asian Wall Street Journal*, 26 April, 1989), a long-term observer of the region, noted that: 'It is ironic that the Japan that has sought for almost a century to distance herself from Asia and establish itself as both a 'unique' power and a member of the white man's club – the Group of Seven – had found that the very act of achieving these goals has thrown her back into Asia.'

Bartu (1993:48) reported that when a Tokyo correspondent of *Asiaweek* magazine researched an *endaka* story, he was struck by the number of Japanese businessmen he encountered who perceived investments in Asia to be more difficult that those in the West because of cultural differences and communication problems. This observation is quite understandable. First of all, all Japanese who finish high school will have studied English for 6 years but few Japanese have studied an Asian language other than their own.

Secondly, modern Japanese do not necessarily have a stronger cultural affinity with Asian countries than with the United States. Though most Japanese recognize the cultural influences from China, they consider modern Japan to be in a totally different league from the other Asian countries. Japanese tend to believe that they have much more in common with modern day Western societies, especially in terms of the material aspects of Japanese society.

Japan is the Germany of Asia or, if you prefer, Germany is the Japan of Europe. Like Germany, Japan is an economic powerhouse feared and respected by its neighbours. Furthermore, in a very negative sense, Japan like Germany has instilled a sense of hatred for its wartime atrocities. For most Asians, Japan's Daitoa, or the Greater East Asian Co-Prosperity Sphere, quickly proved itself to merely be a Japanese euphemism for terror, injustice and human tragedy (Bartu, 1993:25). Unlike Germany, Japan has failed for decades to clearly admit the atrocities it committed, apologize, or even show repentance. The gross misrepresentations of the activities of the Imperial Japanese Army in the textbooks, whose content is closely supervised by the Ministry of Education *(Monbu-sho)*, has led to great anger and protests among the Asians who suffered under their terror.

There are still articles in newspapers discussing issues related to sins committed by the Japanese military against its neighbours and the lack of official apology. The most recent issue covered by the press is the complaints and calls for compensation from 'comfort women,' women from various Asian countries who were forced to serve as sex slaves to Japanese soldiers during the war. These negative attitudes towards the Japanese do have serious consequences for Japanese FDI in Asia. To many Asians the great increase in Japanese FDI is seen as another invasion, the virtual Japanese economic conquest of Asia. This is expressed in a quote from the late president of the Philippines, Ferdinand E. Marcos (*Asiaweek*, 20 May, 1983): 'The unspoken feeling of most of the countries in Southeast Asia has always been that what Japan failed to get during the war, she has obtained by economic conditions.'

4.5.3 Japan and Thailand

Thailand has never been colonized and thus has not experienced the same degree of Western influence as Singapore and Malaysia. Per capita income in Thailand is approaching $2,000 per year. Thailand has a population of nearly sixty million providing an abundant supply of labour. However, rapid economic development during the last decade has led to a tighter labour market and more recently significant shortages have arisen in many of the more skilled and highly trained occupations (Lawler et al., 1995:325). Thailand's infrastructure has also not kept up with the fast pace of economic growth. The population of Bangkok has grown to 8 million and the traffic jams and pollution have become infamous. There are also frequent blackouts during peak demand for electricity. The rapid growth has also caused serious environmental problems. The lure of materialism has pushed many Thai people to seek short-term profit even though their activities causing deforestation and pollution may lead to long-term problems.

Traditionally, Thai society has been highly stratified, with groupings and little mobility across class lines. Buddhism to some extent supports the class system since there is a belief that one's current situation in this life is a consequence of actions taken in previous lives. While those in lower classes may subordinate themselves to those in the upper classes, nevertheless the more privileged have the obligation to treat social inferiors in a kindly and fair manner. The class system is reflected in the organization and management of family-owned enterprises; however, modernization is bringing about changes as explained by Lawler et al. (1995:325-6):

> In such organizations there is little need for highly formalized personnel management systems, as the external social system largely defines patterns of interaction, rights and obligations. Nepotism and social networking have been closely linked to the reliance on external class distinctions as a means of establishing and maintaining control within the traditional Thai organization. However, the pressures of modernization have inevitably weakened the class system. A relatively small, educated elite is increasingly being displaced by an educated and affluent middle class. Entrepreneurial opportunities abound, even for many in the lower classes.

Furthermore, Lawler et al. (1995:327) point out that Thailand's rapid economic growth over the past decade has resulted in significant changes in traditional organizational forms. As family enterprises have increased in size and scope, it has been necessary to fill high-level management positions with professionals who do not have any ties to the ruling family. Moreover, the Thai capital market has also greatly expanded and many firms have relied on the market as a source of capital to fuel further expansion. Publicly traded firms have increasingly sought professional managers. Lawler *et al.* (1989) found that publicly held Thai corporations tended to follow human resource strategies that are a hybrid of Western rationalism and the traditionalism of the family enterprise.

As in many countries in Southeast Asia, Chinese families own many of the largest and most powerful organizations in Thailand. One characteristic of the Chinese way of conducting business is a heavy reliance on family connections and inter-family networks for developing and maintaining external relationships. These networks often extend across national boundaries to form international trade systems. Thus, Chinese entrepreneurs play an important role in the economic development of Southeast Asia. Therefore, when considering the cultural environment in the business world of Southeast Asia it is important to include relevant Chinese cultural characteristics.

It is said that Confucian values have played an important role in shaping management practices in organizations dominated by Chinese. Confucianism as management ideology demands the loyalty of those lower in the organizational hierarchy to those at the top. In exchange for their loyalty, subordinates can expect organizational leaders to take care of their basic needs. Since national culture also shapes management practices, there are national variations in the management practices of Chinese-dominated organizations in Southeast Asia. However, the management systems of most Southeast Asian countries stress harmony, conformity, hierarchy and the avoidance of direct conflict (Putti, 1991).

The Thai government has demonstrated a positive attitude towards FDI in Thailand; however, their policies have changed reflecting changing conditions. During the 1960s the government followed a policy of import substitution and encouraged FDI in the corresponding sectors, while in the 1970s, facing a growing external trade deficit, the government welcomed foreign investment in export generating industries. Presently Thailand's foreign investment policies seek to encourage the following types of investments (Toyo Keizai, 1996:28):

1. investments that raise the level of the country's industrial technology;
2. investments that use domestic materials and utilize the country's supporting industries to generate foreign currency earnings through exports;

3. investments that promote the development of areas outside of Bangkok;
4. investments that develop and/or support domestic infrastructure;
5. investments that protect natural resources and help alleviate environmental problems.

The Thais and the Japanese have been trading for many years, long before the opening of Japan in the second half of the 19th century. The memories of the Pacific War are not as strong as in other countries in the region. However, there have been expressions of anti-Japanese sentiment, such as the anti-Japanese riots during the Tanaka visit in 1974. On the other hand, Emperor Akihito was well received during his visit to Thailand in 1991. Perhaps the oldest, strongest bond between Thailand and Japan is their history. Neither country has ever been colonized and both countries consider themselves as civilized and established in an area of neophyte nations. Thome and McAuley (1992:180) claim that there is a natural cultural affinity between Japan and Thailand:

> Both nations are Buddhist (Japan more in name than in practice, whilst Thais practise their religion as a natural part of their daily life). Both are relatively homogeneous ethnically, and there is a high regard for ritualized politeness, etiquette and maintaining face and harmony.

Japan has become the largest foreign investor in Thailand, accounting for more than half of all investment inflows. The great increase in Japanese investment in Thailand occurred between 1987 and 1990. Thailand is becoming an important offshore base for the Japanese automotive industry. Japanese manufacturers are investing heavily to upgrade their operations, and firms like Honda, Mazda, Mitsubishi, Nissan and Toyota are starting to see Thailand as part of their core operations. Japanese investment in Thailand is not limited to the automotive industry. Manufacturers from many other Japanese industries such as electronics and consumer products are also well represented in Thailand. However, it appears that not everyone in Thailand is pleased with the growing dependence on Japan. This sentiment is expressed in a quote from the former Prime Minister of Thailand, Chatichai Choonhavan (quoted in Bartu, 1993:255): 'You [Americans] don't compete enough with the Japanese. I do not want my children to speak Japanese. I want them to speak English.'

In spite of the fact that Japan and Thailand share certain cultural, religious and historical traits, and even though the relationships between Japanese and Thais are harmonious they are not intimate according to Thome and McAuley (1992:190). Thais tend to be much more individualistic than Japanese in spite of showing a higher degree of collectivism in Hofstede's analysis. Socializing between Thai and Japanese managers is made difficult due to language barriers. Japanese managers seem to prefer to limit their associations after work to recreation with other Japanese PCNs. Japanese are infamous for forming Japanese ghettos wherever there is notable Japanese FDI and numerous Japanese PCNs. The Japanese even have their own section of the red-light district in Bangkok where there are clubs serving only Japanese clients.

Thai and Japanese culture also differ fundamentally in terms of work-related attitudes and behaviours. As previously discussed, Japanese managers often put the needs and demands of their job before personal and family considerations and the line between their private and public life at the company often becomes blurred. On the other hand, Thai managers seek a balance between their careers and family life and do not allow the firm to impinge on their personal or family life. Lawler *et al.* (1995:300–1) observed that: 'Although Thais may be dedicated to their work, career advancement is not often a dominant consideration. Rather, they prefer some moderate path that balances career and family life.'

K. Yoshihara (1990) carried out a comparative study of Japanese and American subsidiaries in Thailand. He concluded that Japanese PCNs made a greater effort to accommodate the subsidiary to the Thai managerial climate than their American counterparts and had better relations with the unions. However, Yoshihara found that it was difficult to implement Japanese management practices and suggested two reasons to account for the difficulties encountered. First, since many of the fundamental Japanese management practices are passed on through the company culture of the parent company and are not encoded in work rules or job descriptions, it is difficult to communicate management techniques to the Thai HCN managers without misunderstandings. Second, Thai HCN managers are not willing to accept Japanese group-oriented management practices that are viewed as egalitarian management techniques because they believe that egalitarianism is against Thai middle class consciousness.

Thome and McAuley (1992:194–5) report the mutual impressions Japanese and Thai managers have of each other as gathered during their interviews at four Japanese subsidiaries in Thailand. The Japanese managers felt that Thais were more controlled and less likely to show their feelings than other Asians. However, several managers commented on the volatility of Thai workers, with long periods of placid co-operation punctuated with extreme outbursts, such as labour disputes. On the other hand, Thai managers complained about insufficient delegation of authority and decision-making.

There were also some other interesting observations reported by Thome and McAuley (1992) concerning decision-making. Japanese managers found it difficult to adjust to the Thai tradition of top-down decision-making, and, in joint ventures, family involvement in decision-making. Japanese also wanted Thai managers to have a more professional approach to decision-making by adopting more rigorous methods rather than rely on gut feeling. On the other hand, one Thai manager expressed a cynical but comical, and in some cases perhaps close to the truth, view of the *ringi* system of decision-making (see Chapter 5 for a detailed discussion of this system). The manager stated (Thome and McAuley, 1992:196) that if you want to do business with the Japanese go to the top and get a decision since the boss will order his subordinates to write a report supporting the decision

4.5.4 Japan and Malaysia

Malaysia's population is currently around 18 million. The people come from a number of different ethnic groups – Malay, Chinese, Indian (mainly Tamils), indigenous Orang Asli (original people) and the various tribes of Sarawak and Sabah. It is reasonable to say the Malays control the government while the Chinese have their finger on the economic pulse. Approximately 85 per cent of the population lives in Peninsular Malaysia and the remaining 15 per cent in the much more lightly populated states of Sabah and Sarawak. The eastern part of Peninsular Malaysia is dominated by cities where there is often a majority of Chinese such as Penang, while the western part is more rural and the vast majority of the inhabitants are ethnic Malays.

Though Malaysia may seem very multicultural, the government policy is not. Malaysia is for the Bumiputra (literally 'sons of the soil,' often abbreviated to Bumi) first, other Malaysians second and foreigners only out of necessity (Thome and McAuley (1992:162). That is to say, there is preferential treatment of Bumiputra and discrimination against Chinese and Indians as well as the other ethnic groups in Malaysia. Foreigners are accepted as long as they contribute to economic development and international trade. There is a dark history of relations between the Bumiputra and Chinese. In 1969 only 1.5 per cent of company assets in Malaysia were owned by Bumiputra and per capita income amongst Bumiputra was less than half that of non-Bumiputra. Under these conditions, violent intercommunal riots broke out in 1969, the riots were particularly violent in Kuala Lumpur and hundreds of people were killed. Thereafter, legislation was drafted granting many privileges to Bumiputra and requiring firms to follow quotas in hiring and promoting employees.

The official language of Malaysia is Bahasa Malaysia or 'Bahasa.' However, English is often used for communication between the various ethnic groups. English was once the main language of instruction at higher levels of education but Bahasa Malaysia is now the sole language of instruction at all levels. The consequence of this policy seems to be leading to a decline in the proficiency of English among younger Malaysians.

Ever since Mahathir Mohamad became Prime Minister in 1981 he has worked towards industrializing Malaysia. Mahathir admired the economic development of Japan, South Korea and Taiwan. He exhorted the Malaysians to emulate the industrious and diligent people of these countries by initiating the 'Look East' campaign. His appeal was directed at the indigenous Malays, who for many reasons had not been able to compete successfully with the more business-minded Chinese minority. However, the Malays seemed to lack many of the essential ingredients of his recipe for turning Malaysia into a second Japan (Bartu, 1993:54).

According to Clad (1991) the 'Look East' campaign of Mahathir was not a success. Cultural antagonisms were never overcome. The East Asian companies were soon criticized for their aggressive attitudes towards their local employees. Cases were reported of Korean supervisors physically assaulting their Malay subordinates. Only second-level technologies were being transferred, and engineers returned from supposed training in East Asia complaining that they had been treated as a source of cheap manual labour. The Koreans and Japanese were correspondingly unenthusiastic about their counterparts. According to a Japanese university survey (Clad, 1991:63), Japanese managers gave Malaysians a five per cent approval rating in the 'care taken in work' category, and not one Japanese manager gave Malaysian workers a good rating to a question probing assessment of 'ability to adapt to changing situations.'

As of 1995 there were approximately 1100 Japanese firms with operations in Malaysia. More than 600 of these firms are involved in manufacturing and are contributing significantly to the development of the Malaysian economy. In particular, due to the rising costs of production in Japan, these companies are shifting production to Malaysia and the number of firms establishing research and development capabilities at their Malaysian subsidiaries is increasing at a rapid rate.

Furthermore, in response to the major manufacturers shifting more production to Malaysia, the related small and medium size suppliers of parts and services are also moving to Malaysia to service their traditional Japanese customers. Goods and services of Japanese subsidiaries in Malaysia account for 15 per cent of the GDP and the high growth rate of the Malaysian economy over the past few decades is in no small part due to the FDI of Japanese and other foreign firms. Government policy is still directed towards encouraging FDI in manufacturing to fuel economic growth and offers numerous incentives to foreign investors such as tax breaks (Toyo Keizai, 1996:26).

The Malaysian government also offers the possibility of 100 per cent foreign ownership of subsidiaries in Malaysia under certain conditions. In the case of manufacturing firms, if 80 per cent of the production is exported then 100 per cent foreign ownership is allowed. Investment in certain industries automatically qualifies. These industries include aerospace, biotechnology, and other high-tech industries. Even though the government seeks to promote the employment of HCN managers, it is relatively easy for foreign subsidiaries to obtain work visas for their PCN managers who will be in positions such as; president, general manager, R&D manager, international marketing manager, and the like (Toyo Keizai, 1996:27).

The economic growth in Malaysia has led to a labour shortage. Shortly before the economic crisis in Asia, unemployment was below three per cent, which indicates that the economy was in a state of full employment. In particular there is a shortage of HCNs qualified for managerial positions or with technical expertise. It is common for such HCNs to change jobs when offered better conditions. There is an impression among Malaysian HCNs that, compared to the situation at American and European subsidiaries, the pay at Japanese subsidiaries is low, there are linguistic and cultural barriers, it is difficult to be involved in the management of the subsidiary and promotions come slowly. It also has been getting difficult to attract enough workers when a few hundred or more are required. When necessary the Malaysian government has allowed (before the economic crisis) the importation of labourers from Indonesia and Bangladesh, but the government prefers that manufacturers first seek to automate production or introduce labour saving production systems instead. Companies must also follow the legislation concerning the mix of ethnic groups employed (Toyo Keizai, 1996:27).

There are strong cultural and linguistic barriers to socializing between Japanese PCN and HCN managers. In the case of the Bumiputra, religion is the main reason they seldom go out with Japanese managers after work. Japanese socializing is strongly based on the consumption of alcoholic drinks and obviously not appealing to the Islamic Bumiputra.

The historic relationship between Japan and Malaysia is strongly tainted by the war. Malaysia was a major battleground and the Japanese committed many atrocities during the war such as cutting off the heads of locals and hanging them in the main square to scare the population into submission. There may be admiration of Japan's technological and industrial achievements but under the surface there is still a lot of tension.

Thorne and McAuley (1992:172) also report the mutual impressions Japanese PCN and HCN managers have of each other as gathered during their interviews at three Japanese subsidiaries in Malaysia. The HCN managers in Malaysia complain about ceilings on promotion, poor communication, arrogant attitudes, a lack of respect for woman's abilities, and a lack of delegation from Japanese managers and from Tokyo to local offices. The Japanese comment that the Bumiputra put personal and social considerations before business considerations. In general the Japanese PCN managers prefer to work with Chinese HCNs. The Japanese tend to view the Bumiputra as lacking ambition and diligence. While the Bumiputra view the Japanese as too preoccupied with trying to look busy even when they do not have any work to do.

4.5.5 Japan and Singapore

For the past 20 years Singapore has sustained phenomenal growth rates with an annual average of about eight per cent. This steady high growth rate and the continuous shifts to higher value-added economic activities have earned Singapore the status of being one of Asia's four 'dragons' along with Hong Kong, Taiwan and Korea. Singapore has been a net creditor, inflation is low and unemployment is virtually nonexistent. Singapore's economy is a based on trade, shipping, banking and tourism with a programme of light manufacturing. It also has a major oil refining business producing much of the petroleum for Southeast Asia. Other important industries include shipbuilding and maintenance, and electronics. Singapore's port is the fourth busiest in the world.

Singapore may seem like a model free-market economy but in reality the government is closely involved in regulation of not only the economy but the society too (examples include: prohibiting the chewing of gum, and forcing fat school children on diets and exercise regimes). While tariffs are low or nonexistent and FDI is encouraged with few restrictions, Singapore still fits the capitalist-development model of development, an approach to development similar to the pattern followed in Japan. For example, the government provides direction by targeting industries for development and offering tax incentives. The government also controls unions and the labour market and there is tough legislation against strikes.

Singapore has a population of about 2.7 million consisting of 76 per cent Chinese, 15 per cent Malay (Bumiputra), seven per cent Indian, and two per cent from a variety of races. The city-state has a strong Chinese flavour as would be expected since two-thirds of the residents are Chinese. However, unlike Malaysia which only recognizes Malay as the official language in light of the Malay majority, in Singapore the Chinese majority has accepted four official languages; Chinese, Malay, Tamil and English. English is the main language of business and administration. It is also the language used by the various ethnic groups to communicate with one another. Furthermore, English was officially adopted as the first language of instruction in schools in 1987.

Many Singaporeans, particularly elder citizens, have bitter memories of the Japanese invasion and occupation of Singapore during the war. The occupation was particularly brutal. Estimates of the Chinese slaughtered by Japanese soldiers slaughtered range between 40,000 and 100,000. The civilians also suffered humiliation and beatings. More than 100,000 Australian, British and soldiers of other nationalities were taken prisoner, and Changi became a massive holding camp for Allied prisoners. From Changi thousands were sent to work camps, such as the notorious Burma Railway, where, along with even larger number of local labourers, they suffered unimaginable brutality from Japanese and Korean guards. After the Pacific War Singapore was slow to turn to Japan.

Thome and McAuley (1992:150–9) report the mutual impressions of Japanese and Singaporean managers have of each other as gathered during their interviews at thirteen Japanese subsidiaries in Singapore. Concerning decision-making the Japanese find the Chinese to be patriarchal and authoritarian. On the other hand, the Singaporeans feel that they are left out of the decision-making process and the Japanese PCN managers allow the parent company to make all the important decisions and consult too much with the head office concerning all matters. Some Singaporean HCN managers felt so excluded that they left the company.

Thome and McAuley also report that Japanese PCNs are upset at the Singaporean individualism and lack of any sense of teamwork. In addition, there are conflicts concerning loyalty; Chinese tend to be loyal to their family while Japanese loyalty is the firm or occupation. An important question for the Japanese PCN managers to consider is how can they expect to gain the loyalty of the HCN managers if they do not allow them to fully participate in the managing of the business and offer better career opportunities. This view is reflected in the advice Singaporean HCNs had for other Singaporeans who are working for a Japanese subsidiary (Thome and McAuley, 1992:156):

> Singaporeans' general advice to their compatriots in Japanese firms is to understand they offer jobs, not careers. For people with technical skills, not seeking advancement, there are good jobs available. On joining a Japanese firm one should learn their ways, learn the language, and adapt; accept that the Japanese will not adapt. Those seeking promotion ladders or rewards for genius or individual effort, however, would do well not to work in Japanese firms.

4.5.6 Japan and Australia

Japan has been an important trading partner with Australia. Japan has been Australia's largest export market since the late 1960s and Australia's second largest source of imports since the 1970s. However, only recently has Japanese FDI in Australia begun to match its trading pattern. Since the early 1980s, the Japanese share total FDI in Australia has risen to 30 per cent making Japan Australia's third largest investor after the US and UK. Japanese FDI has been concentrated in agriculture, mining, transport equipment and finance, with a great increase in investment in tourism and real estate (Nicholas *et al.*, 1995).

Japan's investment in manufacturing in Australia has been relatively small compared to that in Thailand, Malaysia and Singapore. According to the data in Toyo Keizai (1996), at the end of 1994 the total number of Japanese subsidiaries registered in Australia was 510. Of these firms there were: 92 involved in manufacturing, 186 in wholesale distribution, 7 in retail, 8 in restaurants, 30 in finance and insurance, 21 in securities and investments, 44 in real estate, 12 in transportation and communication, 40 in various services, and 24 holding companies. Thus, Japanese subsidiaries involved in manufacturing represent only 18 per cent of all Japanese subsidiaries in Australia. On the other hand, the percentage of the Japanese subsidiaries involved in manufacturing is 57 per cent in Thailand (545 out of a total of 960), 61 per cent in Malaysia (415 out of a total of 681), and 30 per cent in Singapore (278 out of a total of 941).

There seems to be great sensitivity among many Australians concerning Japanese FDI, especially when the FDI involves the acquisition of an existing Australian firm. Such investments often cause a lot of public outcry. Some people express concerns that Australia is being taken over by foreigners, particularly Japanese. This fear of FDI is much stronger when the company investing is Japanese compared to investment from a European or American company. Perhaps these attitudes are related to racist sentiments or bitter memories of the war that exist among certain segments of the Australian population. Another possibility is that Australians are concerned about their dependence on Japanese trade and investment. Furthermore, in the minds of the average person in Australia Japan may appear to be an unstoppable economic powerhouse intent on dominating all industries.

4.6 REFERENCE GROUP THEORY

How a PCN manager feels about an overseas assignment and the degree the manager identifies with the parent company may greatly affect the manager's ability to identify with the foreign subsidiary and the host-country environment. Iida (1984) reported that there was communication gap between Japanese PCNs and Australian HCNs in Japanese subsidiaries located in Australia. The main cause was that Japanese PCNs tend to adhere to the rigid orders and values of

Japanese society and organizations even while assigned to foreign subsidiaries.

Iida (1984) explains these findings in terms of the reference group theory. The reference group is the group with which an individual identifies as a basis for self-evaluation, comparison, and normative guidance. The reference group theory stipulates that if the PCN manager's dominant reference group is the parent company or particular individuals and groups at the parent company, the PCN manager will tend not to identify strongly with HCN managers and be greatly influenced by the reference group in terms of managerial thinking and action. Iida (1984:46) stated:

> If workers in Japan are the reference group affecting and controlling the managerial thinking of Japanese expatriates, the latter will be likely to conform to managerial norms which are observed in Japan and employ them as a basis for managerial practices which are to be carried out in the Japanese subsidiaries in Australia. Similarly, if local nationals in Japanese overseas subsidiaries consider their local managerial milieus as their reference group, it is assumed that they are not likely to feel the need to be incorporated and assimilated into organizational milieus in the subsidiary to which they belong, whereas they will create managerial behaviour like that in their local business environments.

Iida (1985) further suggests that most Japanese PCNs view postings to subsidiaries in Australia as part of job rotation by their parent companies and the relatively short term (usually three to five years) reinforces the temporary nature of the position. He claims that while working in Australia Japanese PCNs have anxieties about whether they can catch up with management systems and practices in the parent company after they are sent back. Yoshino (1976:172) argues that there is a great deal of strenuous effort by Japanese PCN managers to maintain personal ties with relevant groups at the parent companies. Furthermore, a report on Japanese PCN managers in overseas subsidiaries (Trapedia, 1980) reveals that the most worrisome problems for Japanese PCN managers are whether they will lose their identity during the appointment, and whether they will suffer from a counter-culture shock after they are sent back home, as previously discussed in relation to repatriation.

5 Communication and Decision-making

The focus of this chapter is on the variables of communication and decision-making in the Conceptual Model of Factors Affecting HCN Integration. First of all, language, culture and behaviour issues affecting communication are discussed. The concept of high and low context cultures is presented to help explain some of the challenges Japanese face in communicating with non-Japanese. It is pointed out that certain cultural attitudes such as the belief in the uniqueness of Japanese language and culture *(nihonjinron)* negatively affect intercultural communication. Next, there is a discussion of organizational communication and the flow of information in Japanese MNCs. Common reasons for misunderstandings between Japanese PCN and HCN managers are given.

In addition, how problems in communication between PCN and HCN managers as well as problems in the flow of information to HCN managers inhibit the participation of HCN managers in the decision-making process is covered. Thereafter, a general overview of organizational decision-making is followed by a description of typical American and Japanese decision-making practices. The typical American decision-making practices are offered as a contrast to those of Japanese MNCs. Subsequently, the discussion focuses on decision-making at Japanese foreign subsidiaries. The data indicate domination of decision-making at the subsidiaries by Japanese PCNs. The consequences of the lack of HCN participation in decision-making are also discussed.

5.1 THE IMPORTANCE OF INTERPERSONAL COMMUNICATION IN ORGANIZATIONS

In the last decade increased attention has been paid to interpersonal networks in organizations and to their contribution to managerial success and organizational effectiveness (Erez, 1992). Binnis and Nanus (1985) proposed that communication is the only way any group can become aligned behind the goals of the organization. In addition, Kotter (1988 and 1982) identified network building as one of the two major factors in leadership effectiveness. Furthermore, communication provides the means for transcending differences of interpretation in advance of organized action, as well as for the retrospective sense making about actions that have been taken (Donnellon *et al.*, 1986). As discussed later in this chapter, in the case of Japanese companies it is very important for all managers to build up an interpersonal communication network *(jinmyaku)* This informal communication network is important because effective decision-making in Japanese corporations is based on extensive informal discussions among managers throughout the organization.

5.2 LANGUAGE, CULTURAL AND BEHAVIOUR ISSUES AFFECTING COMMUNICATION

This section deals with cross-cultural communication issues. Namely, it investigates how language, culture and behavioural patterns affect communication between members of different cultural, ethnic and national groups. The main goal is to provide essential information and concepts for understanding the communication problems between Japanese PCNs and HCNs at Japanese overseas subsidiaries. First, the relationship between culture and communication is discussed. Second, language as a barrier to communication in Japanese subsidiaries is explored. Third, how Japanese cultural nationalism can negatively affect communication between Japanese and non-Japanese is explained. Finally, the concept of high context cultures vs. low context cultures is presented and applied in an analysis of communication between Japanese and non-Japanese.

5.2.1 The Relationship Between Culture and Communication

Patterns of interpersonal communication reflect the culture of the participants, and interpersonal communication is an implicit part of organizational communication. The concept that culture is a system of shared values, norms in symbols, is a central part of some of the definitions of culture presented in Chapter 2. For example, D'Andrade (1984) views culture as a pattern of symbolic discourse and shared meaning that needs interpreting and deciphering in order to be fully understood. Furthermore, Shweder and LeVine (1984) view culture as a set of shared meaning systems wherein members of the same culture are likely to interpret and evaluate situational events and practices in a similar way.

According to Donnellon *et al.* (1986) the relationship between culture and communication is reciprocal; the communication network forms the connecting links among group members, transmitting the social values and facilitating their sharing. Conversely, shared meaning and values facilitate the flow of communication. Both shared meaning and shared communication mechanisms facilitate collective action. Furthermore, the degree of shared meaning and values determines the degree of shared context and the degree of explicitness required in communication. This idea forms the basis of Hall's (1976) high-context/low-context view of communication discussed later in this chapter. It is the lack of shared context that makes cross-cultural communication problematic. Comical situations occurring in movies in which one culture meets another are always based on this theme of miscommunication as a result of the lack of shared context.

5.2.2 Language as a Barrier to Communication in Japanese Subsidiaries

Communication is greatly facilitated when the people involved all share the same mother tongue. However, this is often not the case when communication takes place between PCNs and HCNs in the overseas subsidiaries of MNCs. American PCNs have a great advantage over Japanese PCNs since English is not only the dominant language in many countries throughout the world, it is often studied as a second language by non-native speakers. On the other hand, Japanese is the dominant language of only one country, Japan. Furthermore, even though the number of non-Japanese studying the Japanese language has greatly increased in recent years, the number of non-Japanese who can conduct business in the language is still extremely small. In spite of the fact that English is taught for a total of six years during Japanese secondary school, years of experience in Japan allow me to argue that few Japanese can actually communicate in English with a non-Japanese. In school English is treated as an object to be analysed and discussed in Japanese rather than practised for the purpose of communicating with foreigners.

5.2.3 Cultural Nationalism as a Barrier to Communication

As previously discussed, Japanese cultural nationalism is manifested in the doctrines of *nihonjinron*. Language and culture are at the core of the claim of Japanese uniqueness advocated in *nihonjinron*.

Kunihiro (1976) argues that the difficulty of communicating with a Japanese person is considered to be closely associated with the Japanese people's particular view of language and mode of language usage, the unique patterns of cognition and perception, and the system of logic. The tacit, implicit, emotive and non-logical modes of Japanese communication are pointed out in *nihonjinron* literature. An example of such is the model dialogue found in a cross-cultural communication handbook published by Nippon Steel (1987:405):

> Mr. J (American): I don't think I could ever learn to make the subtle distinctions you need in Japanese.
>
> Mr. S (Japanese): It's so tied in with the whole culture. It's difficult to master for someone who grew up in another country.

In the *nihonjinron* literature such as the example above, linguistic and communicative culture in Japan always tends to be discussed as an obstacle to communication between Japanese and foreign businessmen. They stress the differences rather than the similarities. As stated by Yoshino (1992:181): 'If the attempt at "international understanding" is made through the conscious assertion of Japanese uniqueness or through the extreme version of cultural relativism, the unintended consequence of such an "internationalizing" attempt can ironically be the enhancement of cultural nationalism because it fails to stress the commonalty shared by different peoples.' He also notes that the businessmen's concern to improve intercultural communication and their cultural nationalism are often two sides of the same coin.

Bartu (1993:22) also discussed how Japanese seem to not like being understood too easily. He quoted an episode of a Japanese explaining Japan to a Westerner:

> The Japanese takes great trouble and time to describe in detail the most important aspects of Japanese way of life, work and decision-making. In the end, he asks the Westerner politely: 'Do you understand?' When the foreigner replies: 'Yes, I do,' the Japanese exclaims in disappointment: 'Well, in that case I must have explained it wrongly!'

Even when foreigners acquire a high level of proficiency in Japanese, there is an attitude on the part of Japanese that they must overcome. Many Japanese believe that Japanese language and culture are genetically based and have certain irreducible essences that define their uniqueness. That is to say, foreigners, who are not 'genetically' Japanese, are precluded from being considered Japanese in spite of their ability in the Japanese language and their familiarity with the culture. This attitude is a stark contrast to countries that are populated mainly by immigrants such as the United States or Australia where language proficiency and cultural assimilation usually earns recognition as a 'normal' member of the respective society.

In understanding the essence of what it means to be Japanese, proponents of the uniqueness of Japanese stress the importance of such concepts as: *kokoro* (heart), *seishin* (spirit), and *tamashi* (soul). That is to say that there is a Japanese heart, a Japanese spirit and a Japanese soul (referred to as Yamato *damashi*). These are considered attributes that a foreigner cannot acquire, as if they were transmitted genetically and not through the process of socialization. This line of reasoning also infers that non-Japanese cannot understand Japanese aesthetics, which are largely based on the concepts of *wabi* (taste for the simple and quiet), *sabi* (elegant simplicity), and *mono no aware* (sensitiveness to beauty). Mannari and Befu (1991:37–8) point out that through the sharing of these and other essential and unique characteristics, the Japanese claim to possess certain uncanny non-verbal abilities to communicate with one another, often expressed as *ishin denshin* (from mind to mind) or *haragei* (belly-art or reading one's mind). The implication is that foreigners, lacking these abilities, are hindered in communicating with the Japanese.

5.2.4 High-Context Cultures vs. Low-Context Cultures

Context is so important in communication that words and phrases sometimes have completely different meanings depending on the context. For example, the phrase 'Mary had a little lamb,' has numerous different meanings depending on the context or frame of reference. Context is not just restricted to the spoken word. Non-verbal communication is also contextual and tends to differ among cultures. The Japanese, like the Thai, tend to smile in many situations in which it would be inappropriate in most Western cultures. However, there are differences in the characteristics of the various smiles, and people who share the same culture understand these differences.

The more familiar people are with one another in terms of having similar knowledge, values and beliefs, that is to say, the same general cultural background, the less context is needed for communication.

Thus, culturally heterogeneous populations such as that of the US require greater context than culturally homogeneous populations such as that of Japan. Hall (1976) explains that high-context messages are placed at one end and low-context messages at the other end of a continuum. A high-context communication or message is one in which most of the information is either in the physical context or internalized in the person, while very little is in the coded, explicit, transmitted part of the message. A low-context communication is just the opposite; the mass of the information is vested in explicit code.

Hall (1976:91) also proposes that the level of context determines everything about the nature of communication and is the foundation on which all subsequent behaviour rests (including symbolic behaviour). From the practical viewpoint of communication strategy, one must decide how much time to invest in contexting another person. A certain amount of this is always necessary, so that the information that makes up the explicit portions of the message is neither inadequate nor excessive.

According to Hall (1976:111–13), in Japan, the over-all approach to life, institutions, government, and the law is an approach in which one has to know considerably more about what is going on at the covert level than in the West. High-context cultures make greater distinctions between insiders and outsiders than low-context cultures do. People raised in high-context systems expect more of others than do the participants in low-context systems. When talking about something that they have on their minds, a high-context individual will expect his interlocutor to know what is bothering him, so that he doesn't have to be specific.

The argument of Japan having a high-context culture, a tenet of *nihonjinron*, is supported by the idea of Japanese uniqueness and homogeneity. As previously discussed, some scholars argue ardently against the idea of Japanese uniqueness (for example: Dale, 1986; and Kashima, 1974) and question the true extent of homogeneity in Japan. However, Kunihiro (1976:272) argues that in spite of disagreements on these matters, most people would agree that present-day Japan is more homogeneous than any other major country in the world. It is what anthropologists call an endogamous society, meaning that the members share a great many aspects of their daily life and consciousness. Therefore, explanations through the medium of language often become unnecessary, and the intuitive, non-verbal communication of the sort that develops among family members living under the same roof spreads throughout the society.

In contrast, Americans as well as people from similar cultures favour explicitness over indirection. The thrust is on communicating the facts, even when they may constitute negative feedback. The cultural preference is for clarity in communication, since it conveys sincerity and directness. Communication problems in an organization are largely resolved by establishing formal networks, whose effectiveness is measured in terms of speed and, more important, accuracy of information. Individual satisfaction with the social aspects of the communication process is of secondary importance (Sethi et al., 1984:134).

5.3 COMMUNICATION AND FLOW OF INFORMATION IN JAPANESE MNCs

This section focuses on organizational communication and the flow of information in Japanese MNCs. However, first the concept of information as a source of power is presented to establish that the effectiveness of HCN managers may be inhibited by poor communication and flow of information. Thereafter, interpersonal communication in Japanese organizations is explained. Next, common causes of miscommunication between Japanese and PCN managers and HCN managers are discussed. Finally, the flow of information between PCNs and HCNs at Japanese subsidiaries is explored

5.3.1 Information as a Source of Power

There is a communication system in all organizations that serves in the formulation and implementation of organizational goals as well as to meet the organization's demand for the co-ordination of its diverse activities. Communication systems are also carriers of power. Since there is differential access to the flow of communications during a decision-making process, information access and control is a source of organizational power. Several authors have researched the concept of control over information as a source of power. Mechanic (1962) studied the sources of power of lower participants in complex organizations and argued that within organizations dependency can be generated with others by controlling access to the resources of information and instrumentalities. Pettigrew (1972) examined the increased possibilities for filtering information under the conditions of an innovative decision. He demonstrated that decisional outcomes reflect the interests that are communicated most effectively on the administrative level at which decisions are made.

According to Pettigrew, the analysis of organizational power requires some attempt to map the distribution and use of resources and the ability of actors to produce outcomes consonant with their own or their system's goals. Following Easton's analysis of throughput of demands in his model of political systems, Pettigrew views the process of decision-making as a set of interactions through which demands are processed into outputs. He states (1972:189):

> A major assumption is that the demands do not flow randomly through a system; they have a directional force towards the locus of power in the organization. Gatekeepers, those who sit at the junction of a number of communication channels, are in position to regulate the flow of demands and potentially control directional outcomes. Easton suggests that gatekeepers may not only open and close communications channels, they also collect, combine and reformulate information.

In Japanese foreign subsidiaries where Japanese PCN managers hold positions of authority they most likely function as gatekeepers regulating the flow of information from the parent company to the HCN managers. In the same way, HCN managers in lower level managerial positions may be able to regulate the flow of information from the bottom of the organization to the top. However, if the parent company exercises substantial control over the subsidiary then PCN managers may regulate the degree of HCN managers' participation in decision-making by consciously or unconsciously withholding information.

5.3.2 Interpersonal Communication in Japanese Organizations

Erez (1992) studied interpersonal communication systems in Japanese corporations and their relationship to cultural values, productivity and innovation. She examined two propositions; (1) the Japanese corporate communication systems are anchored in the socio-cultural values of the society, and shaped by the values and patterns of the interpersonal communication system of the society as a whole and (2) the effective corporate communication system is related to the high level of productivity and technological innovation. The former proposition was confirmed without too much difficulty.

On the other hand, the latter proposition suggests a cause and effect relationship that cannot be statistically proved, thus Erez

(1992:59) simply infers a relationship between effective communication and productivity/innovation by citing numerous factors:

It can be argued that the communication system is one of the factors which facilitates the rising level of productivity and innovation for the following reasons: (a) communication allows for information sharing and for an increasing level of knowledge and understanding; (b) it enhances the diffusion of innovation and provides the infra-structure necessary for utilizing past inventions and developing them into future innovative products and services; (c) technology transfer seems to be a necessary condition for doing advanced research and development today; (d) bottom-up communication stimulates additional sources of innovative ideas of employees, who are familiar with the nature of their own work perhaps more than anyone else; (f) interpersonal communication improves the co-ordination between different organizational units, which is necessary for organizational effectiveness; and (g) interpersonal communication enhances employees' motivation by clarifying companies' goals and strategies, and making them meaningful, and by enhancing employees' self efficacy as they improve their knowledge no how to perform their jobs.

Erez (1992:50) describes the communication network identified in the course of interviews with managers at ten major Japanese companies as consisting of highly complex formal and informal systems with top-down, bottom-up, horizontal and diagonal channels. Furthermore, Ballon (1988) states that in contrast to the linear pattern with a definite point of origin for the communication flow and the decision-making process, in the Japanese case the pattern is circular, whereby any single point in a circle can become the origin.

Channels of informal communication play a central role in the communication and decision-making processes in Japanese firms. As is discussed later in detail, before any formal meetings are held to address a given issue informal discussions take place as the first steps in building a consensus through a process known as *nemawashi*. It is important for a manager who advocates a certain position to contact key individuals in the relevant sections and/or departments to communicate his opinions and seek support.

Thus, managers gain power by developing connections to and from which information and favours flow. This communication system is known as *jinmyaku*, which literally means human veins. It is similar to the phrase in English 'to be well connected' but in Japan the emphasis is more on the communication aspect. The phrase *'kare wa jinmyaku ga oi'* (he has a lot of *jinmyaku*) connotes that the person is kept well-informed and can find out information on just about any matter. The entertaining after hours between managers of the same company is another way to exchange opinions and discuss matters informally and develop stronger relationships or strengthen their *jinmyaku*.

5.3.3 Miscommunication Between Japanese and HCN Managers

Goldman (1994) claims that differences in language and culture account for most of the organizational communication difficulties experienced between Japanese PCNs and HCNs. Oyama (1994:71) studied Japanese intercultural communication strategies in subsidiaries of Japanese MNCs in the US. In the analysis of his results he reported major themes concerning problems and miscommunication between Japanese PCN and US HCN managers. First, there is the formality factor. Japanese workers preferred to be formal and not give a large amount of personal information about themselves. Second, there are social hierarchical distinctions. Japanese workers often interacted with American workers differently depending on job relationship, status, age, and gender, whereas American workers tended to minimize differences that might suggest inequality. Third, there are ambiguous communication strategies. Japanese workers preferred ambiguous communication strategies that include general, tentative, and indirect expressions. This ambiguous presentation of their ideas functioned so as to minimize conflicts. However, it created problems and miscommunications in the intercultural workplace. Fourth, there are language attitudes. The Japanese language provided a cue for in- and out-group membership and expressed the heart of ethnic identity. Occasionally Japanese language functioned so as to isolate the Japanese speakers from the English language environment since it created distinctive linguistic boundaries between in- and out-groups.

Obviously the degree to which formality is an intercultural barrier to communication depends on the differences between Japanese customs and those of the host country. In the case of America, where the customs concerning formality sharply contrast those of Japan, Oyama found that the formality of the Japanese PCN managers made the US HCN managers feel uncomfortable. Likewise, the informality of HCNs can make Japanese PCNs feel uncomfortable. For example, it is difficult for a Japanese PCN manager to adjust to addressing others in the office by their first name (not doing so would be impolite in the case of Thailand where one's first name is always used). In Japan it is not even common to use the last name of senior managers when talking directly to them. Instead, Japanese usually address superiors by their title such as *kacho* (section chief) or *bucho* (department chief). Initiating interactions usually requires addressing someone by their name. Thus, even this seemingly small difference in customs can substantially hinder communication since it may discourage interaction between Japanese PCN and HCN managers.

Oyama also found (1994:78) that in America, the Japanese PCN managers appeared to be reluctant to offer or seek personal information and develop a personal relationship with HCN managers. Consequently, American managers often felt discomfort and considered the Japanese managers to be cold and uncaring. In actuality it is important in Japan to develop close relationships between managers working together in the same office. However, developing these relationships takes place outside the office and not during normal working hours. Even though a superior may act very informal and be friendly with subordinates while out drinking together in the evening, the next day at the office a formal atmosphere will be maintained. The lack of English ability on the part of some Japanese PCNs may also account for their hesitation in engaging in more informal conversations about personal matters without which a friendly rapport may not develop.

Oyama (1994:83) found another aspect of hierarchical distinction in initiating interaction. That is, when Japanese managers tried to initiate work to be done by Americans some of them conveyed their instructions to the workers indirectly by having it filter down through the intervening layers of the hierarchy instead of communication directly to the person responsible. Again, this practice may or may not cause friction in the workplace depending on the local customs of the host country.

The third theme, ambiguous communication strategies, may account for a large portion of communication problems between Japanese PCN and HCN managers. As discussed earlier, Japan has a very high context culture and in Japan managers tend not to be explicit and rely on mutually shared knowledge and perceptions in communicating with their fellow co-workers. Furthermore, Japanese prefer to avoid open disagreement and confrontation, or simply said, they find it difficult to say no. Therefore, even though Japanese may disagree with what someone is saying they may utter unenthusiastic positive reactions. The disagreement or negative response is usually indicated in a subtle manner by certain body language, tone of voice, or the careful selection of words.

In some cultures, such as in that of the US, the norm is 'say what you mean and mean what you say,' otherwise it is 'double-talk' and considered deceitful. Conversely, in Japan it is acceptable to engage in *tatemae* and not mean literally what you say. For example, the phrase *'kore wo maemuki ni kento itashimasu'* (literally: I will give forward-looking consideration to that) usually means that whatever has been said is totally impossible and won't be given any consideration at all. Japanese also prefer tentative expressions in order to soften their statements and avoid decisive judgments that may threaten the harmony of the workplace. However, in certain non-Japanese cultural contexts such tentative expressions may be interpreted as signs of indecisiveness and/or a lack of competence.

The fourth theme deals with language attitudes. Oyama (1994:104–5) reported that Japanese and American workers established that there were Japanese and English language territories in the workplace. Japanese PCNs reacted nervously when US HCNs spoke in Japanese in their interactions. Japanese language served to maintain ethnic boundaries. In addition, the attitude among Japanese PCN managers that it is difficult to discuss problems in English leads to getting together with only other Japanese PCNs to discuss issues and develop an initial consensus before discussing the issues with HCN managers. Such practices may engender strong resentment among HCN managers who feel insulted by being left out of the preliminary discussions.

There are other differences in communication patterns that cause misunderstandings. For example, in Japan silence plays a very important role in communication. However, in most Western and many non-Western cultures people are usually not comfortable with silence during a conversation and may become agitated. Another example is the custom in Japan of constantly saying *'hai'* (which means 'yes' in Japanese) when in a conversation with another person. In Japan it is clear that the person does not necessarily agree by repeating *'hai'* it just indicates that the person is listening, it is a way of being polite in a conversation.

5.3.4 Information Flow Between PCNs and HCNs

Having accurate and timely relevant information is essential in order to make effective decisions. When more than one individual is involved in the decision-making process, which is usually the case in organizations, it is important that all the participants share information openly amongst themselves so that all approach the problem under consideration with all the information available. In the case of Japanese foreign subsidiaries there is usually a great deal of communication taking place between the parent company and the subsidiary. Most of this communication takes place in Japanese and is not translated. HCNs also tend to lack sufficient access to communication channels with PCN managers at the parent company. As a result many HCN managers often do not receive sufficient information in order to fully participate in the decision-making process (Keeley and Doi, 1996 and 1995; Yoshihara, 1996; Nishida, 1991).

There are serious consequences resulting from insufficient communication between PCN and HCN managers. On the one hand, the HCN managers may become frustrated leading to reduced performance or even their resignations. On the other hand, the PCN managers may miss out on important information or expertise that can only come from the HCNs. For example, Wingrove (1997) reported that at a Japanese subsidiary in the UK, the PCN managers' company ignored the HCN managers in the consensus process although they practised it among themselves and in liaison with Tokyo. Because they failed to consult the local experts, decisions were taken that were felt to be inappropriate. HCN managers consequently had to run around and correct the mistakes.

Differences between the ways information is communicated among Japanese compared to the customs in the host country may also lead to conflicts between Japanese PCNs and HCNs. For example, once a task has been assigned to a subordinate, the Japanese manager expects the onus to be on the subordinate to give the supervisor frequent progress reports. If this is not the local custom in the country where the subsidiary is located such reports may not be as forthcoming as expected. The supervisor may then make inquiries, which the HCN subordinate may interpret as interference in the job or as lack of trust.

Japanese managers see themselves in the role of a co-ordinator and it is common to see Japanese managers involving themselves in the detail of subordinates' work. A frequent complaint among HCN managers is that Japanese managers fail to explain the whole context of the issue or problem when assigning tasks. They sometimes simply ask someone to do a small task and another person a related task. This type of management can be frustrating to HCN managers who feel that it robs them of ownership and a feeling of managerial responsibility.

5.4 DECISION-MAKING IN MNCs

There are inherent conflicts in the decision-making process whenever decisions involve or affect a number of people. As decision makers strive for a mutually acceptable choice, differences among them in perceptions, cognitions, values, interests, needs, and preferred alternatives give rise to conflicts (Pettigrew, 1973). The potential for conflict increases with organizational size and diversity. Furthermore, the probability of conflicts in the decision-making process increases greatly when dealing with members of various cultures. The ways conflicts are handled vary from culture to culture on a macro-scale and from organization to organization on a micro-scale. However, in all cases a decision should be acceptable to those responsible for authorizing and implementing it. Furthermore, the decision needs to look reasonable, to have face validity. Finally, it needs to contain built-in justifications and excuses if it results in unexpected outcomes.

In most cultures authority, responsibility and power are associated with the types of decisions managers participate in making and approving. While at one extreme, in some cultures, the power and the authority of an individual is demonstrated by making decisions independently, at the other extreme there are cultures in which those in positions of authority are expected to delegate the decision-making authority to a defined group or at least reach a consensus. In either case, final decisions that emerge reflect the different amounts of power mobilized by the parties in competition. Decision-making may be viewed as a political process in which outcomes are a function of the balancing of various power vectors.

Another source of conflict is due to the way information flows in the organization. As previously mentioned, control of the flow of information can be a source of power. In general, organizations have explicit channels and procedures established for the flow of information. However, regardless of the organization, information often does not flow in an orderly, upward or downward manner through the hierarchy. Instead, information flow follows a grid of communications made up of overlapping, often contradictory and elusive channels. Individuals may not be able to influence an organizational decision because they lack access to the locus of decision-making. Power may be a matter of location or the openness of communication flow in an organization. Thus, Bass (1983) declares that whoever controls the communication channels, whether superior or subordinate, has the power to decide.

Still another source of friction is the balancing of the interests of the parent company and the subsidiary when making decisions. If the firm adopts a global approach then it will try to make decisions in terms of what is good for the multinational as a whole. There have been numerous reports from various researchers that Japanese firms tend to always put the interests of the parent company first even when the decision may have considerable negative effects on the subsidiary. For example, Thome and McAuley (1992:153) studied Japanese subsidiaries in Asian countries and made such an observation:

> In all our interviews, in Singapore and elsewhere, there is no notion of the relationship between Tokyo and the periphery evolving into one of mutuality, or interdependence, as it has in many multinationals of other national origins. The assumption remains one of Tokyo being in control, a hub periphery model. This failure to let go leads to friction and divided loyalty. We hear, for example of Japanese managers in Singapore branches of large firms having to bear large losses to satisfy a client who is important in Tokyo. This is hard for local managers to fathom, who have no identity in the larger corporation. If they are autonomous units, then they should be given autonomy, and allowed to operate as independent profit centres with local staff involved in the corporate decisions. Local staff complain of having neither inclusion nor autonomy.

5.5 CHARACTERISTICS OF DECISION-MAKING AT US MNCs

Though the focus of this research is on HCN managers' participation in decision-making in Japanese foreign subsidiaries, decision-making in American firms is presented here to provide a contrast. First of all, the so-called top-down decision-making that is usually associated with US MNCs is discussed. Secondly, the assignment of authority and managerial discretion is explored. Thirdly, the formal group process in decision-making at US MNCs is examined. Finally, there is a discussion of rational decision-making.

5.5.1 Top-Down Decision-making

American corporations generally bear the strong imprint of their top management. It inevitably follows that decision-making is essentially a top-down phenomenon in American corporate life. Explicit in the manager's power to lead is the authority to make decisions. American business schools perpetuate this view with their academic emphasis on decision execution rather than on decision formulation and on professional leadership instead of consultative processes. All elements of the institution operate in a contractual capacity. Downward communications consist primarily of orders for implementation, and upward communications consist of reports on performance and accomplishment.

Sethi et al. (1984:131–2) point out that the top-down approach to decision-making is also greatly influenced by the American view of how to respond to the element of uncertainty in the decision-making process. Uncertainty is not considered a desirable state of affairs, but a problem to be reduced efficiently or eliminated through the use of analytical rationality, aggressive decisiveness, and a thrust toward predetermined outcomes. The system of rewarding and promoting employees on individual merit also strengthens this tendency toward top-down decision-making. In contrast, Hasegawa (1986) and other authors claim that the traditional tendency in Japan has been to make corporate decisions from the bottom-up rather than the top-down. They argue that the aim of the Japanese method is to raise the morale of all employees by using a method of decision-making that allows everyone to feel they are participating. However, I assert many employees and HCN managers in Japanese overseas subsidiaries in particular, do not participate fully in the decision-making process in a bottom-up fashion.

5.5.2 Assignment of Authority and Managerial Discretion

Sethi et al. (1984:132) claim that one of the ways large American corporations accomplish the goal of ensuring that its plans and decisions will be carried out exactly as envisioned is by converting a large body of otherwise discretionary decisions into a set of rules and procedures that everyone at lower levels is expected to follow. The success of a large corporation often depends on the extent to which top management can make decision-making a routine function, thereby assuring that, in a given situation, lower-level employees will follow a particular course of action predetermined by top management. However, there are also innovative decisions that require discretion on the part of the manager and thereby expose the corporation to an element of risk. Therefore, the higher the degree of discretion allowed a manager, the greater will be that manager's authority to commit the corporation to a binding contract or risk exposure, and the higher up that manager will be in the corporate hierarchy.

Individualism in America is expressed in the individual-based decision-making process and employee evaluation process of American corporations. Individual employees seek to demonstrate their ability by the decisions they make and therefore individual responsibility and explicit accountability are important elements of the system. According to Pascale and Athos (1981:144) there are few problems that vex younger American managers more than the dilemma of how to advance the boss's credibility while retaining their own. They stress that American society attaches great weight to what is plainly visible and that is not attuned to thinking very much about what goes on backstage. On the other hand, in Japanese organizations where group effort is the norm and the role of the superior is to guide the efforts of subordinates, achievements are attributed to the group as a whole.

The above observations illustrate differences in performance evaluation between Japanese organizations, where individual recognition is a secondary factor, and those of the US and other countries where individual recognition is a primary factor. These differences may lead to difficulties in motivating HCN managers in Japanese subsidiaries operating in foreign cultural environments. The greatest difficulties occur when HCN managers are placed in positions of apparent managerial responsibility but do not possess what they consider should be the corresponding decision-making authority.

5.5.3 Formal Group Process in Decision-Making at US MNCs

In spite of the strong individualism in the US, group activities or collective meetings are still important in US organizations. There are functional-command groups specified by the organizational structure or task-project groups specifically established by top management to solve a designated problem. Groups operate subject to a specific agenda and interaction often consists of individual members advocating their solution to the problem and defending it before the group. The group explores the various alternatives till one is found that satisfies the majority of the group, or satisfies the most powerful member(s).

Sethi *et al.* (1984:135) argue that American business values demand that the group confront its differences and work through its disagreements in order to arrive at a genuine integrative solution. Maintenance functions, such as harmonizing and compromising, are considered to be of limited value, since they are useful only in reducing types of disagreement among group members. Groupthink is the phenomenon that occurs in highly cohesive groups where the need to conform to group norms pressures members towards a consensus that may not represent the 'best' solution to the problem. Groupthink is an undesirable consequence of the group function by American standards, since the primary function of the group is not to achieve commitment by the group members to the group solution, but to afford each member the opportunity to be heard in the group process and to arrive at a solution that will satisfy management.

5.5.4 Rational Decision-making

The analytical approach to seeking the truth is a basic tenet of Western science and philosophy. Frederick Taylor followed the analytical approach in seeking greater efficiency when he developed his time-and-motion studies. Modern management techniques involve the application of this approach in formulating management strategy. In decision-making, following the analytical approach means dissecting all elements of a problem, assessing each factor objectively, and then calculating the advantages and disadvantages of a course of action (cost–benefit analysis). According to Hayashi (1989:72), many Japanese companies still do not use this process, in spite of the fact that some Japanese management specialists recommend US-style decision-making, finding it inexplicable that Japanese companies can use less rigorous methods and still be reasonably successful

5.6 CHARACTERISTICS OF DECISION-MAKING AT JAPANESE MNCs

The aim of this section is to present the typical characteristics of decision-making at Japanese MNCs. Obviously there are always exceptions to the rule and the actual characteristics of Japanese MNCs should vary. However, the generalizations given here are useful in understanding the typical environment in which HCNs at Japanese MNCs work. First of all, the informal organizational structures and their relation to decision-making in Japanese firms are presented. Secondly, there is a summary of the relationship between collectivism and consensus decision-making. Thirdly, the *ringi-sho* or formal proposal that is commonly employed in the decision-making process at Japanese firms is explained. Finally, the advantages and disadvantages of Japanese-style making are discussed.

5.6.1 Informal Organizational Structures and Decision-making

Examination of an organizational chart of a typical Japanese MNC will not reveal any substantial differences from the formal structure of Japanese MNCs and those of their American and European counterparts. However, the formal organizational structure of Japanese MNCs does not reflect the important informal links between individuals of different sections and departments that have formed over the years mainly due to the practice of frequent rotation of employees. Informal structures surely exist in non-Japanese organizations as well; however, the importance of their function in Japanese organizations may be greater. Japanese organizations often differ from their American counterparts in that role boundaries are vague so employees may be actually performing tasks that would not appear to be in their realm of responsibility according to the organizational chart.

The bottom-up style of decision-making is claimed by many Japanese and non-Japanese writers to be the most common form of decision-making in Japanese organizations (for example: Hasegawa, 1986; Pascale and Athos, 1981; Sasaki, 1981; Abegglen, 1958). However, whether or not the bottom-up decision-making process is widely practised or not depends on the definition or understanding of what this process actually is when measuring the degree it is practised. If the understanding of the process is that middle management plays the central role in making day-to-day decisions and has considerable influence in the formulation of strategy then perhaps it is commonly practised. On the other hand, if the process is understood to mean that workers and low-level managers are making significant decisions than it is definitely not practised. March (1992b) follows this line of reasoning in discussing the difference between participation and power in Japanese factories.

To understand how the bottom-up decision-making process functions in its ideal form it is necessary to examine how the flow of information determines how decisions are made. The information required for making decisions usually creates a flow of information from lower levels of management to higher ones. Top management relies on information from middle management, who in turn may consult with their subordinates. In this consultation process middle management and lower management are exposed to corporate strategy.

Nemawashi plays a central role in this consultation process in Japanese organizations. *Nemawashi* is the informal discussion that precedes formal decision-making in Japanese corporations. It is also an integral part of bottom-up decision-making. Effective *nemawashi* presupposes smoothness in human relations. No matter how brilliant an employee's proposal, it would be difficult to gain acceptance for implementation if the person proposing it has not established adequate human relations within the organization. Establishing amicable relations with key members of the company's management organization is the only means to make one's voice effective in the company's decision-making.

One of the main responsibilities of middle management is to gather information and achieve consensus among peers and subordinates. This is achieved through the process of *nemawashi*. Only when the *nemawashi* is concluded and a project or proposal declared feasible by all those concerned is the written proposal or *ringi-sho* (discussed below) submitted. Give-and-take is the implicit rule behind interdepartmental relations, and *nemawashi* requires that middle managers keep in mind a balance sheet of favours owed and favours due (Hasegawa, 1986:42–3).

Nemawashi is a universal trait of all Japanese organizations; however the extent to which it is practised appears to vary among companies and industries. Hayashi (1989) surveyed Japanese companies concerning their use of *nemawashi* and the centralization/decentralization dichotomy of decision-making. First he asked the questions; 'When a decision is made, is a general discussion of the issue important? Or is private consultation *(nemawashi)* preferable?' Light-industry employees and wholesalers expressed more support for the open-discussion method of decision-making, while support for *nemawashi* was notably stronger in heavy industry. Next, Hayashi asked the question; 'Should company decisions be made by the top echelon/head office, or should decision-making be decentralized to lower levels and branch offices?' The results revealed that wholesalers generally supported the top-level/head-office style, while the finance industry showed a marked preference for the lower-echelon, decentralized pattern (Hayashi, 1989:32).

There are rarely open disputes during official meetings in Japanese companies. Important decisions are most often already determined before the meeting is called. If participants do disagree in such meetings they use moderated language acknowledging an alternative position or an opponent's contention as they proceed with expressing their own position. As Hayashi (1989:134–5) pointed out, the dialogue advances an inch at a time; much like sappers clearing a minefield, and meeting participants do not demolish each other's arguments or attack another person's opinion.

Decisions are usually by unanimous agreement, not by majority vote. Although no objections or dissent are expressed at a formal meeting when a course of action is ratified, there are always some members with strong objections who have been forced to go along. A party where people can be candid and express their *honne* or true feelings often follows official meetings in Japan. At the party the group leader placates the disgruntled minority. This effort to console an unhappy faction usually continues with a *nijikai* or a second party after the official party. This process ensures that new policies will be smoothly implemented.

Hayashi (1989) believes that the primary reason Japanese want to avoid formal meetings, as a decision-making method, is a dread of personal responsibility. Whether it is recognition of outstanding achievement or blame for failure, there is an aversion to making a specific individual accountable. The entire group carefully makes policy and the result is the responsibility of all members collectively, not of a single individual. Even if an official record is kept of the meeting, it does not indicate who was really the prime mover in the group's action (Hayashi, 1989:132). In his book, *The Enigma of Japanese Power*, van Wolferen (1992) argues that one of the greatest weaknesses of Japanese society in general is the Japanese trait of not taking individual responsibility for decisions.

5.6.2 Collectivism and Consensus Decision-making

Consensus style decision-making in Japan appears to be related to the collectivist nature of Japanese society. Through the process of consultation and sharing of information, the parties confirm that they are members of the same organization and share responsibilities for its actions. The complexity involved in exchanging information is multiplied as the number of members in a given organization grows. Japanese firms spend a great amount of energy in developing a consensus since, as previously argued, there is a strong tendency to desire group rather than individual decisions.

The criticism that Japanese managers in their foreign subsidiaries are over-concerned about their head office's reactions is often heard.

In fact, however, this concern on the part of the PCN managers is a direct result of the consensus-forming process between the key managers at head office and the PCN managers at the subsidiaries. In the homogeneous society of Japan it is vital for each member to keep harmony with other members of his organization (Sasaki, 1981); thus the PCN managers do not want to be perceived as ignoring the key managers at the parent company. This consultation takes place regardless of the degree of authority delegated to the subsidiaries. Nevertheless, it also implies that the management of the foreign subsidiaries is centralized at the parent company since the PCNs function as an extension of the in-group based at the parent company.

Collectivism in Japanese organizations is also expressed in the way that roles are designed and performed. Sasaki (1981) uses the dichotomy of set of roles versus set of people to contrast Japanese decision-making with that of Western-based organizations (also discussed in Chapter 4 in relation to control mechanisms). Sasaki views the firm as a set of people, and at the same time it is a set of roles to be performed by this set of people. Each of the two sets is an organized complex whole. One system is the sum of the roles that the people perform (relationship A) while the other is the sum of the people (relationship B). In relationship A the role system dominates the people system. The functioning of the firm is partitioned into individual roles for individual members to perform. The acceptance of the role by an individual represents a contract to perform the specified duties of the role, no more and no less.

On the other hand, in relationship B the people system dominates the role system. A set of people is formed, which then explores what it can and/or should do. Although the result is the same in that the people perform individual roles, the boundaries of the individual roles are vague. This relationship can be described as *gemeinschaftlich*. In the West relationship A is prevalent while in Japan relationship B dominates. If the existing principles and concepts of organizational behaviour, that have been developed in the West relating to the decision-making process, are re-examined in contrasting relationship A with relationship B, light is shed on the decision-making mechanisms of Japanese firms which otherwise may appear incomprehensible to the Westerner. Sasaki (1981:59–60) maintains that relationships A and B demand different value systems for their base. Therefore, in order to understand relationship B a drastic inversion of Western value criteria is necessary.

Communication and Decision-making

Sasaki's observations overly stereotype Western organizations; surely co-operation and the desire to perform above and beyond one's specified duties exist in Western organizations. However, the concept serves well in explaining the connection between collectivism and decision-making in Japanese organizations. Even though Sasaki does not explicitly describe the above concept in the context of a discussion on collectivism, it is implied since collective societies value group efforts over individual efforts. In group efforts individual roles and responsibilities are usually not well defined.

Almost all Japanese decisions in any organization are a product of group thinking, and a consensus among the group is demanded by the value system of Japanese society, which is basically collectivistic. An individual decision is understood to be the product of the individual's value system and knowledge. In order for a group to reach consensus members must have the similar values and information. The practice of long-term employment and the homogeneity of Japanese society along with the pressure to conform to group behavioural patterns have led to a converging of values among members of the same organization in Japan. Accordingly, people in a given organization should be able to easily come to a consensus on a decision if they had the same information. In practice, even in the homogeneous Japanese society, individual value systems are found to differ. Where the difference is relatively great, the information exchange process becomes more subtle and delicate, and each member of the group has to manipulate information to achieve agreement with the others.

It should be noted that even though the term 'consensus' is often used in reference to decision-making in Japanese firms, unanimity is perhaps more appropriate. It is absurd to think that the managers in a given Japanese firm can always come to a consensus when making decisions. Unanimity may be achieved because managers who actually may disagree with a decision will still indicate agreement if the majority of managers or certain important executives agree with the decision. In this way decision-making in the Japanese context may differ from that of the US in that Japanese are more likely to not publicly express disagreement with a decision if they judge that their view is not that of the majority or significant individuals.

5.6.3 The *Ringi-sho* or Formal Written Proposal

The *ringi-sho* is a written recommendation or proposal urging a specific course of action. The word *sho* means document while the word *ringi* is the act of obtaining approval on a proposed matter through the vertical, and sometimes horizontal, circulation of documents to the concerned members in the organization. The proposal process begins when the initiators discuss the issue at hand with all the sections and departments concerned *(nemawashi)*, and prepare the necessary documents and materials. Once an informal agreement among these parties is obtained the formal circulation procedure starts. The document is passed up through the administration to the top managers. If there are objections along the way the *ringi-sho* is returned to the initiators. The objections must be overcome by persuasion or the *ringi-sho* must be rewritten.

When managers accept the proposal they affix their seal to it as a sign of agreement. Thus, some scholars have labelled the *ringi* system a 'consensual understanding,' and a 'confirmation-authorization' process of decision-making. The *ringi*, in this context, is used to confirm that all elements of disagreement have been eliminated at the *nemawashi* stage. When the *ringi-sho* reaches the top of the organization it may receive formal authorization and the final go-ahead.

Sometimes higher-level managers initiate a *ringi-sho* by giving it to subordinates to propose. In relation to this observation, Yoshimura and Anderson (1997:165) believe that the bottom-up decision-making process as manifested in the *ringi* system is actually just an illusion that Japanese companies create in order to motivate employees. They claim that when the subordinates learn what the superior wants, the subordinates will formally write up the *ringi-sho* and begin circulating it. In such a case other managers will feel obliged to affix their seal of approval regardless of whether or not they completely agree with the proposal.

There are conflicting opinions on the origin of the *ringi* system. According to Hasegawa (1986), the *ringi* system was already in operation in the 17th century during the Tokugawa period. However, Sasaki (1981:56-7) states: 'The feudal political order in Japan during the middle of the 19th century gave birth to the *ringi* system where the substantial job of policy-making was left to the lower-upper or upper-middle level members of the hierarchy in order to make it possible for the top to escape from taking the responsibility by imputing to those who made the drafts of the policies.' Thereafter, Sasaki claims that the *ringi* system was incorporated into the new bureaucracy of the Meiji government.

Abegglen (1958) pointed out the merits of the *ringi* system. The greatest merit he found was participation, in the Japanese way. Under the *ringi* system many people including lower management automatically participate in the decision-making process. In addition to this, Kaufmann and Felix (1970:1) assert that there are four primary advantages: fewer aspects of the decision are overlooked; the trauma that accompanies change is reduced; participants feel committed to implementing a decision they have helped to formulate; and far bolder decisions can be made. Furthermore, they claim that the *ringi* system nurtures an employee's knowledge of how the organization functions since the system forces an individual employee to think through a decision or proposal in the context of how it affects each part of the organization.

Nevertheless, there are disadvantages as well as advantages to the *ringi* system, one of which is the problem of assigning responsibility. The generator of a proposal is an employee of low rank who bears little company responsibility, while his superiors are cast in the essentially passive role of consenting to the *ringi-sho*. As a result, the greater the number of superiors involved, the more the responsibility for the decision is blurred. Since it is impossible to assign responsibility when it is so widely diffused, the end result is that those truly responsible for a failure escape answering for their errors.

Matsushita provides an example of the amorphous nature of the *ringi* responsibility in its decision to halt R&D on mainframe computers in 1964 (Hasegawa, 1986:34). Perhaps the most prevalent complaint about the *ringi* system is the amount of time required to make decisions. Kenneth Courtis, senior economist of Deutsche Bank Capital Markets in Tokyo, (Schlender, 1994:97) commented:

> The white-collar problem is an existential question for corporate Japan. With the technology available today, companies have the ability to collect and analyze data and make decisions so rapidly that traditional vertical management structures just get in the way. If Japanese companies insist on staying with the old hierarchical ways, it won't matter how good their factories are.

Sasaki (1981) claims that there were efforts to purge the feudal *ringi* system for the following reasons:

1. There was a lack of leadership at the top and the drafts drawn by middle management were inflexible or narrow compared with those of top management;
2. There were vague boundaries of authority and responsibility. The prior co-ordination, which takes into account as many comments, advice and opinions as possible from other departments concerned, would often make the final plan a product of compromise.

3. The formality of the system was apt to be inefficient.
4. The excess of *ringi-sho* for the top management to check made them only a stamping machine.

These criticisms appear to still be valid in modern Japanese organizations that continue to employ the *ringi* system. Accordingly, some scholars argue that the traditional *ringi* system is now disappearing. Perhaps the use of the *ringi-sho* is decreasing, but it is unlikely that the underlying spirit of the system is dying. It may be time-consuming and politically delicate but it is very appropriate for the Japanese organization based on and protected by seniority. Hasegawa (1986) believes that consensus and the *ringi* system work smoothly and effectively as long as there are no violent changes that cannot be foreseen. The panic buying during the first oil shock is an example of the consensus of herd mentality of the Japanese.

5.6.4 Advantages and Disadvantages of Japanese-style Decision-making

As discussed above in relation to the *ringi* system, the proponents of decision-making by consensus claim that the strength of Japanese-style decision-making lies in its deliberativeness and in the involvement of all those who will be responsible for the implementation of decisions. However, according to Sethi *et al.* (1984:236), Japanese companies are confronting new conditions that make some of the virtues of the existing systems also their main drawbacks:

1. The rapid rate of technological growth and change introduces new risks and uncertainties, calling for different types of inputs into the decision-making process, ones that do not fit the organizational structure. In fact, the most important skills necessary to evaluate risks may not even be available in the organization.
2. The nature of markets, competition, and lead times for making decisions is becoming increasingly shorter, requiring fast reaction times.
3. The need to protect all those involved creates a bias toward risk avoidance.

Furthermore, Sethi *et al.* (1984:237) argue that companies with the greatest exposure to new technologies and new competition, such as Sony, are also the ones breaking away from the conventional systems by reducing the length of decision-making time by sidelining excess middle managers and limiting the number of people involved in the decision process. In addition, they state that other companies encourage senior executives to work closely with middle and lower-level managers, to inform them of the overall strategies of the firm and management's thinking, thereby providing those below with a clearer indication of the types of actions that will receive top management's approval. In this process of streamlining decision-making, these companies are likely to confront difficulties due to the prevailing cultural behaviour patterns. Sethi *et al.* claim that the result is alienation and the erosion of employee loyalty.

In addition, Woronoff (1992:50–1) contrasted some of the advantages and defects of Japanese-style decision-making. As for the advantages he listed:

1. It provides for some degree of democracy and spontaneity in that lower levels can initiate measures.
2. It provides for greater participation, especially when combined with meetings, since all those even remotely involved in an issue will be invited to attend and present their views.
3. A decision adopted on the basis of consensus, or so it is claimed, will meet with general acceptance.
4. The process reinforces harmony within the company and should encourage all to give their unstinting support to implementation of new measures.

On the other hand, the disadvantages pointed out by Woronoff focus on the amount of time it takes to make a decision, the excessive number of people who must be involved, and the excessive number of meetings that are held wasting the time of managers who are not directly concerned with the matter. As a consequence of the inordinate amount of time it takes some Japanese firms to make decisions, Woronoff cites examples of lost business opportunities and questions whether or not the *ringi* system truly empowers lower-level managers (1992:52–3):

The final decision, however, will result from the basic power relationship between the participants. Although lower ranking staff is also invited, they know better than to sponsor proposals without backing from higher up. So those below will rarely impose the decisions. That being so, why go through all the rituals and formalities when everyone knows they are a sham?

5.7 DECISION-MAKING AT JAPANESE FOREIGN SUBSIDIARIES

Negandhi and Serapio (1991:26) studied 27 Japanese manufacturing subsidiaries in the US. They found that the subsidiaries depended very little on written policies and manuals from the parent company to guide their decision-making. Only ten subsidiaries in the sample reported relying on written policy manuals from the parent company to guide their decision-making. The manuals mainly dealt with matters of production, finance and matters involving Japanese PCNs. Instead of written policies, the MNCs use other forms of control such as visits from parent company executives to the subsidiary, formalized reporting to the parent company, centralized decision-making at headquarters and appointing numerous PCNs to key management positions at the subsidiary.

Negandhi et al. (1987) also studied sixty-five Japanese subsidiaries in Malaysia, Singapore and Thailand. Their conclusions concerning decision-making at these subsidiaries in Southeast Asia are similar to those they made concerning decision-making at Japanese subsidiaries in the US. They found that in order to ensure centralization of decision-making and maintain the influence of the parent company on subsidiary management, most top positions were staffed by Japanese PCNs. Likewise there were frequent visits to the subsidiary by executives from the parent company and frequent written reports on all aspects of the subsidiary's operation.

Sethi et al. (1984) also claim that Japanese companies have great difficulty integrating foreigners into their decision-making process, which requires a common sharing of cultural norms, a knowledge of the political workings of the organization, and an intuitive feeling about the corporate culture. They stress that as long as the Japanese parent company does not substantially change its internal workings, comparatively larger numbers of Japanese expatriate managers will be needed for the communication and watchdog functions in their US operations. Sethi et al. claim that Japanese affiliates have used either the top-down decision-making style or a hybrid system combining elements of both the American and the Japanese styles. They express doubt about the possible implementation of Japanese-style decision-making in Japanese foreign subsidiaries at the management level (1984:258):

> There is also tremendous reluctance on the part of Japanese companies to broaden the scope of consensus-style decision-making.

Consultation is practised largely at lower levels of the organization and involves shop floor or other routine decisions. At middle and upper management levels, the scope of consensus-style decision-making involving American managers is quite narrow, and often practised in form rather than substance.

A consensus-style decision-making process confined to a foreign subsidiary and its operations is unsatisfactory because Japanese subsidiaries are closely controlled by their parents in Japan. Thus, HCN managers must be able to effectively communicate their opinions to the key managers in Japan who strongly influence the outcomes of decisions concerning issues with which the HCN managers are dealing. The important role in-groups play at the parent company in making decisions that directly affect the management of the foreign subsidiary is inimical to the successful integration of HCN managers. Under the present IHRM policies and practices at most Japanese firms, which tend not to promote contact between the HCN managers and the Japanese managers at the parent company, the HCNs are unlikely ever to become part of these in-groups. Due to this lack of contact with the in-groups at the parent company, it seems to the HCN managers that their recommendations are ignored or rejected without apparent reason or rational justification. Thus, they may become frustrated and dissatisfied with the decision-making process at the subsidiary.

Another serious problem in instituting consensus-style decision-making lies in the sharing of responsibility, which is directly or indirectly tied into the reward system. An individual performance-based reward system is in direct conflict with a consensus-style decision-making system. The Japanese executive is rewarded on the basis of shared responsibility and group-oriented compensation, and the success of the entire organization. However, it is difficult to evaluate the performance of HCNs when they are not part of the company-wide decision-making process.

A number of other researchers have reported data indicating the lack of integration of HCN managers into the decision-making process involving management issues that directly affect the foreign subsidiaries where they work. Pucik *et al.* (1989) studied the management culture and effectiveness of HCNs in Japanese subsidiaries in the US. The US executives inform them that the primary responsiblility for most decisions rests with Japanese PCNs in the US, with heavy involvement of PCNs at the parent company in Japan. On the other hand, the HCN managers are responsible for only a small proportion of decisions. Pucik *et al.* report that the decisions where the HCNs are heavily involved are primarily in the marketing area, for example: product pricing, sales and profit targets, and sales promotion. In contrast, HCNs are least involved in decisions concerning R&D in Japan, establishment of new subsidiaries, factories and branches, and borrowing from local sources.

Elashmawi (1990) also discussed the lack of HCN participation in the decision-making process of Japanese overseas subsidiaries. He indicated that in overseas subsidiaries the Japanese tend not to include HCNs in their participatory style. This is due the existence of two separate lines of management: the Japanese PCN managers in one group and the HCN managers in the other group. Elashmawi declares that although they appear to share the work, the Japanese usually control the decision-making process and the HCNs provide the information gathering. He also stresses that most decisions are made in consultation with the parent company in Japan, a process that frustrates the HCNs and makes them feel that their opinions are not valued. He concludes that eventually HCNs will withdraw completely from any decision-making responsibility, thereby giving full control to the Japanese team.

Negandhi, Eshghi and Yuen (1985) made a number of interesting observations concerning decision-making in Japan based on several empirical studies of Japanese overseas subsidiaries undertaken by the authors and their colleagues as previously discussed. They concluded that, in general, research on management of Japanese overseas subsidiaries has found that the prevalent style of decision-making is the autocratic style and there is no evidence of the practice of the consensus style. A comparative study of MNCs in Taiwan indicated that all major decisions are made by Japanese PCNs or by headquarters.

Later, Negandhi, Yuen and Eshghi (1987) reported that other studies on management of foreign subsidiaries of Japanese MNCs have revealed little evidence of a 'bottom-up' decision-making process. Furthermore, they claim that centralized decision-making in its extreme is prevalent in Japanese subsidiaries in the less-developed countries. On the other hand, the authors believe that in developed countries, market conditions and the existence of industrial democracy have forced Japanese subsidiaries to make some modifications in their approach to decision-making. However, they still assert that Japanese managers, at best, simply inform the lower-level employees of issues and the management's decisions.

In the literature on management in Japanese overseas subsidiaries there are numerous quotes from HCN managers expressing their frustration with the communication and decision-making processes at the Japanese firms where they are employed. The main theme is usually the lack of HCN participation in decision-making and the frequent exclusion of HCNs in the consultation. For example, in Oyama's study (1994:70) a HCN employee reported:

> First, Japanese workers discussed some issues among themselves in Japanese. Afterwards we were brought in for the same issue, which was interpreted by the Americans as very insulting because they asked why were we not included in the first place. This is because in a Japanese company if you are not Japanese, you are not included in the decision-making. Americans felt very frustrated. If a Japanese group meets and talks a while, they will probably establish a consensus. The mood is already set. When an American goes to the meeting, he realizes that the consensus is already made. In that situation, he wonders why he is here and he feels insulted even if they ask his opinion. You already reached your consensus.

It appears that this type of situation described by the HCN in Oyama's study is not unique to Japanese subsidiaries in the United States. Rather, regardless of where the Japanese subsidiary is located, there is a high probability that HCN managers will express dissatisfaction with their lack of involvement in decision-making. Indeed the data collected for this research reveals a similar pattern of the lack of HCN managers' involvement in decision-making at Japanese subsidiaries in Southeast Asia and Australia, as is demonstrated in the following chapter. Other researchers have reached similar conclusions for this region. For example, Thome and McAuley (1992:152) found in their study of Japanese subsidiaries in Asia that Japanese PCNs controlled decision-making at the subsidiary and constantly consulted with the parent company in Japan:

> Many Singaporeans believe the Japanese overdo consultation, and some suggest they consult with locals only on minor issues, while major issues are settled in consultation with Tokyo. As in other countries the degree of influence, perhaps interference, exercised by central office in Tokyo is a source of continuing irritation. In most cases decision-making has been almost entirely removed from the local office, relying on almost continuous communication with Tokyo from where detailed control is exercised.

6 A Study Clarifying HCN Integration in Japanese MNCs

The previous four chapters have introduced and elaborated on the variables in the Conceptual Model of Factors Affecting HCN Integration. This chapter focuses on my qualitative and quantitative study, which is used to test this model. First, the qualitative data obtained during interviews as well as written comments by the questionnaire respondents are presented. Second, the data obtained from the questionnaires completed by human resource managers are presented. Thereafter, the data obtained from the questionnaires for PCN and HCN managers are presented.

Following the presentation of the data, hierarchical regression analysis is employed to analyse and test the Conceptual Model of Factors Affecting HCN Integration. The goal of this analysis is to examine the relationships between the factors that are postulated to influence or predict the integration of HCN managers in the management process at Japanese overseas subsidiaries in terms of their participation in decision-making.

6.1 RESEARCH METHODS

This section describes the research instruments, data collection, demographics, and the scales developed for measuring the variables in the Conceptual Model of Factors Affecting HCN Integration.

6.1.1 Research Instruments

In the pilot study, two questionnaires were developed, one in English to be completed by HCN managers employed at Japanese subsidiaries in Malaysia and Australia as well as one in Japanese to be completed by the PCNs at the same companies. I developed the questionnaires with the co-operation of Kazuo Doi, a colleague of mine at Kyushu Sangyo University in Fukuoka, Japan. The English and Japanese versions of the questionnaires fundamentally ask the same set of questions. However, there are certain questions that logically apply to only HCN or PCN managers and these types of questions were also included.

The pilot study served to validate the research instruments and offered insights into how the study could be improved. A number of questions employed in the pilot study that did not provide particularly useful insights were omitted from the questionnaire used in 1996. While considering the results of the first study, additional questions were formulated to seek more precise data. For example, additional items to be used in the scale for HCN participation in decision-making were added to the 1996 questionnaire. In addition, I developed a separate questionnaire concerning the staffing of the subsidiary and various IHRM policies and practices to be filled out by human resource managers.

6.1.2 Data Collection

Data collection for the pilot study was carried out over a period of about 10 weeks beginning 17 July 1994 while data collection for the study took place from 5 June 1996 for a period of about 16 weeks. The target subsidiaries were selected from the list of Japanese subsidiaries in foreign countries published in *Kaigai Shinshutsu Kigyo Soran* (Guide to Japanese Foreign Direct Investment). The 1994 edition was used for the pilot study and the 1996 edition for the main study.

In the pilot study, priority was given to what appeared to be the largest Japanese subsidiaries in Australia and Malaysia based on the number of employees. However, care was taken to include companies from both service and manufacturing sectors. In the 1996 study, questionnaires were sent to a greater number of Japanese subsidiaries in Australia, Malaysia, Singapore, and Thailand.

In the pilot study, interviews were carried out at nine Japanese subsidiaries in Malaysia (seven manufacturing, two non-manufacturing) and one subsidiary in Australia (manufacturing). At least two Japanese managers and two HCN managers at each subsidiary were interviewed for an average of 70 minutes for each individual. Questionnaires were sent or hand-delivered to 29 subsidiaries in Malaysia and 20 in Australia for a total of 49 firms. HCN managers received the English version of the questionnaire while Japanese managers answered the Japanese version. By the deadline of 30 September 1994, 34 companies returned usable questionnaires yielding a response rate of 69 per cent.

174 *International Human Resource Management*

The high response rate in the pilot study is due to the fact that many firms were contacted by phone before sending the questionnaires. No firms contacted by phone refused to receive the questionnaires but not all of them returned questionnaires. The total number of individual questionnaires from Japanese managers was 120 (22 from Australia, 96 from Malaysia, and two from Singapore) while the total number returned by HCN managers was 128 (23 from Australia, 103 from Malaysia, and two from Singapore).

In the 1996 study, interviews were carried out at eight Japanese subsidiaries in Australia (one manufacturing, seven non-manufacturing). Questionnaires were sent to a total of 476 Japanese firms (114 in Australia, 96 in Malaysia, 145 in Singapore, and 121 in Thailand). By 30 September 1996 83 companies returned usable questionnaires yielding a response rate of 17.4 per cent. The lower response rate compared to that of the pilot study might be due to the fact that very few firms were contacted by phone to request co-operation in the study due to the cost burdens involved. The total number of individual questionnaires from Japanese managers was 133 (37 from Australia, 20 from Malaysia, 43 from Singapore, and 33 from Thailand) while the total number returned by HCN managers was 123 (37 from Australia, 23 from Malaysia, 41 from Singapore, and 22 from Thailand).

Furthermore, questionnaires concerning general human resource practices were sent addressed to the human resource managers at Japanese subsidiaries in Australia, Malaysia, Singapore, and Thailand. Thirty-seven companies completed the human resource questionnaire (11 from Australia, six from Malaysia, 15 from Singapore, and four from Thailand).

6.1.3 Demographics

The demographics in this sub-section describe the respondents and their companies for the 1996 study. There were 105 male HCN respondents and 18 female HCN respondents, while the gender for PCN respondents was 129 male and two female (no response = two). The average age of the HCN respondents was 40 ($SD = 7.31$), while the average age of the PCN respondents was 45 ($SD = 7.31$). The majority of the HCN and PCN respondents held either a high-level or mid-level management position. The levels held by the HCN respondents were 39 high-level, 70 mid-level and seven low-level (no response = seven), while for PCN the numbers were 62, 51, and nine, respectively (no response = 11).

The average number of years the HCN managers had been working at the subsidiary at the time of the study in 1996 was 9.76 years (SD = 6.88). The majority (76 or 62 per cent) had been working there for two to ten years. The PCNs tend to rotate from the parent company to the subsidiaries. Thus, as could be expected, the average, 3.37 (SD = 2.18) was much lower. The majority to the PCNs had been working there for one to three years (82 or 62 per cent). The average size of the companies where the respondents were employed was 742 employees with a range of 43 to 3,800. The average number of years that companies had been in operation was 15 years (SD = 9.37).

As reported in the previous section, a total of 37 human resource managers at Japanese subsidiaries in Australia (11), Malaysia (six), Singapore (15), and Thailand (five) completed the questionnaires concerning general human resource practices. Ten of these subsidiaries have less than 200 employees, twelve have 200 or more and less than 501 employees, six have 501 or more and less than 1,001 employees, and nine have 1,001 or more employees. The subsidiaries have been in operation for an average of 16 years (SD = 8.43).

6.1.4 Scales Developed for Measuring Model Variables

In order to measure each of the elements of the model, scales were developed to specifically tap issues relevant to Japanese subsidiary companies. There are no generally accepted existing scales for these elements that perform the function adequately. The pilot study identified the issues of relevance and provided the opportunity to develop instruments that tapped directly into the key points relating to HCN's involvement in the management process of Japanese subsidiaries. All items in the scales are shown in Appendix A.

Target variable: The dependent variable, the integration of local managers in decision-making (referred to as integration), was measured using a 16-item scale. Respondents were asked who mainly made decisions, local managers or Japanese managers, in relation to a list of issues. A five-point Likert scale was used, anchored at one 'completely Japanese' and five 'completely local.' The scale includes questions related to decisions concerning such issues as: hiring of new employees, employee benefits, production schedules, purchase of production inputs, local advertising, new facilities, and sales goals. The scale had very good reliability for both the HCN data set (Cronbach alpha = 0.93) and the PCN data set (Cronbach alpha = 0.90). This approach is effective in determining the extent that HCNs participate in the decision-making process. There are no published research results, besides those of the author (Keeley and Doi, 1996 and 1995) that specifically demonstrate to what extent decisions are made by PCNs and HCNs at Japanese overseas subsidiaries.

Explanatory Variables: International human resource management (referred to as IHRM) was measured using a five-item scale. The essence of this measure is the extent to which HCN managers are incorporated in the company as international managers and not just employees of the subsidiary. The concept reveals how respondents felt the company developed HCN managers for growth in the subsidiary and other parts of the parent company. This is an important factor, as discussed in Chapter 3, since the distinction between *seishain* and *non-seishain* modulates the role of employees. The scale includes such items as: 'This company offers local managers the opportunity to work at the parent company in Japan or at a subsidiary in another country,' 'There are clear career paths for locally hired employees,' 'There are good management development programmes for locally hired employees.' The items were anchored using a five-point Likert scale where one is 'strongly disagree' and five is 'strongly agree.' The scale had moderate reliability for both HCN (Cronbach alpha = 0.69) and PCN data (Cronbach alpha = 0.61).

Communication was measured using a 14-item scale focusing on communication, information sharing, and language barriers within the subsidiary and between the subsidiary and the head office. A five-point Likert scale was used where one is 'strongly disagree' and five is 'strongly agree.' There are seven items that deal with the communication between HCN managers and PCN managers at the parent company, and seven items that deal with the communication between HCN managers and PCN managers at the subsidiary. The questions relate to the existence of communication difficulties, language barriers, HCN access to communication channels to the PCN managers at the parent company, the existence of sufficient trust for smooth communication, the degree information is openly shared, informal communication during after-hours socializing, the flow of information between HCN and PCN managers at the subsidiary, and whether or not important information is withheld from HCN managers.

The questions reflect the importance of communication between the subsidiary and the parent company. As discussed in Chapter 5, decision-making in Japanese companies usually involves a lot of consensus building and networking. In order for HCN managers to fully participate in the decision-making process at the subsidiary there must be sufficient communication and networking with not only the PCN managers at the subsidiary but also those at the parent company. The scale had good reliability for both the HCN data set (Cronbach alpha = 0.80) and the PCN data set (Cronbach alpha = 0.83).

An eight-item scale was used to measure issues related to business practices and culture (referred to as business culture). This concept focuses on HCN understanding of Japanese business practices and culture as well as PCN understanding of local business practices and culture. There are also questions concerning the extent to which the company endeavoured to familiarize PCN and HCN managers with these cultural issues. Furthermore, there are questions that deal with cultural conflicts and the concept of *nihonjinron* discussed in Chapter 3. A five-point Likert scale was used with a range one 'strongly disagree' to five 'strongly agree.' The scale had good reliability for the HCN data (Cronbach alpha = 0.73) and moderate reliability for the PCN data (Cronbach alpha = 0.66).

Control variables: Demographic variables are also included in the analysis since they might affect the dependent variable in this study. It is possible that older managers, due to respect for their age and work experience, are more integrated in the decision-making process than are younger, less experienced managers. Similarly, it is possible that longer serving managers are more familiar with the operations of the company and their input in decision-making, compared to newer managers, is more highly valued by the company. Managers' position in the organizational hierarchy might also influence HCN integration since, by virtue of their positions, senior managers might be more extensively involved in decision-making than more junior managers. Accordingly, age, years employed at the subsidiary, and level in the hierarchy are included as control variables in the analysis.

Standard multiple regression analysis was selected to analyse and test the model using SPSS. Such analysis provides insight into the relationships between the variables in the model.

6.1.5 Scales Developed for Human Resource Questionnaire

A group of six questions concerning IHRM policies was employed in the questionnaire completed by human resource managers to further clarify to what extent HCN employees are considered global human resources (referred to as global HRM scale). Four of these questions are the same as those employed by Kopp (1994a) for the same purpose (see Chapter 4). However, Kopp simply allowed for a yes/no response. On the other hand, the items in this scale were anchored using a five-point Likert scale where one is 'strongly disagree' and five is 'strongly agree.' Furthermore, two additional questions were added to the scale. The questions used in the scale are also listed in Appendix A. The scale had good reliability (Cronbach alpha = 0.77). A high score on this scale indicates that a company is co-ordinating its human resources on a global scale (or, conversely, a low score would indicate ethnocentric IHRM).

In addition, the data for five other questions were used to develop a scale for measuring HCN satisfaction with evaluation and remuneration process as perceived by the human resource manager (referred to here as evaluation and remuneration Scale). These questions included in the scale are also listed in Appendix A. The items were anchored using a five-point Likert scale where one is 'strongly disagree' and five is 'strongly agree.' The scale had good reliability (Cronbach alpha = 0.87). A high score on this scale indicates that HCNs are satisfied with the evaluation and remuneration policies and practices.

6.2 PRESENTATION OF THE QUALITATIVE DATA

The format for presenting the qualitative data follows that of the Conceptual Model of Factors Affecting HCN Integration. The dependent variable, integration of HCN is discussed first, followed by a discussion of the three independent variables: IHRM, communication, and business culture. However, qualitative data are not easily confined to one element in the model. The comments often deal with more than one issue, and are thus discussed in the most relevant section.

6.2.1 Qualitative Data Related to HCN Integration

The main goal of the interviews was to ascertain to what extent HCN managers are integrated into the management process of the subsidiaries, as measured by the HCN managers' participation in decision-making. The variable HCN integration in decision-making appeared woven into many of the comments dealing with the three other variables in the model, particularly IHRM and communication. For example, IHRM policies such as staffing would logically appear to be

HCN Integration in Japanese MNCs 179

a determining factor of HCN integration since policies that favour staffing key management positions with PCNs would limit HCN integration. However, even when HCN managers are in key management positions it is possible that their decision-making authority will be limited by other factors.

Furthermore, effective communication, as discussed in Chapter 5, is an important part of the decision-making process. The literature indicates that there is a great deal of communication between Japanese parent companies and overseas subsidiaries in relation to decisions made at the subsidiaries. Thus, HCN managers would have to be involved in this communication loop to obtain the necessary information to participate in making decisions, particularly important decisions. However, the comments of the HCN and the PCN managers indicated that the HCN managers did not usually participate directly in the communication between the subsidiary and the parent company.

Concerning HCN participation in making decisions, the managing director of a large Malaysian manufacturing subsidiary stated that HCN managers were given enough opportunity to participate. However, he added that the decision-making responsibility of HCNs is limited by their position in the organizational hierarchy. He stressed that the PCN managers in consultation with the parent company usually made the strategic decisions since these decisions must be made in the context of the parent company's overall strategy. He claimed that the HCN managers did not have a sufficient understanding of the parent company's strategy and goals to make such decisions.

The issue of parent company involvement in decision-making appeared to be an important factor limiting HCN integration at a number of the companies in the research. For example, along with the lack of access to information from the parent company, it was the most important factor limiting participation in decision-making cited by a group of four HCN managers interviewed at a Japanese manufacturing subsidiary in Australia. At that time the subsidiary was still introducing new products and production processes which required a lot of input from the parent company and the PCN managers. Three of the managers felt that the situation was improving and that over time they would be promoted and have more decision-making responsibility. The remaining HCN was not so optimistic and was not satisfied with his job.

There were also problems associated with the decision-making process itself at Japanese subsidiaries. A HCN manager at a *sogo-shosha* (general trading company) was frustrated with how decisions were made and his lack of opportunity to take independent action:

> Sometimes I cannot believe what it takes to get a deal approved in this company. We really miss out on a lot of good opportunities. What usually happens is someone like me will get involved in negotiations for some new business and our Japanese bosses keep asking for more information. They want to make sure that there is no risk. They are afraid something may go wrong and that they will, you know 'lose face.' They really analyse some deals to death. Really, that is what happens, either the client loses interest or some other faster competitor gets the business. This type of decision-making may work in Japan but not in Australia.

In addition, the manager in charge of wool trading at another *sogo-shosha* in Australia said that he left the company two years ago out of frustration with his job but was persuaded to return when they offered him a large increase in pay. He claimed to be one of Australia's leading authorities in wool trading. In spite of his knowledge and experience, whenever he set a price for a trade a young PCN trader who was his subordinate showed it to a PCN manager at a higher level for approval. He said he had learned to just laugh and shrug it off.

In the interviews, I noted that conflicts between HCN and PCN managers concerning decisions sometimes occurred due to the different perspectives the two groups have in their respective positions within the companies. The PCN managers worked for the Japanese MNC as a whole while the HCN managers worked solely for the subsidiary. Thus, the PCN managers appeared to place the interests of the parent company ahead of those of the foreign subsidiary when there is conflict between the two. On the other hand, the HCN managers appeared to be mainly aware of the interests of the foreign subsidiary where they were employed. A concrete example was given by one of the HCN employees at a *sogo-shosha:*

> My job is to oversee the shipping of the goods purchased in Australia to Japan and other destinations. From my previous experience, I judged that we were being charged too much by the Japanese transportation company we were using so I began to look for alternatives. I gathered all the necessary information and showed Mr. X [his superior, a Japanese PCN manager] how we

could reduce our costs by 40 per cent yielding a significant savings on an annual basis. He said he would consider my plan, but three months passed and nothing happened. Finally, he admitted that they did not want to change because the parent company has a close relationship with this company.

As previously mentioned, staffing key management positions with PCNs would logically limit the integration of HCNs. However, there was one case in which, even though it appeared that PCNs occupied most of the management positions, a HCN manager experienced a high degree of integration in decision-making. This HCN manager was working at a Japanese subsidiary in Malaysia that operates department stores. Although the general manager (PCN) did not provide an organizational chart, it appeared that the majority of the people at the main office in Kuala Lumpur were PCNs (there was a total of 11 PCN managers). When asked why there seemed to be so many Japanese working at the subsidiary, the general manager responded that there was a need for a lot of communication with the parent company in Japan and Japanese suppliers. In addition, PCNs worked together with HCN buyers to ensure that local suppliers met company standards concerning quality, delivery, as well as terms and conditions. In spite of these conditions, the HCN mentioned above reported that the PCNs respected her opinion and involved her in many aspects of managing the subsidiary. She had a number of years experience in the retail industry in Malaysia before joining the subsidiary and acted as a consultant on various issues.

There was one case where even though language barriers were not a problem there was still a lack of integration. Two HCN managers at a medium-size Japanese manufacturing subsidiary in Malaysia had both been hired in Japan right after finishing their studies at Japanese universities. Before returning to Malaysia, they worked at the headquarters of the parent company in order to learn about the companies' products and management culture. They were optimistic about obtaining positions of substantial responsibility at the Malaysian subsidiary since they were fluent in Japanese, had a good understanding of Japanese culture, and even had experience at the parent company. However, after four years working at the subsidiary they were somewhat disillusioned as may be confirmed from a comment by one of the managers:

> We thought we were going to become the main liaison between the parent company and our subsidiary. However, Japanese managers

hold all the important positions. We rarely have direct contact with the parent company in Japan. Mainly they use us as interpreters. Instead of being involved in shaping the management of the subsidiary, we are just telling the locals what the Japanese managers want them to do and telling the Japanese managers what the locals think. It is frustrating because we really don't think the Japanese understand the way the local people think. The Japanese don't understand our culture.

6.2.2 Qualitative Data Related to IHRM

The pattern of staffing of management positions in Japanese overseas subsidiaries is one the key IHRM issues which I sought to understand during the interviews since it has such an important impact on HCN integration. In all the subsidiaries in which interviews were held, a Japanese PCN occupied the top management position. In the case of three of the companies interviewed, I was able to obtain organizational charts. Examination of these charts reveal that in all three cases at least 70 per cent of the positions in the first three layers of the charts are occupied by Japanese PCNs. In addition, all the companies reported that there were no TCN managers employed at their subsidiaries.

However, it appears that some Japanese MNCs are seeing the need for developing a more geocentric approach. For instance, a high-level Japanese PCN manager interviewed at a *sogo-shosha* in Australia was particularly interested in the issue of employing TCN managers (my translation from Japanese):

> Our company has realized that we must effectively use the expertise of our managers throughout our world-wide organization. Our transactions often involve a number of different countries. Managers gain expertise in a certain product or market and they should be given the opportunity to use their knowledge at our subsidiaries in other countries when there is an opportunity to do so. Recently, we have taken our first step in implementing our new policy toward allowing local managers to be transferred to subsidiaries in other countries. Two local managers from our Singapore office were sent abroad, one to our office to Taiwan and the other to our office in Hong Kong. It's just a start, but I hope it is a sign of a new trend in our company.

On the other hand, at one Japanese manufacturing subsidiary of a parent company that operates 17 subsidiaries in Malaysia, none of the HCN managers had been offered the opportunity to transfer to another subsidiary. The reason given was that the HCNs are employees of the subsidiary and not employees of the parent company. PCNs working at the subsidiary are still considered employees of the parent company. The pay scale and benefits for the PCN employees are determined by the parent company in Japan while those for HCN employees are determined at the subsidiary.

All of the PCN managers at the above-mentioned Malaysian subsidiary had extensive experience working in various management positions at the company's foreign subsidiaries. It was reported that, on the average, the PCNs are assigned to a foreign subsidiary for a period of three to four years. However, the managing director had already been at this particular subsidiary for five years and was scheduled to return to Japan later that year. When asked if they would consider a HCN for the position of managing director, he responded (my translation from Japanese):

> The position of managing director requires much knowledge of how the parent company operates and relationships with managers in Japan. Also, we often hesitate to train and develop local managers because after learning a lot about our operations they may leave to work for another company. I realize that it is really kind of a vicious circle *(aku-junkan)*. We don't give local managers more responsibility because we think they will leave, but they leave because they do not get more responsibility. Actually, I think that if we Japanese managers were here longer then we could get to know who are the best candidates for promotion. We could develop better human relations and trust, we could nurture them, but when we leave the Japanese managers replacing us have to develop new relationships with them. Even if we tell our replacements which locals are the best managers, they still need to develop relationships themselves with these local managers before they can really trust them.

The HCN managers interviewed at the same subsidiary confirmed that there were difficulties associated with the rotation of PCNs. They felt that whenever a new manager came from Japan to replace an existing manager, the HCN managers had to start all over again convincing the new manager that they can perform well in their jobs and should be trusted. In this regard, one of the HCN managers said, 'we always have to train the new PCN managers, let them know how things are here in Malaysia and at this subsidiary.'

At the time of the interview, the subsidiary of a *sogo-shosha* in Australia had been in operation for 33 years and employed 85 people. There were a total of 30 management positions, 22 of which were filled by PCNs. When asked why there was such a high ratio of PCN managers, the general manager (PCN) claimed that they had not had sufficient time to develop HCN managers. The type of trading the managers supervised required experience and knowledge of the trading company's activities in Japan as well as in other foreign subsidiaries. This seemed to be a strange response given that the company had been in operation for 33 years. The human resource manager (a HCN) at the same *sogo-shosha* made the following comment while discussing the careers of HCN managers:

> The high-level management positions in this company are always filled by Japanese who come to Australia for a period anywhere between three to seven years and then are replaced by another manager from Japan. The Australians who are ambitious and want to advance usually quit after a couple of years. I think they realize that they can never have much independent authority and get frustrated. But, I think some people come here just for the experience, just to say they have worked for a Japanese company and then try to leverage this experience in getting another job.

Some of the HCN managers interviewed felt very frustrated by the perceived limitations on their careers at Japanese subsidiaries. Perhaps one of the extreme examples was a mid-level HCN manager at a large Japanese manufacturing subsidiary in Malaysia who wrote the following comment on the questionnaire he completed:

> I strongly believe that the Japanese management for overseas would never allow local management to run or manage their overseas facilities or offices anytime in the future. They believe only Japanese can manage and no others are capable or better than they are. Please highlight the fact that many local managers are facing many difficulties due to the fact that many Japanese expatriates hardly ever utter a word besides Japanese.

Many of the managers interviewed expressed satisfaction with their jobs at the subsidiaries in spite of limits on their career opportunities (most of them agreed that their promotions were limited since higher level positions were usually filled by PCNs). One of the main reasons given for their satisfaction was good pay and benefits compared to those offered by local companies (this response was much more frequent at interviews at Japanese subsidiaries in Malaysia compared to those in Australia). However, one manager at a Japanese subsidiary in Malaysia had been employed by an American company before and said that he received better pay and more responsibility but left because he did not get along with his boss (a HCN).

I was also interested in determining to what extent HCN managers had contact with PCN managers at the parent company. In order to have more influence on the outcome of decisions, it is essential for HCNs (PCNs as well) to develop and maintain close working relationships with key managers at the parent company. This is due to the strong influence/control over decision-making at the subsidiary exercised by managers at the parent company. Those HCN managers interviewed who had visited the parent company and met with the managers in Japan with whom they regularly communicate by fax, mail, or even phone, reported improvements in communication and job satisfaction. For instance, a mid-level Malaysian HCN manager commented:

> Before visiting our company's headquarters in Japan, there were a lot of things I did not understand about how things are done. It is also important to know who is in charge of what, and who is the best person in Japan to contact for particular information. It is a burden to always have to ask the Japanese managers here for help in communicating with Japan. Not everyone I met there could speak English well but now I have a couple of good contacts with whom I can communicate well enough. Anyway, when they write kanji I can usually understand what they mean.

Thus, though the expenses involved in sending HCN managers to the parent company are considerable it appears that the benefits may offer justification for such expenditures. The top manager (Japanese PCN) at a large manufacturing subsidiary in Malaysia stated that his company must seriously consider sending more HCNs more often to the parent company in order to improve their ability to manage the subsidiary.

Another item of interest was how well the IHRM policies concerning the evaluation and remuneration were functioning at the Japanese subsidiaries. A *sogo-shosha* in Australia had concluded that they must significantly revise their system for employee evaluation and remuneration. The human resource manager (HCN) who had recently been instructed to establish a new system stated:

> We are now in the process of developing a completely new approach to appraising the performance of our employees. The present system lacks concrete measurements and there are not sufficient incentives offered for improved individual performance. Some of our managers are really pushing for a new system while there are others who are comfortable with the present system and are resisting changes. I think these managers are afraid because they just muddle through; they are not really contributing significantly.

As the above quote demonstrates, Japanese subsidiaries sometimes experience difficulties at foreign subsidiaries with IHRM policies that are borrowed from the parent company. In the case of this *sogo-shosha*, the IHRM policies engendered complacency among the HCN managers and discouraged those managers who had a lot of ambition and drive. As a general observation, it appears that the IHRM policies and practices of the Japanese subsidiaries interviewed were not conducive to fostering ambitious HCN managers to take over key management positions at the subsidiaries where they were employed.

The HCN managers interviewed were never offered positions outside their respective subsidiaries. In contrast, as discussed in Chapter 3, most Japanese firms implement a policy of rotating their parent company employees to various divisions, sections, and locations throughout the company. The goal of this policy is to increase the general understanding of how the company operates as well as improve the communication between managers throughout the company in order to facilitate co-ordination in decision-making. It can be postulated that Japanese companies see a connection between IHRM policies and communication as well as between these two factors and decision-making.

6.2.3 Qualitative Data Related to Communication

There appeared to be a number of major factors impeding effective communication between HCN and PCN managers at the subsidiaries

HCN Integration in Japanese MNCs   187

where interviews were conducted. The most important of these factors was the language barriers between the two groups of managers. The only foreign language spoken (or at least studied) by the Japanese PCN managers interviewed was English, and the proficiency in English of these managers varied greatly. Most of the PCN managers at the trading companies all had extensive experience abroad and could comfortably communicate in English. However, as seen in the quote in the above section from one Malaysian manager at a Japanese manufacturing subsidiary, none of the PCN managers at the subsidiary in question could effectively communicate in English.

On the other hand, only three HCN managers out of the all the HCN managers interviewed in Australia and Malaysia spoke Japanese well enough to use the language in a business setting. Two of these HCNs were the Malaysians mentioned in the above section who had graduated from a Japanese university before being hired to work at the Japanese subsidiary in Malaysia. However, it was pointed out that they did not experience a high level of integration in spite of their proficiency in Japanese and understating of Japanese culture. The other HCN proficient in Japanese worked at the subsidiary of a Japanese trading company in Australia. However, he was a legal expert acting more as a consultant than a manager.

Though language barriers appeared to impede communication between HCN and PCN managers at the subsidiaries, it was an even greater impediment between HCN managers and managers at the parent company. For example, the general manager (PCN) at a large manufacturing firm in Malaysia reported that communication between the subsidiary and the parent company was mainly carried out in Japanese. Even though their company employed staff to translate documents sent from the parent company into English for the benefit of HCN managers, they stated that it was only possible to have a small portion of the documents translated.

All of the HCNs' managers interviewed were asked if they had direct contact on a regular basis with PCN managers at the parent company. Only the Malaysian HCN manager who visited Japan, mentioned in the above section, indicated having regular direct contact. A few other HCN managers indicated that they had communicated directly with certain PCN managers at the parent company in relation to special projects or certain business transactions. However, these were not cases of sustained regular contact. In fact, in most of these cases the HCN managers were responding to requests for information. In addition, usually a PCN manager working at the subsidiary had initiated the contact by requesting the HCN manager to provide the information to the PCN manager at the parent company. Thus, this communication between these HCN managers and PCN managers at the parent company did not clearly constitute communication for consensus decision-making between the two parties.

Communication and its relation to decision-making were reported to be an important issue at a Japanese manufacturing subsidiary in Australia. All four HCN managers interviewed at this subsidiary were enthusiastic about the study since they had all filled out questionnaires for the pilot study and had received the results before being interviewed in 1996. The human resource manager (HCN) stated that he had discussed the results with the participants and there was a consensus among them that apparently HCN managers at Japanese subsidiaries of other companies face similar issues. In particular, they felt there were significant communication problems and a need for greater participation in the consultation involved in making decisions.

The PCN managers interviewed at this subsidiary were positive about the development of the subsidiary. The PCN production manager claimed that they had already achieved a high level of quality and production efficiency. However, all of the PCN managers agreed that the flow of information to the HCN managers must be improved. Language barriers were cited as the greatest impediment to better communication. Three of the four PCN managers said their ability in English was limited which made communication difficult. Furthermore, almost all the documents received from Japan were written in Japanese.

Differences in communication styles of PCNs and HCNs also appeared to cause problems. For example, it appears that Japanese PCN managers offer less direct feedback about employee performance than some HCNs are accustomed to or expect. For instance, a mid-level Malaysian manager reporting to a PCN manager at one Japanese subsidiary in Malaysia commented:

> I am not often sure if my manager thinks I am doing the right thing. He rarely comments on my performance. If I ask him specifically what he thinks about something I have done or plan to do, he may give me his opinion but even then, it is somewhat vague, not direct. He never says 'you are doing a good job,' or 'you need to improve this or that.' I am not comfortable because I don't know what he thinks about me. If I need to change the way I am doing

HCN Integration in Japanese MNCs 189

my job I want to know, I want to improve, but I need more clear feedback.

One PCN manager at a small Japanese manufacturing subsidiary in Australia expressed a high level of satisfaction with the communication between himself and the HCN managers. He also claimed that the PCN and HCN managers shared equally in making decisions. However, the opinions of the two HCN managers interviewed at this subsidiary contrast. They felt that there were serious communication difficulties between themselves and the PCN managers. They said that the PCN managers often ignored their opinions and did not justify their decisions. One of the HCN managers stated:

> Managers must have confidence in an organization. The people sent from Japan are not always able to adapt and assist in pulling an organization together. They often choose the wrong people for overseas positions. These in turn have no idea how to evaluate/assess local people and in turn accumulate the wrong people locally as well. In short, they create 'a dead letter office.' Anybody with any skill must quickly lose confidence and leave. The Japanese staff cannot hear all that happens and again miss the important communication that generates good company progression. The Japanese do not use locals sufficiently (or trust locals) to evaluate company and people performance. It is so easy for some locals to continually bluff Japanese directors. Japanese directors in turn do not listen or want to listen to an individual who understands the business, is prepared to trust and dedicate all to the organization, and who wants allocation of locals to the position of directors.

In the above example, it appears that not only language is the barrier to effective communication; rather there are other factors such as cultural factors. The HCN manager in this case experiences a cultural gap between himself and the PCN managers. He views HCNs and PCNs as two distinct groups working together, or perhaps it should be said separately, at the same subsidiary. Differences in business and cultural issues are discussed further in the following section.

6.2.4 Qualitative Data Related to Business Culture

As discussed in Chapter 2, differences in business practices and culture add an extra dimension to the management of overseas subsidiaries that is not present in the domestic setting. It has also been pointed out many Japanese consider it difficult, if not impossible, for non-Japanese to fully understand Japanese culture. Many foreigners also appear to hold this view. In the interviews with HCN managers, I often found myself explaining the behaviour of the Japanese PCNs when they said they could not understand why their PCN boss acted in a certain way.

Most of the HCN managers tended to express a stereotypical understanding of Japanese culture in our discussions, with the distinct exception of the one Australian HCN and the two Malaysian nationals who spoke Japanese fluently and had extensive experience in Japan. On the other hand, while some of the PCN managers interviewed had a great deal of experience working abroad, many of the PCN managers had limited experience and training to prepare them for the management positions they held at their respective foreign subsidiaries. For example, the PCN managers at a large manufacturing subsidiary in Malaysia indicated that they were selected for their present positions at the foreign subsidiary on the basis of their experience and knowledge of the product manufactured without much, if any, consideration given to international experience. The managing director of this subsidiary had been in Singapore for four years and the general manager had been in America for three months before being assigned to their positions in Malaysia. When asked if they were given any special training for their international assignments, one of the PCN managers responded (my translation from Japanese):

> We did not have any type of training to prepare us for coming here. It was a shock at first. I find it really hard to communicate in English and the culture here is so different. The biggest problem is that there are three different cultures: Malay, Chinese, and Indian. I can relate to the Chinese culture to a certain extent but the Malay and Indian cultures are so different and difficult to understand.

These PCN managers also indicated that differences in culture hampered communication between PCN managers and HCN managers. Even after 20 years in operation, the subsidiary in Malaysia had not been able to reach a similar level of efficiency in production as factories in Japan. The PCN managers attributed the lack of success in improving productivity to differences in work ethic and attitudes.

As a result, there appeared to be a lot of frustration among the PCN managers in dealing with HCN employees, both managerial and labour. For example, they were having difficulties implementing the multi-skilled, flexible-responsibility approach used at the parent company with the employees on the factory floor. Concerning the Malaysians' attitude towards their job and training the general manager commented (my translation from Japanese):

> We are trying to improve the abilities of our employees through training. But every time we teach them something new they want a raise. Our company cannot continue to give in to these demands. We have to come up with some kind of new system that will give them incentives to improve their abilities without constantly giving them more money.

The HCN managers interviewed at this subsidiary reflected the same sense of frustration between the PCN managers and the HCN managers. They all felt that there was insufficient communication between themselves and the Japanese managers. The comments of the HCN managers indicated that there was a very strong feeling of us-versus-them mentality between the HCNs and the PCN managers. There appeared to be a general lack of understanding and trust between the two groups. The HCN managers complained that though the Japanese managers would often ask for information or their opinions, the PCN managers made the important decisions.

There were also examples of difficulties and conflicts arising from differences in culture and business practices in Australia. For instance, one HCN manager at a *sogo-shosha* commented:

> The Japanese managers seem to be totally dedicated to the company. Not only do they work excessively long hours, they are even willing to be separated from their family for years when they come to Australia. That's fine for them but I would not want the company to control my life like that. The trouble is because we don't make the same sacrifices they don't think we are loyal to the company.

The examples given in this section demonstrate that differences in business practices and culture are related to issues of IHRM policies, communication, and ultimately HCN integration. The above two examples show that these differences influence how PCNs view the attitude of HCNs towards their job. There was a definite tendency among the PCN managers interviewed to view the HCN managers as less dedicated to their jobs and the company compared with Japanese PCNs in general. Such views among the PCNs would not be a positive factor in the promotion of HCN managers to positions of greater responsibility. The data obtained from the questionnaires completed by HR managers at Japanese overseas subsidiaries, presented in the following section, appears to confirm many of the observations obtained in the interviews.

6.3 DATA OBTAINED FROM THE QUESTIONNAIRE FOR HUMAN RESOURCE MANAGERS

Obtaining data concerning the staffing patterns at the Japanese overseas subsidiaries was of one of the main goals of the questionnaire developed for human resource managers. The human resource managers reported that PCNs occupied 75 per cent of the high-level positions, 34 per cent of the middle-level positions, and seven per cent of the low-level management positions. There were no TCNs in management positions at these companies. These data demonstrate a strong tendency towards ethnocentric staffing.

The global HRM scale was employed to measure the human resource policies and practices of the subsidiaries on the ethnocentric–geocentric continuum. The mean for the global HRM scale was 1.86 on a five-point scale (SD = 0.63), which indicates that HCNs are rarely considered global human resources. In addition, 80 per cent of these 37 firms reported that the human resource department of the parent company in Japan is solely responsible for the affairs of the Japanese PCN managers. Only in 14 per cent of the firms is the subsidiary solely responsible. These results reflect the differentiation common in Japanese firms between *seishain* (regular, core, or formal employees) of the parent company and employees of foreign subsidiaries.

As discussed above the evaluation and remuneration scale was also created for the data from the human resource manager questionnaire. The mean for this scale was 3.15 on a five-point scale (SD = 0.75), which suggests human resource managers perceived HCN managers to be fairly satisfied with their evaluation and remuneration.

The data presented in this section indicates that ethnocentric IHRM practices are common in the foreign subsidiaries responding to the questionnaire. The primary indication of ethnocentric IHRM is the domination of higher-level management positions by Japanese PCNs. In addition, the results for the global HRM scale indicate that HCNs are rarely considered global human resources. Nevertheless, the results for the evaluation and remuneration scale suggest human resource managers perceived HCN managers to be fairly satisfied with their evaluation and remuneration. In the following section, the quantitative data obtained from the questionnaires completed by HCN and PCN managers is presented and analysed.

6.4 TESTING THE MODEL AND HYPOTHESES

In this section, the scales are employed to measure each of the variables in the Conceptual Model of Factors Affecting HCN Integration. Thereafter, hierarchical regression analysis is employed to analyse and test the relationships between the variables that are postulated to influence or predict the integration of HCN managers. The data was examined for outliers, skewness, kurtosis, multivariate normality and homoscedasticity using SPSS statistical procedures and plots. Evaluation of assumptions showed that in the HCN data set, the variable YEARS (length of service with the subsidiary) contained one outlier. The analysis was run with and without the outlier and removing the outlier significantly affected the results so it was removed from the analysis. In the PCN data set, for the variable YEARSUB (years with the subsidiary) the analysis was run with and without two outliers and these significantly affected the results and so they were removed from the analysis.

6.4.1 Findings for HCN Data

The means for each of the variables in the models are given in Table 6.1. The four variables of interest were scored on a five-point scale. The relatively low mean for integration, 2.64, supports the view that HCN managers in Japanese subsidiaries are not highly integrated in the management process as measured by the degree of their participation in decision-making. In addition, the relatively low means for IHRM (2.75), communication (2.64) and business culture (2.82) indicate that Japanese overseas subsidiaries are experiencing difficulties with these issues.

Table 6.1 also presents the correlation matrix for HCN managers. In support of the model, there is significant correlation between the

Table 6.1 Correlation matrix, means and standard deviations for HCN data

	Integration	IHRM	Communication	Business culture	Age	Years	Level
IHRM	.46**						
Communication	.41**	.57**					
Business culture	.43**	.57*	.66**				
Age	.30**	.15	.07	.16			
Years	.07	.03	.14	−.02	.38**		
Level	.20*	.23	.03	.08	.21*	.01	
Mean	2.64	2.75	2.64	2.82	39.78	9.05	2.28
S.D.	.70	.83	.63	.64	7.05	6.00	.57

Listwise deletion N = 101, *p ≤ .05, **p ≤ .01

dependent variable integration and the three independent variables IHRM (r = .46), communication (r = .41) and business culture (r = .43). As for the three control variables, the age of the respondent (r = .30) and the respondent's level in the hierarchy (r = .20) are significantly correlated with HCN integration in decision-making, while the number of years in service is not significantly correlated with integration. Thus, it appears that a HCN manager's perception of integration increases with age and the respondent's management level, but not with the number of years in service at the subsidiary. These results agree with the logic that the opinions of older HCN managers may be given more respect and naturally, there should be more decision-making responsibility at higher management levels.

The three explanatory variables, IHRM, communication, and business culture are all significantly correlated amongst themselves. In fact, the correlations among these variables are the highest in the correlation matrix: 0.66 between business culture and communication, 0.57 between business culture and IHRM, and 0.57 between communication and IHRM. Apparently, there is a connection among these three variables. Logically, differences in business practices and culture should affect communication between HCNs and PCNs in the work environment. Furthermore, it should be more difficult to implement IHRM policies that seek to treat HCNs as an integral part of the parent company (as global human resources) if there are perceived differences in business practices and culture as well as communication difficulties between the HCNs and the PCNs.

There are no significant correlations between these three explanatory variables and the three control variables; the age of the respondent and

HCN Integration in Japanese MNCs 195

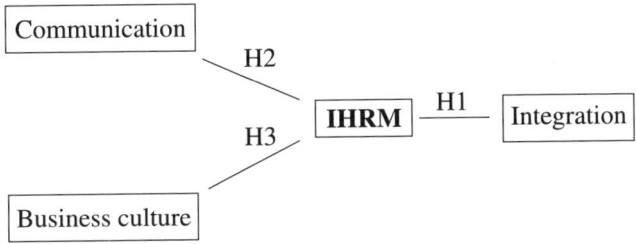

Figure 6.1 Conceptual Model of Factors affecting HCN integration

the respondent's level in the hierarchy, and the number of years in service. On the other hand, among these control variables themselves, the age of the respondent is significantly correlated with years in service ($r = .38$) and with the respondent's level in the hierarchy ($r = .21$). These results indicate that the higher-level management positions tend to be filled by relatively older HCNs while lower positions are filled by relatively younger HCNs. However, since the variable years in service is not significantly correlated with the variable level in the hierarchy, perhaps higher-level positions tend to be filled by relatively older HCNs who may have experience at other companies to qualify them for the positions, and/or internal promotions of HCNs may not be common.

The Conceptual Model of HCN Integration presented in Chapter 1 is shown again in Figure 6.1 with the addition of three hypotheses expressing the relationships between the variables in the model:

1. Hypothesis 1 is: 'high scores indicating IHRM policies and practices that develop and promote HCN managers as well as treat HCNs as international human resources are positively associated with the integration of HCN managers.'
2. Hypothesis 2 is: 'high scores for the variable communication, indicating good communication between HCN and PCN managers, are positively associated with the IHRM scores.'
3. Hypothesis 3 is: 'high scores for the variable business culture indicating that there is a good understanding among the PCNs and HCNs of each other's business practices and culture as well as a lack of cultural-related conflict between the two groups are positively associated with IHRM scores'.

In order to test the model and associated hypotheses, regression analyses were performed with integration as the dependent variable

Table 6.2 Multiple regression reporting standardized coefficients for HCN data

Variables	Dependent Variable: Integration		Dependent Variable: IHRM	
	Full model	Trimmed model	Full model	Trimmed model
IHRM	.22*	.42***		
Communication	.18		.37***	.35***
Business culture	.14		.31**	.33**
Age	.24*	.24**	.05	
Years	−.05		−.04	
Level	.08		.19*	.20*
R^2	.32***	.27***	.44***	.43***
Adjusted R^2	.28***	.25***	.41***	.42***
F	7.36***	17.73***	14.67***	24.71***

$N = 101$. *$p \leq .05$, **$p \leq .01$, ***$p \leq 0.001$

and IHRM as the dependent variable. Table 6.2 presents the regression results including standardized coefficients, R^2 and adjusted R^2. The full model with integration as the dependent variable had an adjusted R^2 of .28 (F = 7.36, p $\leq$ .001). The control variable age (b = .24, p $\leq$ .05) and IHRM (b = .22, p $\leq$ .05) significantly predicted integration.

In the standard multiple regression analysis with IHRM as the dependent variable, the variables communication and business culture were significant at p $\leq$ 0.01, and the control variable level was significant at p $\leq$ 0.05. A model trimming approach was adopted. All coefficients not significant at p $\leq$ 0.10 were assumed to be equal to zero and omitted from the final empirical model. Accordingly, after excluding the variables that were not significant, two more regression analyses were undertaken, one with integration as the dependent variable and one with IHRM as the dependent variable. The results can be seen in Table 6.2 and are shown diagrammatically in Figure 6.2.

The final trimmed model with integration as the dependent variable was significant (F = 14.67, p $\leq$ 0.001) with an adjusted R^2 of 0.25. The final trimmed model with IHRM as the dependent variable was significant (F = 24.71, p $\leq$ 0.001) with an adjusted R^2 of 0.42. Thus, there was support for Hypothesis 1, that IHRM significantly predicts HCN integration (p ≤ 0.05). This indicates that HCN managers are more likely to report that they are integrated in the decision-making process if they have a sense of being international managers. Hypotheses 2 and 3 were also supported. That is, HCN managers' satisfaction with communication significantly predicted their reported sense of being international managers. Similarly, HCN managers' positive responses in relation to business culture was positively related to their reported sense of being international managers.

The decomposition of the relationships shown in the Final Empirical Path Model for HCN respondents (Figure 6.2) is shown in Table 6.3. In addition to the direct effects that can be seen from Figure 6.2, Table 6.3 shows the indirect effects of communication on integration

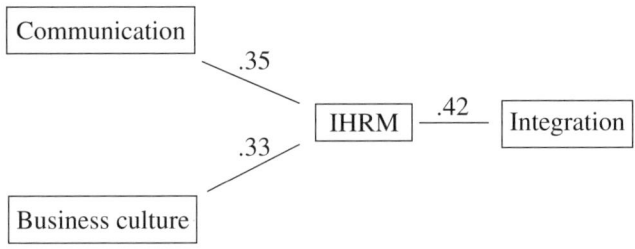

Figure 6.2 Final Empirical Path Model for HCN respondents (standardized coefficients)[a,b]
[a] The control variable age was significantly related (p ≤ .01) to integration as a dependent variable.
[b] The control variable level was significantly related (p ≤ .01) to IHRM as a dependent variable.

Table 6.3 Decomposition for Final Empirical Path Model[a]

Bivariate Relationship	Path		
	Direct	Indirect	Total
IHRM on integration	.42		.42
Communication on integration		.35*.42 = .15	.15
Business culture on integration		.33*.42 = .14	.14
Communication on IHRM	.35		.35
Business culture on IHRM	.33		.33

[a]The control variable age was significantly related to integration as a dependent variable and the control variable level was significantly related to IHRM as a dependent variable.

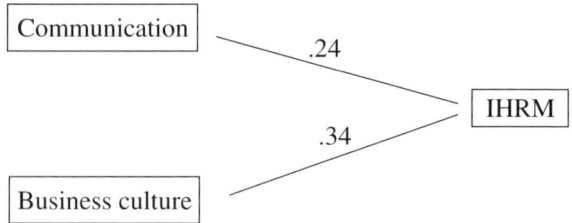

Figure 6.3 Final Empirical Path Model for PCN respondents (standardized coefficients)

and business culture and the total effects for all bivariate relationships. As shown in Table 6.3, there were no direct effects of communication and business culture on integration. The relationship between communication and business culture on integration is fully mediated by IHRM.

Overall, the trimmed model of HCN integration shown in Figure 6.3 accounts for 25 per cent of the variation of integration and 42 per cent of the variation in IHRM (see Table 6.2). IHRM is predicted by communication and business culture and, in turn, IHRM significantly predicts HCN integration. Accordingly, improving communication and business culture appears to be important for developing a sense of being an international manager, which in turn enhances perceptions of integration among HCN managers. As seen below, the data from PCN respondents show similar results when IHRM is the dependent variable, but different results when integration is the dependent variable.

6.4.2 Findings for PCN Data

The descriptive statistics for the PCN managers (refer to Table 6.4) were very similar to those of the HCN managers. The mean for integration (2.38) was even lower than that of the HCN data (2.64). This result suggests that PCN managers on the average feel that HCN managers have less decision-making authority than the HCN managers themselves tend to believe they have. The means for the explanatory variables from the PCN data were: communication 2.76, IHRM 2.79 and business culture 2.83, which were very similar to those of the HCN respondents (2.64, 2.79, 2.82, respectively). These results indicate that the PCN managers and the HCN managers tend to have similar views concerning all these aspects of the environment in which HCN managers work.

HCN Integration in Japanese MNCs

Table 6.4 Correlation matrix, means and standard deviations for PCN managers

	Integration	IHRM	Communication	Business culture	Age	Years sub.	Level
IHRM	.13						
Communication	.13	.38**					
Business culture	.07	.44**	.41**				
Age	.10	.07	−.01	.02			
Years sub.	−.58	.01	−.06	−.02	.12		
Level	.19*	.13	.06	.06	.53**	.04	
Mean	2.38	2.78	2.76	2.84	44.12	3.28	2.44
S.D.	.61	.60	.52	.43	7.28	1.94	.63

Listwise deletion N = 113, *$p \leq .05$, **$p \leq .01$

As shown in Table 6.4, very few variables were significantly correlated in the PCN data. The lack of significant correlations between the explanatory variables implies that PCN managers do not tend to see a connection between IHRM, communication, and business culture with the integration of HCN managers. Only level was significantly correlated with integration ($r = .19$). However, level here refers to the management level of the PCN respondent, not the level of the HCN managers. Therefore, the inference from this correlation might be that PCNs at higher management levels at the subsidiary tend to perceive greater integration of HCNs. This may be due to the fact that they have more contact with higher-level HCN managers than the lower-level PCN managers do and, as seen as seen in the HCN data, the level of HCNs is positively correlated with integration ($.20, p \leq .05$).

Communication ($r = .38$) and business culture ($r = .44$) were related to IHRM, and communication and business culture were related ($r = .41$). These results correspond with those of the HCN managers in terms of the degree of significance; however, the correlations for PCN managers (38, .44, and .41, respectively) are lower than those of HCN managers across the board (.57, .57, and .66, respectively). Thus, the same inferences stated in the presentation of the HCN correlations apply. Namely, differences in business practices and culture should affect communication between HCNs and PCNs in the work environment making it more difficult to implement IHRM policies that seek to treat HCNs as an integral part of the parent company.

Table 6.5 presents the regression results including standardized coefficients, R^2 and adjusted R^2. In order to test the model shown in Figure 6.1 for the PCN data, the first regression equation with

Table 6.5 Standard multiple regression reporting standardized coefficients for PCN data

Variables	Dependent Variable: Integration	Dependent Variable: IHRM	
	Full Model	Full Model	Trimmed Model
IHRM	.08		
Communication	.09	.24**	.24**
Business culture	−.01	.33***	.34**
Age	.01	.02	
Yearsub	−.06	.02	
Level	.17	.08	
R^2	.06	.25***	.24***
Adjusted R^2	.01	.22***	.23***
F	1.08	7.22***	17.59***

[a]$N = 113$, **$p \leq .01$, ***$p \leq .001$

integration as the dependent variable had all independent variables included, namely, communication, IHRM, business culture and the demographic variables, age, yearsub (of service with the subsidiary) and (managerial) level. The full model with integration as the dependent variable had an adjusted R^2 of .01 and the model did not predict integration. Given that none of the variables was significant, it is not necessary to trim the model.

A second regression analysis was then undertaken with IHRM as the dependent variable. As shown in Table 6.5, with the exception of integration, all variables that were in the first regression were included in the second regression. The variables communication and business culture were significant at $p \leq 0.01$. The control variables were not significant. As with the HCN data, a model trimming approach was adopted. All coefficients not significant at $p \leq 0.01$ were omitted from the final empirical model. Accordingly, after excluding the variables that were not significant, the regression analysis was re-run, with IHRM as the dependent variable. The results can be seen in Table 6.5 and shown diagrammatically in Figure 6.3.

The final trimmed model with IHRM as the dependent variable was significant ($F = 17.59, p \leq 0.001$) with an adjusted R^2 of 0.23. Thus, in the PCN data set, there was no support for Hypotheses 1. PCN managers did not subscribe to the view that improvements in communications, understanding the business culture, and HCN involvement in the company as international managers leads to greater HCN integration in decision-making. However, there was support from the PCN data set for Hypotheses 2 and 3. That is, communication ($b = .24, p \leq 0.01$) and business culture ($b = .34, p \leq 0.001$) did predict IHRM in the PCN data set.

Overall, PCN respondents were in agreement with HCN respondents that communication and business culture are important in creating a sense of HCNs being international managers. However, they did not go to the important next step of recognizing that a sense of being an international manager is important for HCN integration. None of the control variables significantly predicted IHRM. The Final Empirical Path Model for PCN respondents is shown in Figure 6.3. Given that the hypotheses were not supported for PCN data, it is not necessary to show a decomposition table of direct and indirect results.

7 Conclusions Concerning HCN Integration in Japanese MNCs

The central focus of this book is the integration of HCN managers in the management process of Japanese overseas subsidiaries as measured by their participation in decision-making. This issue has been addressed by reviewing the related literature in Chapters 2 to 5 and the original study presented in Chapter 6. The Conceptual Model of Factors Affecting HCN Integration in Chapter 1 has also been tested in the previous chapter. This chapter discusses the findings and draws conclusions.

7.1 WHAT DO THE FINDINGS CONCERNING THE VARIABLES IN THE MODEL INDICATE?

The analysis that led to the development of the revised model of HCN integration has provided a quantitative basis for understanding the relationship between the independent variables themselves and how they predict integration. This section further explores the findings for each of the variables in this model. Since to varying degrees these variables are interrelated, at times the discussion of one variable entails the mention of how it is related to one or more of the other variables.

7.1.1 What Do the Results Say about HCN Integration in Japanese Subsidiaries?

As discussed in the introduction, the integration of HCN managers is the most important IHRM issue facing Japanese companies as they continue to expand their operations abroad. The data from the human resource manager questionnaire supports the assertion that there is a shortage of qualified Japanese PCN managers to fill the management positions at foreign subsidiaries. In addition, the high cost of maintaining so many PCN managers at foreign subsidiaries and complaints by HCN employees and local authorities are forcing Japanese firms to consider this issue more seriously. Moreover, there are a number of advantages to be gained by employing HCN managers. These advantages, presented in Chapter 1, include the HCN managers' inherent familiarity with the local culture along with the business and regulatory environment; as well as the HCN managers' inherent language ability. Papers have been published that suggest, based on qualitative findings and some quantitative data, that HCN managers play a limited role in the management of Japanese overseas subsidiaries (for example: Kopp, 1994a and 1994b; Negandhi and Serapio, 1991; Elashmawi, 1990; Pucik *et al.*, 1989; Sethi *et al.*, 1984). The original research presented in Chapter 6 generated the first quantitative definition of the degree of HCN integration in Japanese overseas subsidiaries. The scale used for measuring HCN integration clearly demonstrates who (PCN or HCN) makes what decisions (see scale items in Appendix A).

The mean for integration from the HCN data was 2.64, while that from the PCN data was 2.38 on a five-point scale. These mean values indicate that HCN managers in Japanese subsidiaries are not highly integrated in the management process as measured by the degree of their participation in decision-making. It appears that PCN managers tend to perceive that HCN managers have less decision-making authority than the HCN managers themselves tend to believe they have. This is probably due to the PCN managers' greater awareness of the scope of decisions made. As has been pointed out, there is usually a great deal of communication between the PCN managers at the subsidiary and their counterparts at the parent company to which the HCN managers are not privy. So, naturally, the HCNs would tend not to be aware of the scope of decisions actually made.

The issue of parent company involvement in decision-making appeared to be an important factor limiting HCN integration at a number of the companies interviewed. According to most HCN and PCN managers interviewed, important decisions tend to be made by the PCNs in close consultation with their counterparts and superiors at the head office in Japan. These findings coincide with those of other researchers such as Negandhi and Serapio (1991), Pucik *et al.* (1989), and Negandhi *et al.* (1987). More specifically, Negandhi and Serapio found in a study of Japanese subsidiaries in the US that the forms of control used included visits from parent company executives to the subsidiary, formalized reporting to the parent company, centralized decision-making at headquarters and appointing numerous PCNs to key management positions at the subsidiary. In their study of 65 Japanese subsidiaries in Malaysia, Singapore, and Thailand,

Negandhi *et al.* (1987) reached the same conclusions concerning decision-making and parent company control (see Chapter 5.7). This form of direct control may be related to the desire on the part of the parent company to ensure the wishes of the parent company are always given top priority. As mentioned in Chapter 6, some HCNs reported conflicts between the subsidiaries and the parent company concerning certain decisions. In such cases, the PCNs working at the subsidiary in question always supported the interests of the head office. This finding is in agreement with that of Thome and McAuley (1992) who studied Japanese subsidiaries in Asian countries.

Thome and McAuley (1992:153) claim that there is no notion of the relationship between Tokyo and the periphery evolving into one of mutuality, or interdependence, as in the case of many MNCs of other national origins. They state that HCNs complain of having neither inclusion nor autonomy. This issue is related to the identity of the HCN within the context of the company, an issue covered in the discussion of the IHRM variable below. That is to say, is the HCN's identity anchored in the subsidiary or the company as a whole? From the interviews with HCNs, it appears that their identity is clearly anchored in the subsidiary. Thus, they would naturally be concerned about the interests and profitability of the subsidiary first and foremost. Consequently, cases in which the interests of the parent company and the subsidiary conflict may cause HCNs to feel a lack of integration in the company as a whole, the type of integration that appears to be the norm for PCNs.

The interviews also revealed that there are problems associated with the decision-making process itself at Japanese subsidiaries. The two main issues were frustration in relation to how long it takes to make some decisions and the lack of individual decision-making authority. As reported in Chapter 6, some HCNs expressed the view that their subsidiary sometimes missed business opportunities due to indecisiveness or the slow pace of the decision-making process. Indeed, one of the main criticisms of Japanese-style consensus management made by some researchers is the long time it takes to come to a decision (for example: Woronoff, 1992; Sethi *et al.*, 1984).

The discussions with the HCN managers usually included complaints regarding a lack of decision-making authority. A prime example mentioned in Chapter 6 is the wool trader at a Japanese trading company in Australia whose buying decisions were closely supervised. The interviews with the HCN managers and the PCNs indicated that in most Japanese overseas subsidiaries there is a dual management system. On the one hand, there are the PCN managers who work closely with their PCN counterparts in Japan. On the other hand, there are the HCN managers who interface with the PCN managers at the subsidiary and act as a liaison between these PCNs and the non-managerial HCN employees. It appears that this type of role segregation even occurs when HCNs are fluent in Japanese as seen in the example of the two Malaysians interviewed who graduated from Japanese universities and then were hired to work at a Japanese subsidiary in Malaysia. Elashmawi (1990) also noted that most often in Japanese overseas subsidiaries two separate lines of management exist: one consisting of the Japanese managers and the other of the HCN managers. He argued that though they appear to share the work, the Japanese usually control the decision-making process and the HCN managers' role is limited to gathering information.

Correspondingly, at the Japanese subsidiaries participating in interviews, it did not appear that the HCN managers were an integral part of any consensus decision-making process that might be going on between the subsidiary and the parent company. Some HCNs indicated that most of this consultation took place after they had left the office. Oyama (1994:70) also reported that PCN managers at Japanese subsidiaries in the US tended to reach a consensus amongst themselves before meeting with the HCN managers. Likewise, Sethi *et al.* (1984:258) claim that there is a tremendous reluctance on the part of Japanese companies to broaden the scope of consensus-style decision-making to include HCN managers, and that it is often practised in form rather than substance. Negandhi *et al.* (1987) also found little evidence of a 'bottom-up' decision-making process at foreign subsidiaries of Japanese MNCs.

Some PCN managers indicated that the parent company must staff certain management positions at the subsidiary with PCNs to handle the need to consult often with the parent company. The inference is that HCN managers could not carry out this consultation. This is the most probable conclusion given the importance of in-groups and *jinmyaku* (human networks) in the decision-making process (see Chapter 5) as well as language barriers. These points are discussed in detail in the following sections concerning the variables IHRM and communication.

7.1.2 Are Japanese IHRM Policies and Practices Conducive to HCN Integration?

The PCN and HCN managers appear to have similar views concerning the degree to which IHRM-related issues exist at the subsidiary as measured by the IHRM scale. The mean for IHRM from the HCN data was 2.75, while that from the PCN data was 2.78 on a five-point scale. The testing of the model indicates that IHRM, from the viewpoint of HCN managers, is the most important factor in relation to HCN integration. Since certain characteristics of ethnocentric IHRM impede HCN integration, it is important to ascertain to what degree Japanese MNCs are practising ethnocentric IHRM. Thus, this section examines the quantitative and qualitative data gathered in this study and compares the data with those of other researchers to determine the extent of ethnocentric IHRM at Japanese overseas subsidiaries. According to Perlmutter and Heenan (1979:17–21) as well as Dowling and Schuler (1990:35–40 and 48–51), ethnocentric IHRM includes the following characteristics:

1. The organization of the MNC is highly centralized and there is little decision-making autonomy granted to HCN managers in the subsidiary.
2. PCN managers tend to dominate the key management positions in the foreign subsidiaries.
3. There is a lot of communication between the parent company and the subsidiaries.

First, the data obtained from the survey of HR managers presented in Chapter 6 indicates the existence of ethnocentric staffing patterns at the companies responding to the questionnaire. The human resource managers reported that PCNs occupied 75 per cent of the high level positions, 34 per cent of the middle level positions and seven per cent of the low-level management positions. In addition, there were no TCNs in management positions at these companies (it was pointed out in Chapter 4 that the use of TCNs is an indication of geocentric IHRM). These ethnocentric staffing patterns reflect the patterns found by other researchers, for example: Shiraki (1995), Kopp (1994a), MITI (1991, 1987), Pucik *et al.* (1989), Kobayashi (1985), Tung (1984a), Negandhi (1980), and Tsurumi (1976a:190–3 and 260–1). These studies, which are discussed in Chapter 4, offer a comparison of Japanese staffing practices with those of US and European subsidiaries. It is remarkable that in all these studies the data indicate, without exception, greater ethnocentric staffing practices at Japanese MNCs compared to their US and European counterparts. Furthermore, the data for Japanese companies reflect a continuance of the same pattern over the passage of more than 20 years.

The second indication of ethnocentric IHRM at Japanese subsidiaries is found in the results of the global HRM scale. The scale was employed to measure the human resource policies and practices of the subsidiaries on the ethnocentric–geocentric continuum. As reported in Chapter 6, the mean for the global HRM scale was 1.86 on a five-point scale, which indicates that HCNs are rarely considered global human resources and that their IHRM practices are closest to the ethnocentric end of the scale. In addition, it was pointed out that 80 per cent of the firms responding to the HR questionnaire reported that the HR department of the parent company in Japan was solely responsible for the affairs of the Japanese PCN managers. As previously argued, these results reflect the differentiation common in Japanese firms between *seishain* (regular, core, or formal employees) and non-*seishain*. Only an employee that is considered a *seishain* might be considered a global human resource. In almost all Japanese MNCs, with perhaps the exception of Sony, only Japanese PCNs may be considered *seishain*.

As explained in Chapter 6, the above global HRM scale consisted of a group of six questions concerning IHRM policies. Two of the questions were original but the other four questions identical to those employed by Kopp (1994a) for the same purpose (see Chapter 4). The results coincide with the findings of Kopp's study. She concluded that IHRM policies and practices at Japanese MNCs should be considered ethnocentric compared to those of US and European companies. Kopp also demonstrated an empirical link between ethnocentric policies and practices and the occurrence of IHRM problems. This point is discussed in more detail below in relation to the consequences of a lack of integration of HCNs.

Thus, it appears that the IHRM practices of Japanese MNCs tend to be more ethnocentric than those of their US and European counterparts. Reasons for this phenomenon have been discussed in the previous chapters. First, there is the argument in Chapter 4.1 that many Japanese companies are still in the early stage of internationalization of their organizational structures associated with increased FDI. Most Japanese firms, under conditions of growing trade liberalization, penetrated foreign markets employing a centralized-hub export strategy (Bartlett and Goshal, 1989). Furthermore, the rapid large-scale expansion of Japanese FDI occurred only after 1985 in response to the dramatic rise in the value of the yen upon the implementation of the Plaza Accord.

In addition, as pointed out in Chapter 4.1.3, whenever a firm experiences rapid development of its international operations, regardless of its national origin, the firm can expect to confront difficulties in keeping pace with the corresponding human resource needs. It was reasoned that the difficulties are particularly acute in the case of Japanese firms since they tend to be human resource accumulators rather than human resource deployers (Kagono et al., 1985). This is the same concept as the development of an internal labour market discussed in Chapter 3. It is argued that being a human resource deployer allows for greater flexibility in integrating HCNs into the management process.

In addition, Perlmutter and Heenan (1979:17) claim that ethnocentrism is often not attributable to prejudice as much as to inexperience. However, in the case of Japanese MNCs, others argue (Fernandez and Barr, 1993; Yabe, 1991; Sethi et al., 1984) that ethnocentrism as a style of IHRM in Japanese organizations is also related to the strong ethnocentric attitudes, racism, and xenophobia in Japanese culture and society. There is support for this view in the observation that even at Japanese subsidiaries that have been in operation for many years PCNs still dominated the top management positions. Such was the case in some of the firms interviewed for this study as well as for those firms that responded to the questionnaire for HR managers. Furthermore, in the main questionnaire the average number of years that the company had been in operation was 15 with a range of 4 to 41 (see Chapter 6.3). As pointed out above, studies carried out in the 1970s reveal the same ethnocentric staffing patterns as recent studies carried out in the 1990s.

It has been argued that even when HCN managers attain high level management positions their integration might be limited by the degree to which IHRM policies treat the HCN manager as an international human resource. Familiarity with the parent company as a whole and the development of a network of relationships with managers at the parent company are important factors affecting HCN integration. As discussed in Chapter 5, decisions in Japanese companies usually involve *nemawashi* or consulting with all the parties concerned in making decisions. This process becomes more complicated in the case of decisions involving Japanese overseas subsidiaries since the consultation must take place not just in the subsidiary itself, but also between the subsidiary and the parent company, and even perhaps other overseas subsidiaries as well. PCNs working at overseas subsidiaries may expect to rotate from their positions back to the parent company and perhaps to other foreign subsidiaries, while the HCNs would rarely do so. The critical point here is that the PCNs develop an important network of contacts in the company as a whole, essential for effective participation in decision-making. On the other hand, even though a HCN may attain a relatively high management position at the subsidiary, the lack of a developed *jinmaku* within the company as a whole may limit the HCN's participation in decision-making.

Finally, the discussion of control systems employed in Japanese firms presented in Chapter 4.2.1 is relevant to Japanese IHRM policies and practices. It may also help to explain Japanese MNCs' apparent preference for staffing high-level management positions at foreign subsidiaries with PCNs. It was argued that Japanese firms tend to rely more on elements of culture-oriented control systems than elements of output-oriented control systems. This point is also directly related to the variable business culture and is examined in more detail in that section. The focus here is on 'why do Japanese firms tend to prefer culture-oriented control systems?'

It is argued in Chapter 4 that one possible answer to the above question is found in the role-versus-person dichotomy. Japanese firms may be viewed more as a set of people rather than a set of roles. The emphasis is on developing people who can work together to accomplish the tasks that are not very clearly assigned to any particular roles and individual measurements are not well defined. In addition, though the roles of managers may be formally defined in terms of an organizational chart, the actual roles of managers are often unclear without rigid boundaries. This concept is directly related to the preference of Japanese firms to practise long-term employment and develop managers who are generalists. In addition, this concept ties in with the concept of Japanese firms as resource accumulators rather than resource deployers discussed above. It is much easier to communicate well-defined roles and seek the best HCN manager to perform a given role in an output-oriented control system than to follow an approach of developing a HCN manager as a generalist to function in a culture-oriented control system.

The observations and arguments presented in this section support the assertion that certain traditional Japanese management practices, especially those related to HRM, are difficult to transfer to the foreign environment. As pointed out in Chapter 1, Yoshino (1976) suggested that Japanese management practices would impede the internationalization of Japanese organizational systems. He argued that the Japanese system is closed and too tightly bound to Japanese culture to be well suited for the international environment of the foreign subsidiary (1976:164–5). This concept is further explored in the section of the findings related to the variable business culture. The next section deals with the findings related to the variable communication, one of the two variables that significantly predicted IHRM as a dependent variable.

7.1.3 What Do the Results Suggest Concerning the Variable Communication?

On a five-point scale, the mean for communication from the HCN data was 2.64, while that from the PCN data was 2.76. Of the three independent variables in the original model, communication had the lowest mean for both HCN and PCN data sets. Thus, it would appear that communication is an important problem facing Japanese MNCs. The literature stresses the importance of effective communication in making and carrying out decisions (Erez, 1992; Donnellon et al., 1986; Binnis and Nanus, 1985). The flow of information from the PCN managers to the HCN managers must be improved. This is particularly true in relation to the flow of information from the parent company to the subsidiary. The interviews revealed that PCN managers almost always play the role of the information gatekeeper between the subsidiary and the parent company. Among the HCNs interviewed, there was only one HCN who had the opportunity to visit Japan and establish direct communication links with a few PCN managers in Japan.

Since there is differential access to the flow of communications during the decision-making process, information access and control is a source of organizational power (Pettigrew, 1972). Gatekeepers are in position to regulate the flow of demands and potentially control directional outcomes. Furthermore, these gatekeepers may not only open and close communications channels, they also collect, combine and reformulate information. Whoever controls the communication channels has the power to decide (Bass, 1983:103). The strong parent company control Japanese MNCs tend to exercise over their subsidiaries (Thorne and McAuley, 1992:87) increases the power of this gatekeeper role. This may account for the frustration felt by a number of the HCNs interviewed in relation to decisions made by the PCNs at the subsidiary in consultation with the parent company. HCN managers would naturally wonder if the PCNs at the parent company are actually receiving all the information pertinent to the decisions being considered. Other researchers have also reported similar results concerning the lack of HCN participation in the communication between the subsidiary and the parent company (for example, Wingrove, 1997).

The discussion in Chapters 3 and 5 reveals the important links between communication (particularly *nemawashi* or informal consulting),

Conclusions

jinmyaku and ultimately, participation in decision-making. Communication between managers tends to be very complex and depends greatly upon one's *jinmyaku* (Erez, 1992:50). In contrast to the linear pattern with a definite point of origin for the communication flow and the decision-making process, the pattern is circular, whereby any single point in a circle can become the origin (Ballon, 1988). Thus, HCNs must have a developed *jinmyaku* in order to be part of the communication loop between PCNs at the foreign subsidiary and those at the parent company. However, the findings of this study and the literature indicate that HCNs usually lack the opportunity to achieve a well-developed human network that includes PCNs at the parent company.

Numerous comments by both PCN and HCN managers during the interviews indicated that language was a serious barrier to effective communication between HCN and PCN managers. The ability of Japanese PCNs to communicate in English varies greatly; usually depending on the number of years experience they have working abroad. The problem appears to be more serious in the case of SMEs compared to larger companies that have had a more developed network of subsidiaries overseas for a longer period of time. As reported in Chapter 6, one HCN at a medium sized Japanese subsidiary in Malaysia complained that none of the Japanese PCNs could effectively communicate in English. In addition, PCNs at all the companies interviewed reported that a lot of the written communication from Japan was in Japanese and not all of it was translated for the benefit of HCN managers. Other researchers have also noted the same communication problems associated with language barriers in Japanese MNCs (Goldman, 1994; Oyama, 1994; Nishida, 1991 and 1985).

It is probable that the apparent preference for Japanese PCNs in key management positions is related to potential problems associated with communication when HCNs hold key management positions. Correspondingly, the variable communication is significantly correlated to the variable IHRM ($r = .57$ for the HCN data; $r = .38$ for the PCN data) and in the revised model communication significantly predicts IHRM ($b = .35$ for the HCN data). Communication is greatly facilitated by placing PCNs in key managerial positions at foreign subsidiaries since the language and cultural barriers are avoided. In addition, the PCN manager has most likely developed the necessary *jinmyaku* and knows who must be consulted in making decisions. These observations should help explain the predictive relationship found between communication and IHRM.

There is also a logical relationship between culture and communication and differences in culture may act as a barrier to effective communication. Indeed, there is a significant correlation between the independent variables communication and business culture ($r = .66$ for the HCN data; $r = .41$ for the PCN data). According to Donnellon *et al.* (1986), the relationship between culture and communication is reciprocal; the communication network forms the connecting links among group members, transmitting the social values and facilitating their sharing. Conversely, shared meaning and values facilitate the flow of communication. Both shared meaning and shared communication mechanisms facilitate collective action. In addition, Kunihiro (1976) argues, the difficulty of communicating with a Japanese person is considered to be closely associated with the Japanese people's particular view of language and mode of language usage, the unique patterns of cognition and perception, and the system of logic.

The tacit, implicit, emotive and non-logical modes of Japanese communication are prevalent in *nihonjinron* literature previously discussed. Thus, even when foreigners have some ability to communicate in Japanese, they must overcome the cultural barrier to communication. Sometimes this cultural barrier is merely the attitude of the Japanese participant (Oyama, 1994:104-5). This issue is discussed further in the following section regarding the findings related to the variable business culture.

7.1.4 What Do the Results Say About the Variable Business Culture?

The mean for the variable business culture from the HCN data was 2.82, while that from the PCN data was 2.84 on a five-point scale. These results appear to indicate that both HCN and PCN managers believe that there are problems associated with differences between the business practices and culture of Japan and those of the host countries. Regarding qualitative findings, as discussed in Chapter 6, the understanding of HCN and PCN managers of each other's culture varied according to the experience of the person interviewed. Nevertheless, the majority of managers in each group expressed difficulties in understanding or dealing with the other group's business practices and culture.

The variable business culture was discussed in earlier chapters. In Chapter 2, the importance of culture in determining effective IHRM policies and practices was stressed. In Chapter 3, the particular characteristics of Japanese business practices and culture were presented.

Conclusions

In Chapter 4, the relationship between business practices and culture with IHRM was explored. Finally, in Chapter 5 the effects of culture on communication were examined.

The focus of this section is on the various aspects of the variable business culture that appear to have a direct effect on IHRM policies and practices. It is notable that there is a significant correlation between the variables, business culture and IHRM ($r = .57$ for the HCN data; $r = .44$ for the PCN data) and the regression analysis indicates that business culture as an independent variable significantly predicts IHRM as a dependent variable ($b = .33$ for HCN data). It is argued in Chapter 4 that the control structure of Japanese companies has a negative impact on their ability to integrate HCN managers into the management process of their foreign subsidiaries since Japanese companies tend to rely more heavily on culture-oriented control systems than output-oriented control systems. This preference also may help account for Japanese MNCs' apparent preference for staffing high-level management positions at foreign subsidiaries with PCNs as demonstrated by the data gathered from the HR questionnaire and the data of other researchers presented in Chapter 4.

As described in Chapters 3 and 4, the concepts of *seishain* as well as job rotation for promotion of networking among managers and development of generalists are integral parts of the typical Japanese management system. Under this HRM system, PCN managers absorb the company culture, and in the process learn to make decisions based on what is acceptable and expected, what should and should not be done. Essentially, these HRM practices make it possible for Japanese companies to rely heavily on culture-oriented control systems. However, since HCNs are rarely included in the implementation of these practices they tend not to develop sufficient familiarity with Japanese business practices, Japanese culture, and the corporate culture of the parent company in order to function in a culture-oriented control system.

Thus, culture-oriented control systems create a cultural barrier to entrusting the management of subsidiaries to HCNs. This barrier was evident in various statements made in the interviews by HCN and PCN managers. A case in point is the statement by the Malaysian HCN manager that his company would never allow a HCN to manage the subsidiary because Japanese managers think only they are capable of doing so. However, it is an issue of predictability and trust rather than an issue of managerial competence. As previously discussed, Japan has a tight culture and a high level of uncertainty avoidance while the other four countries included in this study have weak uncertainty avoidance (Hofstede, 1991:113). Hofstede explains that a high ranking in uncertainty avoidance indicates a low degree of tolerance for unpredictable behaviour. In addition, tight cultures are less tolerant of non-conforming behaviour than loose cultures are (Triandis, 1989: 511). The problem is that HCNs do not have the same national-cultural 'programming' as Japanese PCNs, nor do they have the same degree of corporate-cultural 'programming.' Moreover, Yoshimura and Anderson (1997) assert that predictable behaviour and culturally transmitted implicit understanding of what is expected are important aspects of Japanese organizational behaviour.

Conformity and lack of tolerance for non-conforming behaviour is also related to the assertion that Maruyama's nonreciprocal causal model (1984, 1982, 1980) best describes most Japanese MNCs (Adler, 1986) since in most Japanese MNCs there is limited organizational learning and transformation through cross-cultural interaction. In such firms, homogeneity is considered natural, desirable and good, while heterogeneity is viewed as an abnormality and a cause of friction and conflict. The culture of the head office in the parent firm is assumed to apply universally and management believes that there exists one best way to manage the corporation regardless of location and cultural differences. The comments of the PCNs and HCNs presented in Chapter 6 indicate that the attributes of the nonreciprocal causal model are prevalent among the companies studied.

The important social function of the modern-day corporation in Japan in the form of *ie* and the concepts of frame versus attribute in forming groups are discussed in Chapter 3. It was pointed out that in the case of PCNs the frame is the company as a whole, while for HCNs the frame tends to be limited to the foreign subsidiary. This division between the parent company and the foreign subsidiary was clearly apparent in the comments from the interviews presented in Chapter 6 as well as from the HR questionnaire data. The examples given by interviewees of decisions involving conflict between the parent company and the subsidiary are illustrative of this phenomenon.

In addition, even though frame is more important than attribute in the Japanese context, the attribute of being ethnically and culturally Japanese appears to play a very important role in relation to group formation. This is particularly true in the formation of sub-groups or so-called 'in-groups.' Without exception, all the PCNs and HCNs interviewed indicated, directly or indirectly by their choice of words, that there were two distinct groups, the Japanese (PCNs) and the locals (HCNs). As reported in Chapter 6, there is evidence of the 'us-

Conclusions 215

versus-them' attitude at these subsidiaries. Other researchers have also noted the importance of being Japanese ethnically and culturally in relation to group membership. For instance, Yoshimura and Anderson question whether HCNs can really become members of important in-groups in Japanese firms (1997:77–9). The data gathered in this study also indicate that the exclusion of HCNs managers from important management in-groups composed of Japanese PCN managers is common in Japanese overseas subsidiaries.

Furthermore, there is the problem of differences in the value system of Japanese and that of HCNs. Non-Japanese may not have the same attitude towards the company due to differences in value systems concerning frame/attribute-based groups. Even if HCN managers come from a strong collectivist society, it does not mean that they will necessarily be receptive to familism-based policies and practices if the firm is not considered a significant in-group that takes precedence over other affiliations. The conflict between one's private life and the workplace is such an example. While Japanese may sacrifice time with their family in order to spend long hours at the company, such a practice may be unacceptable to HCNs. The comment of an Australian HCN quoted in Chapter 6 reflects this attitude.

Additionally, Ichimura's (1981) survey of Japanese subsidiaries in Southeast Asia illustrates the difference in attitude between Japanese PCNs and HCNs towards the company. As many as 42 per cent of the Japanese managers who responded to Ichimura's questionnaire recommended giving up expecting loyalty to the company on the part of HCN employees. However, it is not that the HCNs are never loyal to the company where they work, rather the loyalty may be expressed differently. For example, while Japanese PCNs may consider staying late at the office even when there is no urgent need to do so as an expression of loyalty, a HCN may consider this behaviour to be a false expression of loyalty. The HCN may consider doing what is best for the interests of the subsidiary to be a true expression of loyalty. However, as previously discussed, what is best for the subsidiary is not always best for the parent company.

7.2 WHAT DOES THE MODEL SAY ABOUT HCN INTEGRATION?

Hypothesis 1 in the model stated that IHRM policies and practices that develop and promote HCN managers as well as treat HCNs as international human resources are positively associated with the integration of HCN managers. The analysis showed that IHRM significantly predicted HCN integration ($p \leq 0.05$) indicating there was support for hypothesis 1. It is important to note that this hypothesis implies that a HCN manager may hold a high-level management position in a Japanese foreign subsidiary but still not feel fully involved in making important decisions. That is, being part of an international management team working closely with the PCN managers at the subsidiary as well as those at the parent company is also important for enhancing HCN integration. HCN managers will experience greater integration if they are part of the consultation with the parent company.

Hypotheses 2 and 3 suggest that problems with communication between PCNs and HCNs as well as differences in business practices and culture may be factors limiting the degree to which HCN managers become part of international management teams. Hypothesis 2 stated high scores for the variable communication, indicating good communication between HCN and PCN managers, are positively associated with the IHRM variable in the model. The analysis confirmed that the variable communication significantly predicts IHRM ($p \leq 0.001$) indicating there is support for hypothesis 2. Hypothesis 3 stated that high scores for the variable business culture, indicating that a good understanding among the PCNs and HCNs of each other's business practices and culture as well as a lack of cultural-related conflict between the two groups, are positively associated with IHRM. The analysis also confirmed that the variable business culture significantly predicts IHRM ($p \leq 0.01$) indicating there was support for hypothesis 3.

In summary, the analysis of the HCN data confirmed all three hypotheses in the model. On the other hand, the PCN respondents also recognize that communication and business culture are related to the implementation of IHRM policies that develop and promote HCNs as well as enhance HCNs' sense of being international managers. However, it is noteworthy that PCNs did not make the important next step to recognize that the development and promotion of HCNs as well as fostering a sense of being an international manager is necessary for HCN integration.

7.3 THE CONSEQUENCES OF A LACK OF HCN INTEGRATION

The consequences of a lack of HCN integration can be discerned from the data gathered in this study as well as the results of other researchers. One important consequence is the difficulty experienced in recruiting and retaining highly qualified HCNs. It is almost a cliché that ambitious non-Japanese should not work for Japanese foreign subsidiaries. There is plenty of evidence from the interviews supporting this contention. For example, the PCN human resource manager at a Japanese subsidiary in Australia indicated that the Australians who are ambitious and want to advance usually quit after a few years. Furthermore, the PCN managing director at a Japanese subsidiary in Malaysia stated that they do not give HCN more responsibility because they fear the HCNs may leave; however, the HCNs leave because they do not get more responsibility. Yoshihara (1996:7–9) also concluded that a high degree of staffing top management positions at Japanese foreign subsidiaries with PCNs, the lack of promotion opportunities for HCNs, and lack of delegation of authority to HCNs make it difficult to attract and retain superior HCNs.

This is an important issue since MNCs are in competition with one another to attract highly qualified HCNs. The competition intensifies in the case of developing countries with a limited cadre of qualified managerial human resources. As discussed in Chapter 4, Negandhi (1980) studied IHRM at US, European, and Japanese MNCs. He concluded that due to the enlightened personnel policies of US MNCs, other industrial and commercial enterprises, including European and Japanese MNCs, have experienced difficulties in attracting and retaining a high-level workforce in the developing countries. In addition, as stated in Chapter 1, US Secretary of Labour Robert Reich (1991:81) believes that problems Japanese MNCs experience in hiring and retaining qualified HCN managers will negatively affect their competitiveness.

Another consequence of low HCN integration is the effect it may have on the profitability of the foreign subsidiary and the parent company as a whole. Yoshihara (1996:7–9) argues that there is evidence of a cause–effect relationship between the comparatively low profitability of Japanese subsidiaries and lack of management localization. In addition, Pucik *et al.* (1989:36–7) report that in many decision-making areas, as well as in the aggregate, the size of the localization gap (lack of HCN integration) was negatively correlated with most performance measures. Firms where executives perceived a smaller localization gap performed better. Specifically, the overall performance and employee morale are affected the most. Product development, pricing decisions, and reward systems for executives are the three areas where the perceived localization gap may have the most impact on the performance of the subsidiary. As for the data gathered from the interviews, there is evidence that the lack of decision-making authority in the hands of HCNs sometimes leads to missed business opportunities.

The consequences of the low HCN integration are related to the general problems associated with ethnocentric IHRM. Kopp's (1994a) survey comparing IHRM policies and practices in Japanese, European, and United States MNCs indicates that these problems include:

1. An inability of the MNC to fully utilize the talents of non-PCNs;
2. re-entry problems for PCNs returning home, general discontent among HCN managers;
3. HCN dissatisfaction with communication and decision-making;
4. HCN frustration with limited promotion opportunities;
5. and high turnover of HCNs.

Kopp's (1994a) regression analysis of all countries in her sample indicates that ethnocentric staffing and policies are associated with higher incidence of IHRM problems. Furthermore, the results reveal that the IHRM policies and practices of Japanese MNCs are more ethnocentric than those of US and European MNCs; and consequently Japanese MNCs experience more IHRM problems than do American and European MNCs. In an earlier study, Zeira (1976) also revealed that MNCs practising ethnocentric HRM policies suffered numerous problems such as low productivity, friction between HCN and PCN managers, and high turnover of HCNs.

There are other problems and costs associated with PCNs themselves as described in Chapter 4. For example, PCNs often suffer from problems related to the adaptation process to the overseas environment. During the adaptation period, PCN managers may not be as effective in their job as they were in the home country environment. In addition, PCNs usually receive much higher incomes and more benefits than HCNs. This gap in compensation often leads to friction between the HCNs and the PCNs.

Finally, there is often a lack of continuity when HCN managers rotate in and out of key management positions. Specifically, as pointed out in Chapter 6, some HCN managers complained that the lack of continuity meant that the PCNs had to be, in a sense, trained by the HCN managers. At the same time, as one PCN manager pointed out, the lack of continuity negatively affects the integration of HCN managers, since the newly arrived PCN managers need time

Conclusions 219

to understand the abilities of the HCN managers. Furthermore, as previously noted, MNCs that fail to integrate HCNs forgo the numerous advantages of having HCN managers in their foreign subsidiaries.

7.4 IMPLICATIONS FOR THEORY AND PRACTICE

The importance of integrating HCN managers into the management process of Japanese overseas subsidiaries should be understood in the context of the increased focus on IHRM as a competitive factor (Mishra, 1994; Pucik, 1992; Evans *et al.*, 1989). Furthermore, the lack of effective IHRM is a primary cause of failure in multinational ventures (Desatnick and Bennett, 1978). In addition, Japanese MNCs have greatly increased the number and scale of their operations overseas during the post-Plaza Accord period. FDI is now an integral part of their competitive strategy. Therefore, now more than ever before, Japanese companies must deal with IHRM issues that include how to effectively integrate HCN managers into the management process of their foreign subsidiaries, and ideally in the company as a whole.

Hopefully, this book fills the gaps in the literature concerning HCN integration in Japanese overseas subsidiaries by clarifying the degree of HCN integration and contributes to the theoretical and practical understanding of the factors related to HCN integration. Likewise, the data analysis should offer Japanese managers an understanding of the perceptions of HCN managers concerning their role in the management process. There are numerous practical applications for Japanese MNCs. The analysis of the model demonstrates that full HCN integration will only take place if and when Japanese companies treat HCNs as international human resources. Japanese MNCs should implement organizational and operational practices to create an environment that will attract and retain HCN managers.

This process implies that HCNs will be given the opportunity to become *seishain*, involved with the operation of the company as a whole, not limited to the arena of the foreign subsidiary. Providing the opportunity for a select group of HCN managers, identified as having high potential, to work at the parent company and possibly other foreign subsidiaries should afford the opportunity for HCN managers to:

1. become familiar with the operations of the parent company as a whole;

2. develop a network among managers necessary for participation in making major decisions;
3. improve communication with PCN managers at the parent company;
4. create a common frame of reference for improved communication with PCN managers at foreign subsidiaries;
5. and finally increase their understanding of Japanese culture and business practices.

Providing HCNs the opportunity to work at the parent company should also have an internationalizing effect on PCNs at the parent company. As discussed in Chapter 4, PCN managers at the parent companies in Japan too often lack an understanding of the overseas environment and tend to be very insular in their attitudes. This is evidenced by the way PCN managers returning from overseas assignments are often viewed with suspicion and considered to be contaminated by their experience in a foreign culture. Japanese companies must overcome these basic ethnocentric attitudes in order to break away from ethnocentric IHRM policies and practices. They must learn to view diversity as a potential strength rather than a weakness or burden.

7.5 FINAL COMMENTS

Insular is an adjective that not only describes the geographic nature of Japan. Insular also aptly describes the national psyche throughout much of Japan's history. Increased interaction with the outside world has always been forced upon the nation by a combination of both internal and external pressures. The threat of colonialism and Perry's black ships represent such external pressures, while internal pressure came from people such as the Daimyo of Satsuma who became a threat to the domestic balance of power when he obtained guns from the Portuguese traders. The people of Japan have demonstrated amazing adaptability when they have been forced to deal with the outside world.

The first major social, political and economic transformation took place during the Meiji period. Since that period, Japan has no longer been able to return to its extreme insular and isolationist policies. However, that is not to say the adjectives insular and isolation no longer have any role to play in describing the psyche of modern Japan.

The rapid expansion of Japanese FDI in response to post-Plaza Accord, rise in the value of the yen and growing trade friction may represent, in a less dramatic fashion, the second major challenge to Japan's insular mentality.

Now the question is how well will Japanese commercial institutions meet the challenge of integrating non-Japanese into their managerial ranks? This study and others demonstrates that Japanese MNCs still have to go through major transformations in organizational behaviour, attitudes, and most important of all, IHRM practices in order to truly integrate HCN managers into the management processes of their subsidiaries and the parent companies as a whole. I hope that for the benefit of Japanese and non-Japanese alike, they will succeed in the near future.

Appendix: List of Questions in Scales

INTEGRATION SCALE

1) Decisions concerning the hiring of new employees.
2) Decisions concerning promotion of employees and wage/salary increases.
3) Decisions concerning employee benefits such as vacation time, etc.
4) Decisions concerning borrowing funds from local banks or financial institutions.
5) Decisions concerning production schedules.
6) Decisions concerning purchase of production inputs.
7) Decisions concerning local advertising.
8) Decisions concerning future products or services offered by the local subsidiary.
9) Decisions concerning investment in new facilities.
10) Decisions concerning pricing of products and services.
11) Decisions concerning production goals.
12) Decisions concerning sales goals.
13) Decisions concerning personnel training for local managers at the subsidiary.
14) Decisions concerning layoffs (dismissar) of employees at the subsidiary.
15) Decisions concerning most minor decisions such as those concerning day-to-day operational issues.
16) Decisions concerning most major decisions such as those concerning strategic of long-term issues.

IHRM SCALE

1) This company offers local managers the opportunity to work at the parent company in Japan or at a subsidiary in another company.
2) There are good management development programmes for locally hired employees.
3) There are clear career paths for locally hired employees.
4) This subsidiary does not discriminate against non-Japanese in favour of Japanese in selecting managers for high-level positions.
5) I (local managers) have sufficient opportunities to visit the parent company in Japan to learn more about the company and make contacts with the people working there.

Appendix

COMMUNICATION SCALE

1) There are no communication difficulties between the local managers here and the Japanese managers at the home office in Japan.
2) There are no communication difficulties between the local managers here and the Japanese managers here at this subsidiary.
3) Language barriers make it difficult for local managers to communicate with the Japanese managers at the head office in Japan (reverse-coded).
4) Language barriers make it difficult for local managers to communicate with the Japanese managers here at this subsidiary (reverse-coded).
5) Local managers are often left out of the communication loop between the head office in Japan and the Japanese managers here at the subsidiary (reverse-coded).
6) Local managers have sufficient access to communication channels with the home office in Japan.
7) The flow of information from the home office in Japan to the local managers here is sufficient.
8) I am satisfied with the communication and flow of information between the local managers and the Japanese managers here at this subsidiary.
9) Information is widely dispersed (openly shared) among all managers at the subsidiary.
10) The home office and the local Japanese managers sometimes withhold important information from the local managers.
11) Socializing after work between Japanese and local managers occurs often.
12) There is sufficient trust between the Japanese managers and the local managers to allow for smooth communication.
13) The home office and the local Japanese managers sometimes withhold important information from the local managers (reverse-coded).
14) Sometimes meetings are held with only Japanese managers participating (reverse-coded).

BUSINESS CULTURE SCALE

1) There is an 'Us versus Them' mentality between the local managers and the Japanese managers (reverse-coded).
2) The Japanese managers have a sufficient understanding of local business practices.
3) The Japanese managers have a sufficient understanding of the local culture.
4) Difference between local values and culture and those of Japan often lead to conflicts (reverse-coded).
5) Japanese culture is so unique that it is impposssible for non-Japanese to fully understand it (reverse-coded).
6) It seems individualism is stronger in this country than in Japan (reverse-coded).
7) Our company has made a sufficient effort to teach local managers about Japanese culture and business practices.

8) Our company has made a sufficient effort to teach Japanese managers about local culture and business practices.

GLOBAL HRM SCALE (HR MANAGER QUESTIONNAIRE)

1) Performance evaluation measures are the same for every employee of our international operations.
2) A training programme has been put in place to groom local nationals for advancement in our company's managerial ranks.
3) Local nationals are often transferred to headquarters or to other international operations for gaining experience and learning about the country as a whole.
4) At headquarters we maintain a centralized roster of all managerial employees (both home-country nationals and foreign nationals) throughout the world in order to facilitate managerial development.
5) Local managers are sometimes transferred to managerial positions at the parent company.
6) Local managers are sometimes transferred to management positions at other foreign subsidiaries.

EVALUATION AND REMUNERATION SCALE (HR MANAGER QUESTIONNAIRE)

1) Local managers are given sufficient opportunity to participate in establishing operating goals for which they are responsible.
2) Local managers receive sufficient recognition for their performance.
3) Local managers clearly understand what their responsibilities are and how their performance is measured.
4) Local managers are satisfied with this company's system of evaluating employee performance.
5) Local managers are satisfied with their salary and benefits.

References

Abegglen, J. and Stalk, G. Jr (1985a). *Kaisha, The Japanese Corporation*. New York: Basic Books.
Abegglen, J. and Stalk G. Jr (1985b). *The Japanese Organization: Aspects of its Social Organization*. New York: Free Press.
Abegglen, J. (1973). *Management and Worker, The Japanese Solution*. Tokyo: Kodansha International.
Abegglen, J. (1958). *The Japanese Factory*. New York: The Free Press.
Adler, N. (1991). *International Dimensions of Organizational Behavior*. Boston: Kent.
Adler, N. (1987). 'Pacific Basin managers: a gaijin, not a woman.' *Human Resource Management* 26 (2), 169–91.
Adler, N. (1986). 'Is Organizational Culture Bound?' *Human Resources Management* 25 (1), 73–90.
Adler, N., Doktor, R. and Redding, S. (1986). 'From the Atlantic to the Pacific Centre: Cross-Cultural Management Reviews.' *Journal of Management* 12 (2), 295–318.
Adler, N. (1983). 'A typology of management studies involving culture.' *Journal of International Business Studies* Fall, 29–47.
Ajiferuke, M. and Boddewyn, J. (1970). 'Culture and other explanatory variables in comparative management studies.' *Academy of Management Journal* 13, 153–63.
Allison, R. E. (1989). 'Neo-Confucianism in human relations of Japanese management.' *Asian Culture Quarterly* 17 (3), 57–70.
Amago, T (1992). *Nihonjin Manager*. (Japanese Manager) Osaka: Sogensha.
Baba, S (1994). 'Kigyo ni okeru ningen to ningenshigen kanri no yakuwari.' (Human resources and the functions of HRM.) *Mita Shogaku Kenkyu* 37 (6), 17–36.
Baba, M. (1984). *Managerial Behaviour in Japan and the USA: A Cross-cultural Survey*. Tokyo: Japan Production Center.
Ballon, R. J. (1988). 'Japanese decision-making: A circular process.' *Business Series No. 117 Tokyo*: Sophia Institute of Comparative Study.
Bartlett, A. and Ghoshal, S. (1989). *Managing Across Borders: The Transnational Solution*. London: Hutchinson Business Books.
Bartlett, C. A. and Yoshihara H. (1988). 'New challenges for Japanese multinationals: is organization adaptation their Achilles' heel?' *Human Resource Management* 27, 19–34.
Bartu, F (1993). *The Ugly Japanese: Nippon's Economic Empire in Asia*. Tokyo: Tuttle.
Bass, B. M. (1983). *Organizational Decision-Making*. Illinois: Irwin.
Beamish, P. W. and Calof, J. L. (1989). 'International Business Education: a corporate view.' *Journal of International Business Studies* Fall, 553–64.
Beechler, S. and Yang, J. Z. (1994). 'The transfer of Japanese-style management to American subsidiaries: Contingencies, constraints, and competencies.' *Journal of International Business Studies* Third Quarter, 467–91.

Berry, W., Poortinga, Y. H., Segall, M. H. and Dasen, P. R. (1992). *Cross-cultural Psychology*. Cambridge: University Press.

Besser, T. L. (1993). 'The commitment of Japanese workers and US workers: A reassessment of the literature.' *American Sociological Review* 58 (December), 873–881.

Binnis, W. G. and Nanus, B. (1985). *Leaders: The Strategies for Taking Charge*. New York: Harper and Row.

Bird, A. and Mukuda, M. (1989). 'Expatriates in their own home: A new twist in the human resource management strategies of Japanese MNCs.' *Human Resource Management* 28 (4), 437–53.

Black, J. S. (1994). 'Okaerinasai: Factors related to Japanese repatriation adjustment.' *Human Relations* 47 (12), 1,489–508.

Black, J. S. Gregerson, H. and Mendenhall, M. E. (1992). *Global Assignments*. San Francisco: Jossey-Bass.

Black, J. S., Gregerson, H. and Mendenhall, M. E. (1991). 'Towards a comprehensive model of international adjustment: An integration of multiple theoretical perspectives.' *Academy of Management Review* 16 (2), 291–317.

Black, J. S. and Porter, L. W. (1991). 'Managerial behaviours and job performance: a successful manager in Los Angeles may not succeed in Hong Kong.' *Journal of International Business Studies* 1st Quarter, 99–113.

Black, J. S. and Mendenhall, M. E. (1990). 'Cross-culture training effectiveness: a review and theoretical framework for future research.' *Academy of Management Review* 15 (1), 113–36.

Boyacigiller, N. (1990). 'The role of expatriates in the management of interdependence, complexity and risk in multinational corporations.' *Journal of International Business Studies* 3rd Quarter, 357–81.

Boyacigiller, N. (1986). *Why Multinational Corporations Use Expatriates: an Organizational and Environmental Study*. Diss. University of California, Ann Arbor: UMI, 1994. 8717908.

Briody, E. K. and Chrisman J. B. (1991) 'Cultural adaptation on overseas assignments.' *Human Organization* 50 (3), 264–82.

Burack, E. H. (1991). 'Changing the company culture: the role of human resource development.' *Long Range Planning* 24 (1), 88–95.

Cascio, W. F. (1989). *Managing Human Resources: Productivity, Quality of Life, Profits*. New York: McGraw Hill.

Caudron, S. (1992). 'Preparing managers for overseas assignments.' *World Executive Digest* Nov., 72–3.

Clad, J. (1991). *Behind the Myth: Business, Money and Power in Southeast Asia*. London: Grafton Books.

Clark, R. (1979). *The Japanese Company*. Tokyo: Tuttle.

Cole, R. E. (1992). 'Work and leisure in Japan.' *California Management Review* Spring, 52–63.

Cole, R. E. and Deskins, D. (1988). 'Racial factors in site location and employment patterns in Japanese auto firms in America.' *California Management Review* 31 (1), 9–22.

Cole, R. E. (1979). *Work, Mobility and Participation*. Berkeley: University of Southern California Press.

Dale, P. N. (1986). *The Myth of Japanese Uniqueness*. London: Routledge.

D'Andrade, R. (1984). 'Cultural meaning systems.' In Shweder R. A. and LeVine R. A. (eds) *Culture Theory: Essays on the Mind, Self and Emotion*. New York: Cambridge University Press.
Deal, T. and Kennedy, A. (1988). *Corporate Cultures*. London: Penguin Books.
do Rosario, L. (1993). 'Out with the oldies.' *Far Eastern Economic Review* April, 22: 74.
Desatnick, R. L. and Bennett, M. L. (1978). *Human Resource Management in the Multinational Company*. New York: Nichols.
Doi, T. (1985). *The Anatomy of Self*. Tokyo: Kodansha International.
Doi, T. (1973). *The Anatomy of Dependence*. Tokyo: Kodansha International.
Donnellon, G., Gray, B. and Bougon M. G. (1986). 'Communication, meaning and organized action.' *Administrative Science Quarterly* 31, 43–45.
Dore, R. P. (1989). *How Japanese Learn to Work*. London: Routledge.
Dore, R. P. (1973). *British Factory, Japanese Factory*. Berkeley: University of California Press.
Dowling, P. J. and Schuler, R. S. (1990). *International Dimensions of Human Resource Management*. Boston: PWS-Kent.
Earley, C. P. (1987). 'Intercultural training for managers: a comparison of documentary and interpersonal methods.' *Academy of Management Journal* 30 (4), 685–98.
Elashmawi, F. (1990). 'Japanese culture clash in multicultural management.' *Tokyo Business Today* 58 (20), 36–9.
England, G. W. (1983). 'Japanese and American management: Theory Z and beyond.' *Journal of International Business Studies* 14, 131–41.
Enz, C. A. (1986). 'New directions for cross-cultural studies: linking organizational and societal cultures.' *Advances in International Comparative Management* 2, 173–89.
Erez, M. and Earley, C. P. (1993). *Culture, Self-Identity and Work*. New York: Oxford Press.
Erez, M. (1992). 'Interpersonal communication systems in organizations and their relationships to cultural values, productivity and innovation: The case of Japanese corporations.' *Applied Psychology: An International Review* 41 (1), 43–64.
Evans, P., Doz, Y. and Laurent, A. (eds) (1989). *Human Resource Management in International Firms*. London: Macmillan.
Fernandez, J. P. and Barr, M. (1993). *The Diversity Advantage: How American Business Can Outperform Japanese and European Companies in the Global Marketplace*. New York: Lexington Books.
Frankel, M. and Takayama, H. (1993). 'The freedom to choose.' *Newsweek*, 51.
Fukutake, T. (1982). *The Japanese Social Structure*. Tokyo: University of Tokyo Press.
Goldman, A. (1994). 'A briefing on cultural and communicative sources of Western–Japanese interorganizational conflict.' *Journal of Managerial Psychology* 9 (1), 7–12.
Goldman, A. (1988). *For Japanese Only: Intercultural Communication with Americans*. Tokyo: Japan Times.
Hall, E. T. (1990). *Understanding Cultural Differences*. Yarmouth, ME: Intercultural Press.

Hall, E. T. (1987). *Hidden Differences: Doing Business with the Japanese*. New York: Anchor Press/Doubleday.
Hall, E. T. (1976). *Beyond Culture*. New York: Anchor Press/Doubleday.
Hamada, T. (1991). 'Winds of change: economic realism and Japanese labour management.' *Asian Survey* 20 (4): 397–406.
Hanada, M. (1989). 'Management themes in the age of globalization.' *Management Japan* 20, 19–26.
Hasegawa, K. (1986). *Japanese Style Management*. Tokyo: Kodansha.
Hatch, E. (1983). *Culture and Morality: The Relativity of Values in Anthropology*. New York: Colombia University Press.
Hayashi, S. (1989). *Culture and Management in Japan*. Tokyo: Tokyo University Press.
Herbig, P. A. and Palumbo, F. A. (1994). 'Karoshi: Salaryman sudden death syndrome.' *Journal of Managerial Psychology* 9 (7), 11–16.
Hodgetts, R. M. and Luthans, F. (1989). 'Japanese HRM practices; separating fact from fiction.' *Personnel* 66 (4), 42–45.
Hofstede, G. (1991). *Cultures and Organizations: Software of the Mind*. London: McGraw-Hill.
Hofstede, G., Neuijen, B., Ohayv, D. and Sanders, G. (1990). 'Measuring organizational cultures: a qualitative and quantitative study across twenty cases.' *Administrative Science Quarterly* 35 (2), 286–316.
Hofstede, G. (1985). 'The interaction between national and organizational value systems.' *Journal of Management Studies* 22 (4), 347–57.
Hofstede, G. (1983a). 'National cultures in four dimensions.' *International Studies of Management and Organization* 13 (1–2), 46–74.
Hofstede, G. (1983b). 'The culture relativity of organizational practices and theories.' *Journal of International Business Studies* 14 Fall, 75–89.
Hofstede, G. (1980). *Culture's Consequences: International Differences in Work-Related Values*. Beverly Hills: Sage.
Hui, C. H. and Triandis, H. C. (1986). 'Individualism–Collectivism: A study of cross-cultural researchers.' *Journal of Cross Cultural Psychology* 17:225–48.
Ichimura, S. (ed.) (1988). *Asia ni Nezuku Nihonteki Keiei*. (Japanese Management in Asia). Tokyo: Toyo Keizai Shinposha.
Ichimura, S. (1981). 'Japanese Firms in Asia.' *Japanese Economic Studies* 10 (1), 31–52.
Ichimura, S. (ed.) (1980). *Nihon Kigyo in Asia*. (Japanese Enterprises in Asia) Tokyo: Toyo Keizai Shinposha.
Iida, T. (1985). *The Relationship Between Management Settings and Organizational Problems in Australian-based Japanese Subsidiaries*. Ph.D. Thesis, Department of Sociology, La Trobe University, Australia.
Iida, T. (1984). 'The reference group of Japanese expatriates.' *Management Update* 50 February, 20–23.
Iida, T. (1983) 'Transferability of Japanese management systems and practices into Australian companies.' *Human Resource Management Australia* 21 (3), 23–7.
Inohara, H. (1990). *Human Resource Development in Japanese Companies*. Tokyo: Asian Productivity Organization.
Inohara, H. (1982). 'Japanese subsidiaries in Europe: Promotion of local personnel.' *Business Series 8*. Tokyo: Sophia University.

Ishida, H. (1990). *Kigyo Guroboru-ka no Jinzai Senryaku*. (Strategies for Globalization of Human Resources) Tokyo: Nikkan Kogyo Shinbunsha.
Ishida, H. (1986). 'Transferability of Japanese human resource management abroad.' *Human Resource Management* 259 (1), 103–20.
Ishida, H. (1985). *Nihon Kigyo no Kokusai Jinji Kanri*. (International Personnel Management in Japanese Enterprises) Tokyo: Nihon Rodokyokai.
Ishida, H. (1981). 'Human Resources Management in Overseas Japanese Firms.' *Japanese Economic Studies* 9, 53–81.
Japan 21st (1995). 'Crumbling Japanese-style personnel management system.' *Japan 21st* April, 67.
Johnson, R. T. (1977). 'Success and failure of Japanese subsidiaries in America.' *Columbia Journal of World Business* Spring, 30–37.
Kagono, T., Nonaka, I., Sakakibara, K. and Okumura, A. (1985). *Strategic vs. Evolutionary Management: A Comparison of Strategy and Organization*. Amsterdam: North-Holland.
Kashima, J. (1974). *Kindaika no Seishin Kozo*. (The Intellectual Structure of Modernization) Tokyo: Hyoronsha.
Kaufmann and Felix (1970). 'Decision-Making Eastern and Western Style.' *Business Horizons* December, 1.
Keeley, T. D. and Doi K. (1996). 'A Study of the Integration of Host Country Nationals in the Management Process at Japanese Subsidiaries in Malaysia and Australia.' *Kyushu Sangyo Daigaku Sangyo Keiei Kenkyusho Nenpo* 28, March.
Keeley, T. D. and Doi K. (1995). 'Nikkeikaigaikogaisha ni okeru keieikankou ni kansuru chousa.' (A study of the management practices of Japanese subsidiaries abroad) *Kokusai Bijinesu Kenkyu Gakkai Nenpo* 1, 135–59.
Kilburn, D. (1994). 'Japan life-time employment, promotion through seniority and single-company unions – are the foundations of Japanese management crumbling?' *Management Today* Jan.: 45.
Kinoshita, A. (1992). *Jinteki Shigen no Kokusai Iten*. (The Transfer of Human Resources Overseas) Kyoto: Keibunsha.
Klein, E. (1992). 'The US/Japanese HR culture clash.' *Personnel Journal* November: 30–8.
Kleinberg, J. (1989). 'Cultural clash between managers: America's Japanese firms.' *Advances in International Comparative Management* 4, 221–43.
Kluckhohn, F., and Strodtbeck, F. (1961). *Variations in Value Orientations*. Westport, CT: Greenwood Press.
Kobayashi, N. (1985). 'The patterns of management style developing in Japanese multinationals in the 1980s.' In Takamiya, S. and Thurley, K. (eds), *Japan's Emerging Multinationals: An International Comparison of Policies and Practices*. Tokyo: University of Tokyo Press.
Kobrin, S. J. (1988). 'Expatriate reduction and strategic control in American multinational corporations.' *Human Resource Management* 27 (1), 62–75.
Koike, K. (1988). *Understanding Industrial Relations in Modern Japan*. New York: St. Martin's Press.
Koike, K. (1981). *Nihon no Jukuren*. (Japan's Skilled Labour) Tokyo: Yuhikaku.
Kopp, R. (1994a). 'International human resource policies and practices in Japanese, European and United States multinationals.' *Human Resource Management* 33 (4), 581–99.

Kopp, R. (1994b). *The Rice-Paper Ceiling*. Stone Bridge Press.
Kotter, J. P. (1988). *The Leadership Factor*. New York: Free Press.
Kotter, J. P. (1982). 'What do effective general managers really do?' *Harvard Business Review* 60, 156–67.
Kunihiro, M. (1976). 'The Japanese language and intercultural communication.' *The Japan Interpreter* 10, 3/4:267–83.
Kurata, Y. (1990) 'Human resource management of foreign staff employees in Japanese companies.' *Hitotsubashi Journal of Social Studies*. 22, 27–36.
Laurent, A. (1986). 'The cross-cultural puzzle of international human resource management.' *Human Resource Management* 25 (1), 91–102.
Lawler, J. J., Jain, H. C., Ratnam, C. S. and Atmiyanandana, V. (1995). 'Human resource management in developing economies: a comparison of India and Thailand.' *The International Journal of Human Resource Management* 6 (2), 319–46.
Lawler, J. J., Zaidi, M. and Atmiyanandana, V. (1989). 'Human resource management strategies in Southeast Asia: The case of Thailand.' In Shaw, B. B. Nedd, A., Ferris, G. R. and Rowland, K. M. (eds) *Research in Personnel and Human Resources Management, Supplement 1*. Greenwich, CN: JAI Press.
Lebas, M. and Weigenstein, J. (1986). 'Management control: the roles of rules, markets and culture.' *Journal of Management Studies* 23 (3), 259–72.
Leung K. and Bond M. H. (1984). 'The impact of cultural collectivism on reward allocation.' *Journal of Personality and Social Psychology* 47, 793–804.
Lim, H. S. (1994). *Japan's Role in Asia*. Singapore: Times Academic Press.
Lim, H. S. (1991). 'Features of Japanese direct investment and Japanese-style management in Singapore.' In Yamashita, S. (ed.) *Transfer of Japanese Technology and Management to the ASEAN Countries*. Tokyo: Tokyo University Press.
Lincoln, J. R. and Kalleberg, A. L. (1990). *Culture, Control and Commitment*. Cambridge: Cambridge University Press.
Lu, D. (1987). *Inside Corporate Japan: The Art of Fumble Free Management*. Tokyo: Tuttle, 1987.
Luthans, F. McCaul and Dodd, N. G. (1985). 'Organizational commitment: A comparison of American, Japanese and Korean employees.' *Academy of Management Journal* 28 (1) 213–19.
March, R. M. (1992a). *Working for a Japanese Company: Insights into the Multicultural Workplace*. New York: Kodansha.
March, R. M. (1992b). 'The difference between participation and power in Japanese factories.' *Industrial and Labour Relations Review* 45 (2), 250–57.
Mannari, H. and Befu, H. (1991). 'Inside and Outside.' In Finkelstein, Imamura and Tobin (eds) *Transcending Stereotypes: Discovering Japanese Culture and Education*. Yarmouth, Maine: Intercultural Press.
Margerison, A. (1993). 'Japan; Good-bye seniority, hello merit.' *International Journal of Career Management* 5 (1), i–iii.
Markus, H. R. and Kitayama, S. (1991). 'Culture and the self: Implications for cognition, emotion and motivation.' *Psychological Review* 98 (2), 224–53.
Marshall, L. (1993). 'Working with the Japanese: A collision of cultural expectations.' *Human Resource Monthly* July.
Maruyama, M. (1994). *Mindscapes in Management: Use of Individual Differences in Multicultural Management*. Hants, England: Dartmouth.

Maruyama, M. (1984). 'Alternative concepts of management: Insights from Asia and Africa.' *Asia Pacific Journal of Management* 1 (1), 100–11.
Maruyama, M. (1983). 'Japanese management theories and Japanese criticisms.' *Futures* 15 (3), 170–80.
Maruyama, M. (1982). 'New mindscapes for future business policy and management.' *Technology Forecasting and Social Change* 21, 53–76.
Maruyama, M. (1980). 'Mindscapes and science theories.' *Current Anthropology* 21 (5), 389–600.
Maruyama, M. (1973). 'Paradigmatology and its application to cross-disciplinary, cross-professional and cross-cultural communication.' *Dialectica* 29 (3–4), 135–96.
Mead, R. (1994). *International Management: Cross-Cultural Dimensions*. Cambridge, Mass: Blackwell.
Mechanic, D. (1962). 'Sources of power of lower participants in complex organizations.' *Administrative Science Quarterly* 7:349–64.
Mendenhall M. E. and Wiley, C. (1994). 'Strangers in a strange land: The relationship between expatriate adjustment and impression management.' *American Behavioural Scientist* 37 (5), 605–20.
Mendenhall, M. E. and Oddou, Gary (1991). *International Human Resource Management*. Boston: PWS-Kent.
Mendenhall, M. E., Dunbar, E. and Oddou, G. R. (1987). 'Expatriate selection, training and career-pathing: a review and critique.' *Human Resource Management* 26 (3), 331–46.
Mendenhall, M. E. and Oddou, G. R. (1986). 'Accumulation profiles of expatriate managers: Implications for cross-cultural training programs.' *Columbia Journal of World Business* Winter, 73–9.
Mendenhall, Mark E. and Oddou, G. R. (1985). 'The dimensions of expatriate acculturation: a review.' *Academy of Management Review* 10 (1), 39–47.
Ministry of International Trade and Industry (MITI) (1991). *Dai Yon Kai Kaigai Jigyo Katudo Kohon Chosa*. (The Fourth Study of the Activities of Firms Overseas) Tokyo: Okurasho Insatsukyoku.
Ministry of International Trade and Industry (MITI) (1987). *Kaigai Jigyo Katsudo Kihon Chosa, Kaigai Toshi Tokei Soran*. (Basic Survey on Overseas Business Activities, General Statistical Survey on Overseas Investment) Tokyo: Okurasho Insatsukyoku.
Ministry of Labour (Rodo-sho) (1985). *Nihon no ro-shi komyunikeshion no genjyo*. (The present situation of communication between labour and management in Japan.) Tokyo: Ministry of Labour.
Mishra, J. (1994). 'Using human resource management to gain international competitive advantage.' *International Journal of Management* 11 (1) March 604–8.
Miyamoto, M. (1977) 'Local culture and business behaviour in Japan.' *Social Order and Entrepreneurship: Proceedings of the Second Fuji Conference*. Tokyo: University of Tokyo Press, 257–90.
Miyashita, K. and Russell, D. (1994). *Keiretsu*. New York: McGraw-Hill.
Morris, J. and Wilkinson, B. (1995). 'The transfer of Japanese management to alien institutional environments.' *Journal of Management Studies* 32 (6), 719–30.

Mroczkowski, T. and Hanaoka, M. (1989). 'Continuity and change in Japanese management.' *California Management Review* 31 (2) 1989:39–53.
Munchus, G. (1993). 'Discrimination against working women in Japan.' *Women in Management Review* 8 (1), 9–14.
Nakane, C. (1972a). *Human relations in Japan*. Tokyo: Ministry of Foreign Affairs.
Nakane, C. (1972b). 'Social background of Japanese in S.E. Asia.' *Developing Economies* 10 (2), 115–25.
Negandhi, A. R. and Serapiro, M G (1991). 'Management strategies and policies of Japanese multinational companies: A re-examination.' *Management Japan* 24 (1), 25–32.
Negandhi, A. R., Yuen, E. and Eshghi, G. S. (1987). 'Localization of Japanese subsidiaries in Southeast Asia.' *Asia Pacific Journal of Management* 2 (1) 67–9.
Negandhi, A. R., Eshghi, Golpira S. and Yuen E. C. (1985). 'The management practices of Japanese subsidiaries overseas.' *California Management Review* 27 (4).
Negandhi, A. R. (1984). *Beyond Theory Z: Global Rationalization Strategies of American, German and Japanese Multinational Companies*. Greenwich: England JAI Press.
Negandhi, A. R. (1980). 'Adaptability of American, European, and Japanese multinational corporations in developing countries.' In Negandhi, R. (ed.) *The Functioning of the Multinational Corporation*. New York: Pergamon Press.
Nicholas, S., Merrett, D., Purcell, W. and Whitewell, G. (1995). 'Japanese foreign direct investment in Australia in the 1990s: Manufacturing, financial services and tourism.' *International Business Working Papers, University of Melbourne* June.
Nippon Steel Human Resources Development Co. Ltd. (1987). *Talking About Japan: Nihon wo Kataru*. Tokyo: ALC.
Nishida, H. (1991). 'Beikoku Shinshitu Nikkei Kigyo de Hataraku Nichibei Jugyoin no Aida no Communication Gap.' (The communication gap between Japanese and American employees at Japanese companies operating in the US) in *Borderless Jidai no Kokusai Kankei*. Tokyo: Hokuki Shuppan.
Nishida, H. (1985). 'Japanese intercultural communication competence and cross-cultural adjustment.' *International Journal of Intercultural Relations* 9, 247–69.
Okada, K. (1984). *Japanese Management – A Forward Looking Analysis*. Tokyo: Asian Productivity Organization.
Otterbeck, L. (1981). *The Management of Headquarters–Subsidiary Relationships in Multinational Corporations*. New York: St. Martin's Press.
Ouchi, W. G. Jaeger, A. M. (1987). 'Type Z organization: Stability in the midst of mobility.' *Academy of Management Review* 5:305–14.
Ouchi, W. G. (1981). *Theory Z: How American Business Can Meet the Japanese Challenge*. Reading, Mass.: Addison-Wesley.
Oyama, N. (1994). *Japanese Intercultural Communicative Strategies in Multinational Companies*. Diss. Arizona State University, Ann Arbor: UMI, 8907751.

Pascale, R. T. and Athos A. G. (1981). *The Art of Japanese Management: Applications for American Executives*. New York: Simon and Schuster.
Perlmutter, H., and Heenan, D. (1979). *Multinational Organization Development*. Reading, MA: Addison-Wesley.
Perlmutter, H., and Heenan, D. (1974). 'How multinational should your top managers be?' *Harvard Business Review* November–December, 121–32.
Perlmutter, H. (1969). 'The tortuous evolution of the multinational corporation.' *Columbia Journal of World Business* January–February, 9–18.
Pettigrew, A. M. (1973). *The Politics of Organizational Decision-Making*. London: Tavistock.
Pettigrew, A. M. (1972). 'Information control as a power source.' *Sociology* 6, 187–204.
Plath, D. W. (1983). *Work and Lifecourse in Japan*. Albany: State University of New York Press.
Porter, M. E. (1986). *Competition in Global Industries*. Boston Harvard Business School Press.
Pucik, V. (1992) 'Globalization and human resource management.' In Pucik, V, Tichy, N. and Barnett, K. (eds), *Globalizing Management; Creating the Competitive Organization*. New York: John Wiley and Sons, Inc.
Pucik, V., Hanada, M. and Fifield, G. (1989). *Management Culture and the Effectiveness of Local Executives in Japanese-Owned US Corporations*. Tokyo: Egon Zehnder International.
Pucik, V. and Katz, J. H. (1986). 'Information, control and human resource management in multinational firms.' *Human Resource Management* 25 (1), 121–32.
Pucik, V. (1984). 'White collar human resource management: a comparison of the US and Japanese automobile industries.' *Columbia Journal of World Management* 19 (3), 87–94.
Pucik, V. and Hatvany, N. (1983). 'Management practices in Japan and their impact on business strategy.' In Lamb, R. (ed.) *Advances in Strategic Management* Vol. 1, 103–32. Greenwich, Conn.: JAI Press.
Putti, J. (1991). *Management in the Asian Context*. New York: McGraw-Hill.
Putti, J. and Chong, T. (1985). 'American and Japanese management practices in their Singapore subsidiaries.' *Asia Pacific Journal of Management* 2 (2), 106–14.
Ray, C. A. (1986). 'Corporate culture: the last frontier of control?' *Journal of Management Studies* 23 (3), 287–95.
Reich, R. (1991). 'Who is them?' *Harvard Business Review* March–April, 81.
Rohlen, T. P. (1975). 'The Company Work Group.' In Vogel E. (ed.) *Modern Japanese Organization and Decision-Making*. Berkeley: University of California Press.
Rohlen, T. P. (1974). *For Harmony and Strength: Japanese White Collar Organization in Anthropological Perspective*. Berkeley: University of California Press.
Sammapan, N. (1995). 'Japanese multinational management in Thailand: Characteristics and transferability.' *University of Antwerp Centre for International Management and Development Discussion Paper* No. 1995/E/18.
Sasaki, N. (1981). *Management and Industrial Structure in Japan*. Oxford: Pergamon Press.

Sato, H. (1994). 'Employment adjustment of middle-aged and older white-collar workers.' *Japan Labour Bulletin* February, 5–8.
Schein, E. (1987). *Organizational Culture and Leadership*. San Francisco: Jossey-Bass.
Schenk, G. J. (1988). *Japanese and US multinational corporations in developing countries: A study of geocentric aspects*. Diss. United States International University, 1988. Ann Arbor: UMI, 1994. 8816706.
Schlender, B. R. (1994). 'Japan's white collar blues.' *Fortune* March 21, 97–104.
Schneider, S. C. (1988). 'National vs. corporate culture: implications for human resources management.' *Human Resources Management* 27, 231–46.
Sethi, S. P., Namiki, N. and Swanson, C. L. (1984). *The False Promise of the Japanese Miracle*. Boston: Pitman.
Shimada, H. (1993). 'Recession and change in labour practices in Japan.' *International Labour Review* 132 (2), 159–60.
Shimada, H. (1986). 'The perceptions and the reality of Japanese industrial relations.' In Thurow L. C. (ed.) *The Management Challenge: Japanese Views*. Cambridge, MA: The MIT Press.
Shimizu, R. (1989). *Success Factors*. Tokyo: Shobo Chikura.
Shirai, T. (1992). *Gendai Nihon No Romu-Kanri*. Tokyo: Toyo Keizai Shimposha.
Shiraki, M. (1995). *Nihon Kigyo no Kokusai Jinteki Shigen Kanri*. (International human resource management in Japanese firms) Tokyo: Nihon Rodo Kenkyu Kiko.
Shweder, R. A. and LeVine, R. A. (eds) (1984). *Culture Theory: Essays on the Mind, Self and Emotion*. New York: Cambridge University Press.
Sohn, J. H. (1994). 'Social knowledge and the effectiveness of expatriate personnel in controlling overseas subsidiaries: a contingency approach.' *Academy of Management Proceedings* 54th Meeting Dallas August 14–17, 158–62.
Tachibanaki, T. (1984). 'Labour mobility and job tenure.' In Aoki, M. (ed.) *The Economic Analysis of the Japanese Firm*. New York: North-Holland.
Takagi, H. (1984). *The Flaw in Japanese Management*. Ann Arbor: UMI Research Press.
Takamiya, M. (1985). 'The degree of organizational centralization in multinational corporations.' In Takamiya, S. and Thurley, K. (eds) *Japan's Emerging Multinationals: An International Comparison of Policies and Practices*. Tokyo: University of Tokyo Press.
Takashita, T. (1989). 'Reappraising the Japanese work ethic.' *Management Japan* 22 (2), 29–32.
Thome, K. and McAuley, I. (1992). *Crusaders of the Rising Sun: A Study of Japanese Managers in Asia*. Singapore: Longman.
Toba, K. (1981). 'How should we approach the peoples of Asia?' *Japan Echo*. Tokyo: Vol. VIII.
Tobin, J. J. (1991). 'Front and rear (*omote and ura*).' In Finkelstein, Imamura and Tobin (eds), *Transcending Stereotypes: Discovering Japanese Culture and Education*. Yarmouth, Maine: Intercultural Press.
Toyo Keizai (1996). *Gaikoku Shinshutsu Kigyo Soran '95*. (The 1995 Guide to Japanese Foreign Direct Investment) Tokyo: Toyo Keizai.
Trapedia (1980). Kaigai Chuzai Hokoku. (Report on overseas assignments) *Trapedia* Vol. 11 November, 8–39.

Triandis, H. C. (1989). 'The self and social behaviour in differing cultural contexts.' *Psychological Review* 96, 506–20.
Tsurumi, Y. (1978). 'The best of times and the worst of times: Japanese management in America.' *Columbia Journal of World Business* Summer, 56–61.
Tsuriumi, Y. (1976a). *The Japanese are Coming: A Multinational Interaction of Firms and Politics.* Cambridge, Mass: Basic Books 1976.
Tsurumi, Y. (1976b). 'The multinational spread of Japanese firms and Asian neighbors' reactions.' In Apter, David E. (ed.) *The Multinational Corporation and Social Change.* New York: Praeger Publishers.
Tung, R. L. (1995). 'Strategic human resource challenge: managing diversity.' *The International Journal of Human Resource Management* 6 (3) September, 482–93.
Tung, R. L. (1988). *The New Expatriates: Managing Human Resources Abroad.* Cambridge, MA: Ballinger.
Tung, R. L. (1987) 'Expatriate assignments: enhancing success and minimizing failure.' *Academy of Management Executive* 1 (2), 117–26.
Tung, R. L. (1984a). *The Key to Japan's Economic Strength: Human Power.* Lexington, MA: Lexington Books.
Tung, R. L. (1984b). 'Strategic management of human resources in the multinational enterprise.' *Human Resources Management* 23, 129–43.
Tung, R. L. (1984c). 'Human resource planning in Japanese multinationals: A model for US firms.' *Journal of International Business Studies* Fall, 139–49.
Tung, R. L. (1982). 'Selection and training procedures of US, European and Japanese multinationals.' *California Management Review* 25 (1), 57–71.
Tung, R. L. (1981). 'Selection and training of personnel for overseas assignments.' *Columbia Journal of World Business* 16, 68–78.
UNCTC (1992). 'Globalization and developing countries: Investment trade and technology linkages in the 1990s.' *Proceedings of a symposium at The Hague* March, New York: UN.
UNCTC (1991). *World Investment Report 1991.* New York: UNCTC.
US House Committee on Government Operations (1991). *Employment Discrimination by Japanese-Owned Companies in the United States: Hearings before the Employment and Housing Subcommittee of the Committee on Government Operations.* 102nd Congress, 1st Session.
van Houten, G. (1989). 'The Implications of Globalization: New Management Realities at Phillips.' In Evans, P. Doz, Y. and Laurent, A. (eds), *Human Resource Management in International Firms.* London Macmillan.
van Wolferen, K. (1992). *The Enigma of Japanese Power.* New York: Alfred A. Knopf.
Vogel, E. F. (1985). *Japan As Number One: Lessons for America*: Tokyo: Charles E. Tuttle.
Watanabe, S. (1993). 'Lifetime employment system is under threat, experts say.' *Japan Times Weekly* International Edition February 15–21, 13.
Wheeler, T. Finlay, H., Turner, P. and Crowther, G. (1991). *Malaysia, Singapore and Brunei.* Victoria, Australia: Lonely Planet.
White, M. (1988). *The Japanese Overseas: Can They Go Home Again?* New York: The Free Press.
White, M., and Trevor, M. (1983). *Under Japanese Management: The Experience of British Workers.* London: Heinemann.

Whitehall, A. M. (1991). *Japanese Management*. London: Routledge.
Wingrove, T. (1997). 'Should giants cut the apron strings.' *Japan Management Review* 4 (2).
Woronoff, J. (1992). *The Japanese Management Mystique: The Reality Behind the Myth*. Chicago: Probus.
Yabe, T. (1991). *Nihonkigyo wa Sabetsu Suru*. (Japanese Companies Discriminate) Tokyo: Daimond-sha.
Yoshihara, H. (1996). *Mijukuna Kokusai Keiei*. (Immature International Management) Tokyo: Hakuto Shobo.
Yoshihara, H. (1989a). *Genchijin Shacho to Uchi Naru Kokusaika*. (Local Nationals as Presidents and the Internalization of Internationalization) Tokyo: Toyo Keizai Shimpo Sha.
Yoshihara, H. (1989b). 'The bright and dark sides of Japanese management overseas.' In Shibagaki, K., Trevor, M. and Abe, T. (eds), *Japanese and European Management*. Tokyo: University of Tokyo Press.
Yoshihara, H. (1989c). 'Internationalization at the top: Selecting local nationals as overseas presidents and internationalization at Japanese companies.' *Management Japan* 20, 7–12.
Yoshihara, K. (1990) *Japan in Thailand*. Kyoto: Kyoto University Center for Southeast Asian Studies.
Yoshimura, N. and Anderson, P. (1997). *Inside the Kaisha*. Boston: Harvard Business School Press.
Yoshino, K. (1992). *Cultural Nationalism in Contemporary Japan*. London: Routledge.
Yoshino, M. Y. (1976). *Japan's Multinational Enterprises*. Cambridge, MA: Harvard University Press.
Yoshino, M. Y. (1968). *Japan's Managerial System*. Cambridge, MA: Harvard University Press.
Zeira, Y. (1976). 'Management development in ethnocentric multinational corporations.' *California Management Review* (18) 4, 34–42.

Bibliography

Adler, N. and Bartholomew, S. (1992). 'Managing globally competent people.' *Academy of Management Executive* 6 (3), 52–65.
Allison, R. E. (1990). 'Culture value in Japanese management.' *Asian Culture Quarterly* 18 (3), 20–32.
Amano, M. M. (1979). 'Organizational changes of a Japanese firm in America.' *California Management Review* 21 (3), 51–9.
Amante, M. (1993). 'Human resource management in Japanese enterprises in the Philippines: Issues and problems.' *Asia Pacific Journal of Management* 10 (2), 237–45.
Aonuma, Y. (1981). 'A Japanese explains Japan's business style.' *Across The Board* 18, 41–50.
Arai, S. (1971). *An Intersection of East and West: Japanese Business Management*. Tokyo: Rikugei.
Ashton, C. (1995). 'Cross-cultural indicators for human resource agendas.' *Management Development Review* 8 (2), 4–6.
Austin, J. E. (1990). *Managing in Developing Countries: Strategic Analysis and Operating Techniques*. New York: Free Press.
Azumi, K. and McMillan C. J. (1981). 'Management strategy and organizational structure: a Japanese comparative study.' In Hickson D. J. and McMillan C. J. (eds), *Organization and Nation*. Farnborough: Gower.
Babbie, E. (1990). *Survey Research Methods*. Belmont, CA: Wadsworth.
Bacarr, J. (1994). *How to Succeed in a Japanese Company*. New York: Citadel Press.
Baker, J. C. (1984). 'Foreign language training and pre-departure orientation training in US multinational firms.' *Personnel Administrator* 29: 68–70.
Bakke, E. (1992). 'The human resource function.' *Management International Review* 32, 74–82.
Baliga, B. R. and Jaeger, A. M. (1984). 'Multinational corporations: Control systems and delegation issues.' *Journal of International Business Studies* Fall, 25–40.
Balinga, G. M. and Baker, J. C. (1985). 'Multinational corporate policies for expatriate managers: selection, training, evaluation.' *SAM Advanced Management Journal* 50 (4), 31–8.
Banai, M. and Reisel, W. D. (1993). 'Expatriate managers' loyalty to the MNC: Myth or reality?' *Journal of International Business Studies* 24 (2), 233–48.
Bangkok Japanese Chamber of Commerce and Industry (BJC) (1987). *Nihonkigyo no Taijin Jugyoin ni taisuru Ankeito*. (A survey of Thai Employees in Japanese Joint Ventures) Bangkok: BJC.
Bartlett, C. A., Doz, Y. and Hedlund, G. (1990). *Managing the Global Firm*. London: Routledge.
Bates, C. and Renforth, W. (1986). 'Cultural linkages to managerial behaviour: implications for transnational managers.' *Advances in International Comparative Management* 2, 159–72.
Batton, J. (1992). *Japanization at Work*. London: Macmillan.

Beatty, J., McCune, J. T. and Beatty, R. W. (1988). 'A policy-capturing approach to the study of United States and Japanese managers' compensation decisions.' *Journal of Management* 14 (3), 465–74.
Befu, H. (1992). 'Demise of Permanent Employment in Japan.' *Human Resource Management* 29 (3), 231–50.
Benedict, R. (1974). *The Chrysanthemum and the Sword: Patterns of Japanese Culture*. New York: New American Library.
Benson, J. and Enomoto, C. (1994). 'The development of labor-management relations in Japan.' *American Business Review* 12 (1), 53–8.
Benson, J. (1993). 'Strategic labour relations: Management practices in Japanese and Australian manufacturing enterprises.' *Japanese Studies Bulletin* (University of Melbourne) 13 (1), 6–23.
Bhagat, R. S. and McQuaid, S. J. (1982). 'Role of subjective culture in organizations: A review and direction for future research.' *Journal of Applied Psychology Monograph* 67 (5), 635–85.
Billesbach, T. J. and Rives, J. M. (1985). 'Lifetime employment: Future prospects for Japan and the US.' *SAM Society for the Advancement of Management* 50 (4) Autumn, 26–30.
Bird, A. and Beechler, S. (1995). 'Links between business strategy and human resource management strategy in US-based Japanese subsidiaries: an empirical investigation.' *Journal of International Business Studies* 1st Quarter, 23–46.
Black, J. S. and Gregerson, H. B. (1993). 'Resolving conflicts with the Japanese: Mission impossible?' *Sloan Management Review* 34 (3), 49–59.
Bob, D. and SRI International (1990). *Japanese Companies in American Communities*. New York: The Japan Society.
Bolan, D. S. and Crain C. R. (1985). 'Decision sequence: A recurring theme in comparing American and Japanese management.' *Proceedings, Academy of Management* San Diego, CA., 88–92.
Boyacigiller, N. and Adler, N. J. (1991). 'The parochial dinosaur: Organizational science in a global context.' *Academy of Management Review* 16, 262–90.
Brewster, C. (1991a). *The Management of Expatriates*. London: Kogan Page.
Brewster, C. and Tyson, S. (1991b). *International Comparisons in Human Resource Management*. London: Pitman.
Brouthers, L. E. and Werner, S. (1990). 'Are the Japanese good global competitors?' *Columbia Journal of Global Business* Fall, 5–11.
Buckley, P. J. and Mirza, H. (1985). 'The wit and wisdom of Japanese management: An iconoclastic analysis.' *Management International Review* 25(3), 16–40.
Byham, W. C. (1993). *Shogun Management*. New York: Harper Business.
Campbell, N. and Burton, F. (1994). *Japanese Multinationals*. London: Routledge.
Chalmers, N. J. (1989). *Industrial Relations in Japan: The Peripheral Workforce*. London: Routledge.
Chan, T. S. (1994). 'Developing international managers: A partnership approach.' *Journal of Management Development* 13 (3), 39–46.
Chinwano, C. and Tambunlertchai, S. (1983). 'Japanese investment in Thailand and its prospects in the 1980s.' In Sekiguchi (ed.) *ASEAN-Japan Relations: Investment*. Singapore: Institute of Southeast Asian Studies.
Christopher, R. C. (1993). *The Japanese Mind*. Tokyo: Tuttle.

Bibliography

Christopher, R. C. (1986). *American Companies in Japan.* New York: Fawcett Columbine.
Clegg, C. (1986). 'Trip to Japan: A synergistic approach to managing human resources.' *Personnel Management* 18 (8), 35–9.
Cohen, A. M. (1993). 'Japan in transit; Remodeling the Japanese corporation.' *Management Japan* 26 (2), 25–31.
Conner, P. (1993). 'A cross-national comparative study of managerial values: United States, Canada and Japan.' *Advances in International Comparative Management* 8, 3–29.
Cool, K. O. and Lengnick-Hall, C. J. (1985). 'Some thoughts on the transferability of Japanese style management.' *Organization Studies* 6 (1), 1–22.
Corey, A. V. (1991). 'Ensuring strength in each country: a challenge for corporate headquarters global human resource executives.' *Human Resource Planning* 14 (1), 1–8.
Cox, T. (1993). *Cultural Diversity in Organizations: Theory, Research and Practice.* San Francisco: Berrett-Koehler.
Cox, T., Lobel, S. and McLeod, P. (1991). 'Effects of ethnic group cultural differences on co-operative and competitive behaviour on a group task.' *Academy of Management Journal* 34 (4), 827–47.
Cray, D. (1984). 'Control and coordination in multinational corporations.' *Journal of International Business Studies* Fall, 85–98.
Cresswell, J. W. (1994). *Research Design: Qualitative and Quantitative Approaches.* Thousand Oaks, CA: Sage Publications.
Delbridge, R. (1995). 'Surviving JIT: Control and resistance in a Japanese Transplant.' *Journal of Management Studies* 32 (6), 803–17.
De Mente, B. L. (1990). *The Kata Factor.* Phoenix: Phoenix Books.
Doz, Y. and Prahalad, C. K. (1986). 'Controlled variety: A challenge for human resource management in the MNC.' *Human Resource Management* 25 (1), 55–71.
Doz, Y. and Prahalad, C. K. (1984). 'Patterns of strategic control in multinational corporations.' *Journal of International Business Studies* Fall, 55–72.
Dunphry, D. C. and Stening, B. W. (1984). *Japanese Organizational Behaviour and Management: An Annotated Bibliography.* Hong Kong: Asian Research Service.
Durlabhji, S. and Marks, N. E. (1993). *Japanese Business Cultural Perspectives.* New York: State University of New York.
Economist (1994). 'Life-time underemployment.' *The Economist* July 9, 10–12.
Edstrom, A. and Lorange, P. (1984). 'Matching strategy and human resources in multinational corporations.' *Journal of International Business Studies* 15, 125–37.
Elger, T. and Smith, C. (eds) (1994). *Global Japanization? The Transformation of the Labour Process.* London: Routledge.
Eli, M. (1991). *Japan Inc.* Chicago: Probus.
Elmuti, D. (1992) 'Investigation of the human resource management practices of Japanese subsidiaries in the Arabian Gulf region.' *The Journal of Applied Business Research* 7 (2), 82–88.
Employee Development Bulletin (1993). 'A clean slate: is there a Japanese approach to recruitment and training?' *Industrial Relations Review and Report* July, 7–10.

Endo, K. (1994). 'Satei (Personal Assessment) and interworker competition in Japanese firms.' *Industrial Relations* 33 (1), 70–82.

Erden, D. (1988). 'Impact of multinational companies on host countries: Executive training programmes.' *Management International Review* 28 (3), 39–47.

Espinoza, J. A. and Garza, R. T. (1985). 'Social group salience and interethnic co-operation.' *Journal of Experimental Social Psychology* 231, 380–92.

Evans, C. L. (1993). 'Human resource management in the Japanese financial institution abroad: The case of the London office.' *British Journal of Industrial Relations* 31 (3) 347–64.

Evans, W. A., Sculli, D. and Yau W. S. L. (1987). 'Cross-cultural factors in the identification of managerial potential.' *Journal of General Management* 13 (1), 52–7.

Far Eastern Economic Review (1991). *Japan in Asia*. Hong Kong: Far Eastern Economic Review.

Ferraro, G. P. (1990). *The Cultural Dimension of International Business*. Englewood Cliffs, NJ: Prentice-Hall.

Finkelstein, B., Imamura, A. and Tobin, J. (1991) *Transcending Stereotypes: Discovering Japanese Culture and Education*. Yarmouth, Maine: Intercultural Press.

Fish, A. and Wood, J. (1993). 'HRM and international expatriate management.' *International Journal of Career Management* 5 (4), 25–36.

Florida, R. and Kenney, M. (1991). 'Transplanted organizations: The transfer of Japanese industrial organization to the US.' *American Sociological Review* 4, 603–25.

Fontaine, G. (1989). *Managing International Assignments: The Strategy for Success*. Englewood Cliffs, NJ: Prentice-Hall.

French, J. L. (1995). 'Japanese and German human resource practices: convergence of West with East.' *Advances in International Comparative Management* 10, 201–26.

Fruin W. M. (1992). *The Japanese Enterprise System*. Oxford: Clarendcon Press.

Fucini, J. J. and Fucini, S. (1990). *Working for the Japanese: Inside Mazda's American Auto Plant*. New York: Free Press.

Fukuda, J. K. and Chu, P. (1994). 'Wrestling with expatriate family problems.' *International Studies of Management and Organization* 24 (30), 36–47.

Fukuda, J. K. (1993). *Japanese Management in East Asia and Beyond*. Hong Kong: Chinese University Press.

Fukuda, J. K. (1988). *Japanese-Style Management Transferred: The Experience of East Asia*. London: Routledge.

Fukuda, J. K. (1986). 'What can we learn from Japanese management?' *Journal of General Management*. 11 (3), 16–25.

Garby, C. C. and Bullock, M. (1994). *Japan A New Kind of Superpower?* Washington: The Woodrow Wilson Centre Press.

Gertsen, M. C. (1990). 'Intercultural competence and expatriates.' *International Journal of Human Resource Management* 1 (3), 341–62.

Ghoshal, S., Westney, E. (1993). *Organization Theory and the Multinational Corporation*. New York: St. Martin's Press Inc.

Gleave, S. and Oliver, N. (1990). 'Human resources management in Japanese manufacturing companies in the UK: 5 Case studies.' *Journal of General Management* 16 (1), 54–68.

Gordon, D. (1988). *Japanese Management in America and Britain.* Aldershot: Avebury.
Graham, L. (1993). 'Inside a Japanese transplant.' *Work and Occupations* 20 (2), 147–173.
Gregersen, H. B. and Black, J. S. (1992). 'Antecedents for commitment to a parent company and a foreign operations.' *Academy of Management Review* 35 (1), 65–90.
Gregory, K. L. (1983). 'Native-view paradigms: multiple cultures and culture conflicts in organizations.' *Administrative Science Quarterly* 28, 359–76.
Grove, C. L. and Torbiorn, I. (1985). 'A new conceptualization of intercultural adjustments and the goals of training.' *International Journal of Intercultural Relations* 9 (2), 205–33.
Gudykurst, W. B., Hammer, M. R. (1984). 'Dimensions of intercultural effectiveness: Culture specific or culture general.' *International Journal of Intercultural Relations* 8, 1–10.
Guptara, P. (1993). 'Multicultural aspects of managing multinationals.' *Management Japan* 26 (1), 7–14.
Hamada, T. (1992). 'Under the silk banner: The Japanese company and its overseas managers.' In Lebra, T. S. (ed.) *Japanese and Social Organization.* Honolulu: University of Hawaii Press.
Hamaguchi, E. and Kumon, S. (eds) (1982). *Nihonteki Shudanshugi.* (Japanese Collectivism) Tokyo: Yuhikaku.
Hammer, M. R. (1988). 'A cross-cultural comparison of intercultural effectiveness: Japan, Mexico and the United States.' *World Communication* 17(1), 119–44.
Hampton-Turner, C. (1990). *Corporate Culture.* London: Hutchinson.
Hansen, C. D. (1994). 'A review of cross-cultural research on human resource development.' *Human Resource Development Quarterly* 5 (1), 55–74.
Harper, S. C. (1988). 'Now that the dust has settled: learning from Japanese Management.' *Business-Horizons* 31 (4), 43–51.
Hasegawa, N. (1965). *The Japanese Character: A Cultural Profile.* Tokyo: Greenwood Press.
Hatvany, N. and Pucik, V. (1981a). 'Japanese management practices and productivity.' *Organizational Dynamics* Spring, 5–21.
Hatvany, N. and Pucik, V. (1981b). 'An integrated management system: Lessons from the Japanese experience.' *Academy of Management Review* 6, 469–80.
Hattori, I. (1987). *Corporate Structure and Decision Making in Japan.* Tokyo: Sophia University Press.
Hayashi, K. (1994) *I-bunka Intafesu Kanri: Kaigai ni Okeru Nihon-teki Keiei.* (Cross-Cultural Interface Management: Japanese Management Overseas) Tokyo: Yugaikaku.
Hayes, J. and Allison, C. W. (1988). 'Cultural differences in the learning styles of managers.' *Management International Review* 28 (3), 75–80.
Heise, H. J. (1989) 'How Japanese work out as bosses in Germany.' In Shibagaki, K. Trevor, M. and Abo, T. (eds), *Japanese and European Management.* Tokyo: University of Tokyo Press.
Hendry, C. (1994). *Human Resource Strategies for International Growth.* London: Routledge.
Herskovits, M. J. (1955). *Cultural Anthropology.* New York: Knopf.

Hiroshima University Faculty of Economics (1990). *Nihongata Keiei wa Tsuyo Suruka: ASEAN Shokoku tono Kakawari o Motomete*. (Is Japanese-style Management Applicable in ASEAN?) Record of International Symposium. Hiroshima: Hiroshima University.

Hofstede, G. (1994). 'Concerning human resources aspects: Predicting managers' career success in an international setting.' *MIR Management International Review* 34 (1), 63–70.

Horvath, D., McMillan, C. J., Azumi, K. and Hickson, K. (1976). 'The cultural context of organizational control.' *International Studies of Management and Organization* 6, 60–86.

Hunt, D. M. and Bolon, D. S. (1989). 'A review of five versions of theory Z: does theory Z have a future?' *Advances in International Comparative Management* 4, 201–20.

Imai, K. and Komiya R. (1994). *Business Enterprise in Japan*. Cambridge: MIT Press.

Imaoka, H. (1985). 'Japanese Management in Malaysia.' *Southeast Asian Studies* 22(4), 9–26.

Inkpen, A. (1994). 'The characteristics and performance of Japanese–North American joint ventures in North America.' *Advances in International Comparative Management* 9, 83–108.

INSAN (1986). *The Sun Also Sets: Lessons in Looking East*. Petaling Jaya, Malaysia.

IRS Employment Trends (1993a). 'Japanese employment policies.' *Industrial Relations Review and Report* November, 4–5.

IRS Employment Trends (1993b). 'Japanese employers avoid redundancy, despite recession.' *Industrial Relations Review and Report* September, 3–4.

IRS Employment Trends (1993c). 'Work organization is main factor in labour productivity.' *Industrial Relations Review and Report* December, 2–3.

Ishinomori, S. (1988). *Japan Inc*. London: University of California Press, 1988.

Itami, Hiroyuki (1987). *Jinhon-shugi Kigyo*. (Human-capitalistic Enterprise) Tokyo: Chikuma-shobo.

Ito, S. (1985). 'Japanese Management in Taiwan.' *Southeast Asian Studies* 22 (4), 89–108.

Iwami, M. (1992). 'What is Japanese style corporate management?' *Management Japan* 25 (1), 24–6.

Iwauchi, R., Kadowaki, A., Abe, E., Jinouchi, Y. and Mori, S. (1992). *Kaigai Nikkei-Kigyo to Jin-teki Shigen*. (Japanese Overseas Enterprises and Human Resources) Tokyo: Dobunkan.

Jackson, T. (1995). *Cross-Cultural Management*. Oxford: Butterworth-Heinemann.

Jaeger, A. M. (1986). 'Organizational development and national culture: where's the fit?' *Academy of Management Review* 11 (1), 178–90.

Jaeger, A. M. and Baliga B. R. (1985). 'Control systems and strategic adaptation: Lessons from the Japanese experience.' *Strategic Management Journal* 6, 115–34.

Jaeger, A. M. (1983). 'The transfer of organizational culture overseas: an approach to control in the multinational corporation.' *Journal of International Business Studies* Fall, 91–114.

Jain, H. C. (1990). 'Human resource management in selected Japanese firms, their foreign subsidiaries and locally owned counterparts.' *International Labour Review* 129 (1), 73–84.
Jain, H. C. (1987). 'The Japanese system of HRM: Transferability to the Indian Industrial Environment.' *Asian Survey* 27 (9), 1023–35.
Japan Productivity Center (1984). *Managerial Behavior in Japan and the USA.* Tokyo: Japan Productivity Center.
JETRO (1988). *ASEAN ni okeru Nikkei Kigyo Katsudo ni kansuru Chosa Hokoku.* (Report of a Survey on Conditions of Japanese Affiliates in ASEAN) Tokyo: JETRO.
JETRO (1982a). *Japanese Corporate Decision Making.* Tokyo: JETRO.
JETRO (1982b). *Japanese Corporate Personnel Management.* Tokyo: JETRO.
Johnson, C. (1988). 'Japanese-style management in America.' *California Management Review* Summer, 34–45.
Johnson, C. (1993). 'Comparative capitalism: The Japanese difference.' *California Management Review* Summer, 51–67.
Johnson, K. R. and Golembiewski, R. T. (1992). 'National culture in organization development: a conceptual and empirical analysis.' *International Journal of Human Resource Management* 3 (1), 71–84.
Johnson, S. G. (1990). 'Not cut from the same bolt: Underneath the management fabric of Japan and the United States.' *Baylor Business Review* Summer, 18–21.
Johnston, S. (1995). 'Managerial Dominance of Japan's major corporations.' *Journal of Management* 21 (2), 191–209.
Jones, S. (1991). *Working for the Japanese.* London: Macmillan.
Joynt, P. and Warner, M. (1985). *Managing in Different Cultures.* Oslo, Norway: Universitetsforlaget.
Kamata, S. (1983). *Japan in the Passing Lane.* London: George Allen and Unwin.
Karsh, B. (1984). 'Human resources management in Japanese large scale industry.' *The Journal of Industrial Relations* June, 226–43.
Kawaji, K. (1982). *Selection of Personnel for Long-Term Overseas Assignment.* Tokyo: Mitsubishi Electric Company Ltd.
Kearns, R. L. (1992). *Zaibatsu America.* New York: The Free Press.
Keeley, T. D. (1994). 'Beikoku no kigyobunka to sono henkaku: GE wo rei to shite.' (American corporate culture and it transformation: the example of GE) In Yasumuro, K. (ed.), *Takokuseki Kigyo Bunka.* (Culture of Multinationals) Tokyo: Bunshindo.
Keio University IRI (1990). 'Nihon kigyo no jinteki shigen kanri no kokusaiteki tekiosei.' (The international adaptability of Japanese companies' human resource management) In *Ho to Keizai no Kihon Mondai.* (Fundamental issues in law and economics) Tokyo: Keio University Industrial Research Institute.
Kelly, L., Whatley, A., Worthley, R. and Lie, H. (1986). 'The role of the ideal organization in comparative management: a cross-cultural perspective of Japan and Korea.' *Asia Pacific Journal of Management* 3 (2), 59–75.
Kenney, M. and Florida, R. (1995). 'The transfer of Japanese management styles in two US transplant industries: Autos and electronics.' *Journal of Management Studies* 32 (6), 789–802.

Keys, J. (1984). 'The Japanese management theory-jungle revisited.' *Academy of Management Review* 9 (2), 342–53.

Kidahashi, M. (1987). *Dual Organization: A Study of Japanese-owned Firms in the United States.* Unpublished Ph.D. Thesis, Columbia University.

Kim, K. I. (1993). 'The concept of fairness: How the Japanese and the Americans see it.' *Management Japan* 26 (1), 26–9.

Kimbara, T. (1988). 'Kokusaikeiei ni okeru genchika no kanosei.' (Possibility of localization in international management) *The Hiroshima Economic Review* 12 (1).

Kobayashi, K. (1989). 'New globalized challenge for the Japanese business.' *Human Resource Planning* 12 (1): 15–20.

Koike, K. (1981). *Nihon no Jukuren.* (Japan's Skilled Labour) Tokyo: Yuhikaku.

Kojima, K. (1985). *Nihon no Kaigai Chokusetsu Toshi.* (Japanese Foreign Direct Investment Abroad) Tokyo: Bunshin-do.

Kokusai Keizai (1988). 'Nippon Kigyo in Malaysia.' (Japanese Business in Malaysia) *Kokusai Keizai*: Special Issue on Malaysia (August).

Koizumi, T. (1989). 'Management of innovation and change in Japanese organizations.' *Advances in International Comparative Management* 4, 245–54.

Kondo, D. K. (1990). *Crafting Selves: Power, Gender, and Discourses of Identity in a Japanese Workplace.* Chicago: University of Chicago.

Kono, T. (1988). *Corporate Culture under Evolution.* Japan: Kodansha.

Kono, T. (1984). *Strategy and Structure of Japanese Enterprises.* London: Macmillan.

Kono, T. (1982). 'Japanese management philosophy: Can it be exported?' *Long Range Planning* 15, June: 90–102.

Kopp, R. (1993). *Koyo Masatsu.* (Employment Friction) Tokyo: Sanno Institute of Management Press.

Kosiyanon, L. and Yoshihara, K. (1985). 'Japanese management in Thailand.' *Southeast Asian Studies* 22 (4), 374–90.

Kriger, M. P. and Solomon, Esther E. (1992). 'Strategic mindsets and decision-making autonomy in US and Japanese MNCs.' *MIR Management International Review* 32 (4), 327–43.

Kujawa, D. (1986). *Japanese Multinationals in the United States: Case Studies.* New York: Praeger.

Kume, T. (1985). 'Managerial attitudes toward decision-making: North America and Japan.' In Gudykunst, W. P., Stewart, L. P. and Ting-Toomey, S. (eds), *Communication, Culture and Organizational Processes.* RR Beverly Hills, CA: Sage.

Kuwahara, Y. (1993). 'New developments in human resource management in Japan.' *Asia Pacific Journal of Human Resources* 31 (2), 3–11.

Kuwahara, T. (1978) 'An understanding of the international applicability of Japanese management system.' *Kyushu Sangyo University Economic and Business Review* 5, 22–33.

Laurie, D. (1992). *Yankee Samurai.* New York: Harper Collins.

Lee, M. E. and Alston, J. P. (1990). 'Is Japanese style management exportable: evidence from the world's largest firms.' *Advances in International Comparative Management* 5, 197–209.

Lee, S. (ed.) (1982). *Japanese Management.* New York: Praeger.

Levine, S. B. and Kawada, H. (1991). *Human Resources in Japanese Industrial Development*. Princeton: Princeton University Press.

Li, C. L. (1992). 'The strategic design of cross-cultural training programmes.' *Journal of Management Development* 11 (7), 22–9.

Lifson, T. (1992). 'The managerial integration of Japanese business in America.' In *The Political Economy of Japan*. Vol. 3 (231–66). Palo Alto: Stanford University Press.

Lincoln, J. R. (1989). 'Employee work attitudes and management practice in the US and Japan: evidence from a large comparative survey.' *California Management Review* Fall, 89–106.

Lincoln, J. R., Hanada, M. and McBride, K. (1986). 'Organizational structures in Japanese and US manufacturing.' *Administrative Science Quarterly* 31, 338–64.

Maddox, R. C. (1993). *Cross-cultural Problems in International Business: the Role of the Cultural Integration Function*. Westport, CT: Quorum Books.

March, R. M. (1992). 'A research note: Centralization of decision-making in Japanese factories.' *Organization Studies* 13 (2), 261–74.

Matsuki, H. (1980) 'Japanese managers in management in the Western world: A Canadian experience.' In Neghandi, Anant R. (ed.) *The Functioning of the Multinational Corporation*. New York: Pergamon Press.

McCormick, B. and McCormick, K. (1996). *Japanese Companies–British Factories*. Aldershot: Avebury.

McMillan, C. J. (1991). 'Going global: Japanese Science-based strategies in the 1990s.' *Managerial and Decision Economics* 12, 171–81.

McNamara, T. E. and Hayanashi, K. (1994). 'Culture and management: Japan and the West towards a transnational culture.' *Management Japan* 27 (2) Autumn, 3–13.

Mead, R. (1990). *Cross-Cultural Management Communication*. Chichester: John Wiley.

Mihalasky, J. (1992). 'Japanese Management Practices.' *American Asian Review* 10 (4) Winter, 79–127.

Miller, E. L., Beechler, S. and Bhatt, B. (1986). 'The relationship between the global strategic planning process and the human resource management function.' *Human Resource Planning* 9, 9–23.

Minami, H. and Ikoma, A. R. (1971). *Psychology of the Japanese People*. Tokyo: University of Tokyo Press.

Misawa, M. (1987). 'New Japanese-style management in a changing era.' *Columbia Journal of World Business* Winter, 9–18.

Misumi, J. (1984). 'Decision-making in Japanese groups and organizations.' In Wilpert, B. and Sorge, A (eds), *International Perspectives on Organizational Democracy*. 92–123. New York: Wiley.

Moloney, J. C. (1954). *Understanding the Japanese Mind*. New York: Philosophical Library.

Moran, R. T. (1986). 'Who makes rules in cross-cultural conflict?' *International Management* 41 (1).

Mortellaro, J. S. (1989). 'Japan's management imperialism.' *Business Marketing* February, 62–6.

Mouer, R. and Sugimoto, Y. (1986). *Images of Japanese Society*. London: Kegan Paul International.

Mroczkowski, T. and Linowes, R. G. (1990). 'Inside the Japanese corporation abroad: Views of American professionals.' *Management Japan* 23 (2), 28–30.
Murata, K. (1990), 'Personnel management in Japanese business enterprises.' *Hitotsubashi Journal of Commerce and Management* 25, 35–46.
Nakane, C. (1989). 'Principles of humanistic enterprise in Japan.' *Futures* December, 640–46.
Nam, Sang H. (1995). 'Culture, control and commitment in international joint ventures.' *The International Journal of Human Resource Management* 6 (3) September, 553–67.
Naotsuka, R. and Sakamoto, N. (1981). *Mutual Understanding of Different Cultures*. Tokyo: Taishukan.
Napier, N. K. and Peterson, R. B. (1991). 'Expatriates re-entry: What do repatriates have to say?' *Human Resource Planning* 14 (1), 19–28.
Nath, R. (1986). 'Role of culture in cross-cultural and organizational research.' *Advances in International Comparative Management* 2, 249–67.
Naumann, E (1992). 'A conceptual model of expatriate turnover.' *Journal of International Business Studies* 3rd Quarter, 499–531.
Near, J. P. (1986). 'Work and non-work attitudes among Japanese and American workers.' *Advances in International Comparative Management* 2, 57–67.
Negandhi, A. R. (1983). 'Cross-cultural management research: trend and future directions.' *Journal of International Business Studies* Fall, 17–28.
Negandhi, A. R. (1979). *A Quest for Survival and Growth: A Comparative Study of American European and Japanese Multinationals*. New York: Praeger.
Nemoto, T. and Yoshimoto, Y. (1994). *Kokusai Keiei to Kigyo Bunka*. (International Management and Enterprise Culture) Tokyo: Gakubunsha.
Nihon Zaigai Kigyo Kyokai (Japanese Overseas Enterprises Organization) (1989). *Kokusai yoin ikusei kenkyu iinkai hokokusho*. (Report of the committee on development of human resources for internationalization) Tokyo: Nihon Zaigai Kigyo Kyokai.
Nonaka, I. (1988). 'Self-renewal of the Japanese Firm and the Human Resource Strategy.' *Human Resource Management* 27 (1), 45–62.
Oddou, G. R. (1991). 'Managing your expatriates: What the successful firms do.' *Human Resource Planning* 14 (4), 301.
Oishi, T. (1993). 'The internationalization of Japanese firms and their challenges.' *Management Japan* 26 (2), 3–6.
Okubayashi, K. (1989). 'The Japanese industrial relations system.' *Journal of General Management* 14 (3), 67–88.
Ozaki, R. (1992). *Human Capitalism: The Japanese Enterprise System as World Model*. New York: Penguin Books.
Ozaki, R. (1978). *The Japanese: A Cultural Portrait*. Tokyo: Tuttle.
Parsons, T. and Shils, E. A. (1951). *Toward a General Theory of Action*. Cambridge, MA: Harvard University Press.
Pascale, R. T. (1978) 'Communication and decision-making across cultures: Japanese and American comparisons.' *Administrative Science Quarterly* 23 (1), 91–110.
Patterson, G. (1989). 'Mazda's 2 top American aides at plant in US quit, are succeeded by Japanese.' *The Wall Street Journal* Oct. 13, A4.

Peterson, M., Brannen, M. Y. and Smith, P. (1994) 'Japanese and United States leadership: issues in current research.' *Advances in International Comparative Management* 9, 57–82.

Peterson, R. B. and Sullivan, J. (1990). 'The Japanese lifetime employment system: whither it goest.' *Advances in International Comparative Management* 5, 169–94.

Peiper, R. (ed.) (1990). *Human Resource Management: An International Comparison.* Berlin: Walter de Gruyter.

Prahalad, C. K. and Doz, Y. (1981). 'An approach to strategic control in MNCs.' *Sloan Management Review* Summer, 5–13.

Rehder, R. R. (1994). 'Saturn, Uddevalla and the Japanese lean systems: paradoxical prototypes for the twenty-first century.' *The International Journal of Human Resource Management* 5 (1) Feb., 1–31.

Rehder, R. R. (1989). 'Japanese transplants: In search of a balanced and broader perspective.' *Columbia Journal of World Business* Winter, 17–28.

Rehfeld, J. E. (1990). 'What working for a Japanese company taught me.' *Harvard Business Review* Nov.-Dec., 167–76.

Ronen, S. (1986). *Comparative and Multinational Management.* New York: Harper and Row.

Runglertkrengkrai, S. and Engkaninan, S. (1987). 'The pattern of managerial behaviour in Thai culture.' *AsiaPacific Journal of Management* 5 (1), 8–15.

Sakuma, M. (1989). 'A proposal for transferring a Japanese management system overseas.' In Shibagaki, K., Trevor, M. and Abe, T. (eds), *Japanese and European Management, Their International Adaptability.* Tokyo: Tokyo University Press.

Sasaki, Naoto (1993). 'Some prospects for future management of Japanese companies.' *Management Japan* 26 (2), 6–8.

Schwind, H. F. and Peterson, R. B. (1985). 'Shifting personal values in the Japanese management system.' *International Studies of Management and Organization* 15 (2), 60–74.

Seigel, J. S. (1995). 'The hollowing out of lifetime employment in Japan.' *Labour* Issue Quarterly Spring, No, 27, 5–6.

Selmer, J. (1995). 'Expatriate executives' perceptions of their HCN subordinate values in Southeast Asia.' *Advances in International Comparative Management* 10, 43–61.

Seror, A. C. (1994). 'An empirical analysis of strategies for managerial control: the United States and Japan.' *Advances in International Comparative Management* 9, 19–44.

Seto, R. (1989). 'Patterns of internationalization of Japanese firms: new developments and managerial issues.' *Management Japan* 22 (2), 14–19.

Shenkar, O. (1988). 'Uncovering some paths in the Japanese management theory jungle.' *Human Systems Management* 7, 221–30.

Shibagaki, K., Trevor, M. and Abe, T. (1989). *Japanese and European Management, Their International Adaptability.* Tokyo: Tokyo University Press.

Shimabukuro, Y. (1982). *Consensus Management in Japanese Industry.* Tokyo: I.S.S.

Shimizu, N. (1995). 'Today's taboos may be gone tomorrow.' *Tokyo Business Today* 63 (1), 29.

Shimizu, N. (1994a). 'Take advantage of Japanese decision-making or lack of it.' *Tokyo Business Today* 62 (5), 46.
Shimizu, N. (1994b). 'Don't copy Japanese firms' organizational styles.' *Tokyo Business Today* 62 (6), 35.
Simon, J. H. (1991). 'US-Japanese management enters a new generation.' *Management Review* February, 42–5.
Solomon, C. M. (1995). 'Learning to manage host-country nationals.' *Personnel Journal* May, 94–101.
Stening, B. W. and Hammer, M. R. (1992). 'Cultural baggage and the adaptation of expatriate American and Japanese managers.' *Management International Review* 329 (1), 77–89.
Stone, R. (1991). 'Expatriate selection and failure.' *Human Resource Planning* 14 (1), 9–18.
Storey, J. and Bacon, N. (1993). 'Individualism and collectivism: into the 1990s.' *International Journal of Human Resource Management* 4 (3), 665–84.
Sullivan, J. J. (1992). *Invasion of the Salaryman: The Japanese Business Presence in America*. New York: Praeger.
Sullivan, J. J. and Peterson, R. B. (1991). 'A test of theories underlying the Japanese lifetime employment system.' *Journal of International Business Studies* 1st Quarter, 79–96.
Sullivan, J. and Snodgrass, C. (1991). 'Tolerance of executive failure in American and Japanese organizations.' *Asia Pacific Journal of Management* 8 (1), 15–34.
Sullivan, J. and Peterson, R. B. (1989). 'Japanese management theories.' *Advances in International Comparative Management* 4, 255–75.
Sullivan, J. J. and Nonaka, I. (1986). 'The application of organizational learning theory Japanese and American management.' *Journal of International Business Studies* Fall, 127–47.
Sumiya, M. (1990). *The Japanese Industrial Relations Reconsidered*. Tokyo: Japan Institute of Labor.
Suzuki, Y. (1991). *Japanese Management Structures 1920–80*. Hampshire, England: Macmillan.
Takanaka, A. (1986). 'Some thoughts on Japanese management centering on personnel and labor management: The reality and the future.' *International Studies of Management and Organization* 15 (3–4), 17–68.
Takanashi, A. (1995). 'Employment practices and unemployment in contemporary Japan.' *Japan Labour Bulletin* April 1, 5–8.
Tayeb, M. (1994). 'Japanese managers and British culture: a comparative case study.' *The International Review of Human Resource Management* 5 (1), 145–66.
Taylor, M. S. (1991). 'American managers in Japanese subsidiaries: How cultural differences are affecting the work place.' *Human Resource Planning* 14 (1), 43–9.
Terpstra, V. and David, K. (1985). *The Cultural Environment of International Business*. Cincinnati: South-Western Publishing.
Thianthai, C. (1986). *The Implementation of Japanese Management Style in Thailand*. Ph.D. thesis, Nova University, Florida, USA.
Thomas, D. C. and Ravlin, E. C. (1995). 'Responses of employees to cultural adaptation by a foreign manager.' *Journal of Applied Psychology* 80 (1), 133–46.

Thomas, D. C. and Toyne, B. (1995). 'Subordinates' responses to cultural adaptation by Japanese expatriate managers.' *Journal of Business Research* 32, 1–10.
Thompson, A. G. (1989). 'Cross-cultural management of labor in a Thai environment.' *Asia Pacific Journal of Management* 6 (2), 323–38.
Tokyo Business Today (1993). 'What's killing Japanese business? Japanese-style management.' *Tokyo Business Today* July, 24–6.
Tomita, T. (1985). 'Japanese Management in Hong Kong.' *Southeast Asian Studies* 22 (4), 61–75.
Toyne, B. (1987). *Host Country Managers of MNCs*. New York: Arno Press, 1987.
Trapedia (1980). *Kaigai Chuzai Hokoku*. (Report on overseas assignments) Trapedia Vol. 11 November, 8–39.
Trevor, M. (1986). *The Japanese Management Development System: Generalists and Specialists in Japanese Companies Abroad*. London: Wolfeboro.
Trevor, M (1983a). *Japan's Reluctant Multinationals: Japanese Management at Home and Abroad*. New York: St. Martin's Press.
Trevor, M. (1983b). *Under Japanese Management: the Experience of British Workers*. London: Heinemann.
Triandis, H. C. (1982). 'Review of culture's consequences: international differences in work-related values.' *Human Organization* 41, 86–90.
Triandis, H. C. (1972). *The Analysis of Subjective Culture*. New York: Wiley.
Tsuda, M. (1986). 'The future of the organization and the individual in Japanese management.' *International Studies of Management and Organization* 15 (3–4), 89–125.
Ueno, A. (1988). *Shin-kokusai Keieisenryaku-ron*. (New international management strategy) Tokyo: Yuhikaku.
van Wees, L. and Jansen, P. (1994), 'Dual ladder in balance.' *International Journal of Career Management* 6 (3), 11–9.
Vance, C. M. *et al.* (1992). 'An examination of the transferability of traditional performance appraisal principles across cultural boundaries.' *Management International Review* 32, 313–26.
Vogel, E. F. (1975). *Modern Japanese Organization and Decision-Making*. Berkeley: University of California Press.
Watanabe, S. and Yamaguchi, R. (1995). 'Intercultural perceptions at the workplace: The case of the British subsidiaries of Japanese firms.' *Human Relations* 48 (5), 581–607.
Watanabe, K. (1992). 'Co-ordinator support in a nemawashi decision process.' *Decision Support Systems* 8 (2) April, 85–98.
Wellford, W., Hardcastle, A. and Deone, M. (1994). 'Cultural transformation of NUMMI.' *Sloan Management Review* Fall, 99–113.
Werner, J. M. (1995). 'Managing a multicultural team.' *Business and Economic Review* Jan.–Mar., 15–18.
Winfield, I. and Kerrin, M. (1994). 'Toyota and management change in the East Midlands.' *Journal of Managerial Psychology* 9 (1), 3–6.
Wolfe, D. and Arnold, B. (1994). 'Human resource management in Malaysia: a comparison between American and Japanese approaches.' *Journal of Asian Business* 10 (4), 80–103.
Womack, J. P. (1990). *The Machine That Changed the World*. New York: Rawson Associates.

Woronoff, J. (1991). *Japan As Anything But Number One*. London: Macmillan.
Yamada, M. (1981). 'Japanese-Style Management in America: Merits and Difficulties.' *Japanese Economic Studies* 9 Fall, 1–30.
Yamaguchi, I. (1993). 'Perception sharing in Japan–US cross-cultural corporation.' *International Journal of Career Management* 5 (4), 9–18.
Yamaguchi, I. (1991). 'A mechanism of motivation processes in a Chinese, Japanese and US multicultural corporation: Presentation of a contingent motivational model.' *Management Japan* 24 (2), 27–32.
Yamanoue, M. (1982). *Selection of Personnel for Long-Term Overseas Assignments: The Case of Kobe Steel Co*. Tokyo: Kobe Steel Company.
Yamashita, S. (1990). *Transfer of Japanese Technology and Management to the ASEAN Countries*. Tokyo: Tokyo University Press.
Yamashita, T. (ed.) (1992). *Gurobaru Shakai to Nihon Kigyo*. (Global Society and Japanese Firms) Tokyo: Toshibunkasha.
Yamauchi, K. (1995). 'The erosion of the Japanese-style management system.' *Management Japan* 28 (1), 3–13.
Yang, C. Y. (1984). 'Demystifying Japanese management practices.' *Harvard Business Review* Nov–Dec, 172–83.
Yang, J. Z. (1992a). 'Americanization or Japanization of human resource management policies: A study of Japanese manufacturing and service firms in the United States.' *Advances in International Comparative Management* 7, 77–115.
Yang, J. Z. (1992b). 'Organizational and environmental impact on the use of Japanese-style HRM policies in Japanese firms in the US.' *The International Executive* 4, 321–43.
Yeh, R. (1995). 'Downward influence styles in cultural diversity settings.' *The International Journal of Human Resource Management* 6 (3), 626–41.
Yeh, R. (1991). 'Management practices of Taiwanese firms: as compared to those of American and Japanese subsidiaries in Taiwan.' *Asia Pacific Journal of Management* 8 (1), 1–14.
Yeh, R. (1989). 'On Hofstede's treatment of Chinese and Japanese values.' *Asia Pacific Journal of Management* 6 (1), 149–60.
Yuen E. C. and Kee T. (1993). 'Headquarters, host-culture and organizational influences on HRM policies and practices.' *Management International Review* 33 (4), 361–83.
Yoshihara, H. (1994). *Gaishikei Kigyo*. (Foreign Firms) Tokyo: Dobunkan Shuppan.
Yoshihara, H., Hayashi, K. and Yasumuro, K. (1988). *Nihon Kigyo no Gurobaru Keiei*. (Japanese Enterprise Global Management) Tokyo: Toyo Keizai Shinposha.
Yoshihara, H. (1979). *Takokuseki Keieiron*. (Multinational Management) Tokyo: Nihon Keizai Shibunsha.
Yoshimori, M. (1992a). 'Sources of Japanese Combativeness Part I.' *Management Japan* 25 (1), 18–23.
Yoshimori, M. (1992b). 'Sources of Japanese Competitiveness Part II.' *Management Japan* 25 (2), 31–36.
Yoshimori, M. (1989). 'Japanese direct manufacturing investment in France.' In Shibagaki, Kazuo, Trevor, M. and Abe, T. (eds), *Japanese and European Management, Their International Adaptability*. Tokyo: Tokyo University Press.

Yuen, E. C. and Kee, T. (1993). 'Headquarters, host-culture and organizational influences on HRM policies and practices.' *Management International Review* 33 (4), 361–83.

Zachary, P. (1994). 'Trading Places: Malaysians become stars at US electronic firms.' *Asian Wall Street Journal* Oct. 3, 1.

Zeffane, R. and Poole, M. (1994). 'International human resource management: a bibliographical review.' *The International Journal of Human Resource Development* 5 (2), 533–43.

Index

Abegglen, J. 33, 46, 94, 159, 164
Adler, N. 17, 18, 19, 21, 214
Ajiferuke, M. 16
Allison, R. E. 30
Amago, T. 113
Anderson, P. 27
Athos, A. G. 28, 94, 157, 159

Baba, S. 51–2, 74, 88, 97
Ballon, R. J. 149, 211
Barr, M. 10, 57, 102, 208
Bartlett, A. 6–10, 89, 100
Bartu, F. 101, 122, 127, 131, 144
Bass, B. M. 155, 210
Beamish, P. W. 121
Beechler, S. 8, 18, 75, 88, 89, 90
Befu, H. 59, 145
Bennett, M. L. 4, 219
Berry, W. 19, 20, 21
Besser, T. L. 95, 96
Binnis, W. G. 141, 210
Bird, A. 101, 120
Black, J. S. 121, 122, 124
Boddewyn, J. 16
Bond, M. H. 28
Boyacigiller, N. 121
Briody, E. K. 121
bucho (department chief) 52
Burack, E. H. 20

Calof, J. L. 121
Cascio, W. F. 29
Caudron, S. 121
Chrisman, J. B. 121
Clad, J. 134
Clark, R. 46
Cole, R. E. 60, 97
cultural synergy 15, 22–4

Dale, P. N. 41–2, 146
D'Andrade, R. 142
Deal, T. 19
Desatnick, R. L. 4, 219

do Rosario, L. 72, 79
Doi, K. 112, 122, 153, 176
Doi, T. 54–6
Donnellon, G. 142, 143, 210, 212
Dore, R. P. 18, 34, 93
Dowling, P. J. 4, 99, 102, 109, 206

Earley, C. P. 16–18, 28, 29
Elashmawi, F. 170, 203, 205
endaka (high value of yen) 100, 127
England, G. W. 18
Enz, C. A. 21
Erez, M. 16–18, 29
Eshghi, G. S. 170, 203
ethnocentrism
  attitudes 9
  IHRM policies 4, 6–9, 102–3,
    107, 113–15, 206–9, 218–20
  measurement of 178, 192–3
Evans, P. 4, 219

Fernandez, J. P. 10, 57, 102, 208
foreign direct investment (FDI)
  in Australia 138–9
  development of MNCs and
    IHRM 99–109
  by Japanese firms 1–7, 60, 128
  in Malaysia 134–6
  in Singapore 137
  in Thailand 130–1
Frankel, M. 73
Fukutake, T. 43

gaijin (foreigner) 48, 57, 58
Ghoshal, S. 6–10, 207
globalization 1–2, 4–7, 22–4, 98–9,
    101–7, 114–15, 118, 155, 177–8,
    192–3
Goldman, A. 150, 211

Hall, E. T. 143, 146
Hamada, T. 66
Hanaoka, M. 81

Index

Hasegawa, K. 65, 66, 70, 74, 77, 79, 156, 159, 164–6
Hatvany, N. 91
Hayashi, S. 16, 18, 27, 29, 68, 158, 160–1
Heenan, D. 107, 208
Herbig, P. A. 37
Hodgetts, R. M. 94
Hofstede, G. 16, 17, 18, 20, 25, 27–8, 34, 124–8, 132, 213–4
Hui, C. H. 25
host country national (HCN) managers
  Australian HCNs 139
  attitudes towards Japanese subsidiary 37–8
  benefits of employing 1–2
  communication 141–5, 150–2, 210–12
  cultural effects 18–22, 26–31, 44–5, 48, 51, 53–4, 56–7
  disagreements with PCN managers 92
  employee commitment 96–7
  information flow 152–4
  integration 1, 3–5, 7–13, 109–12, 115–21, 168–71, 209, 215–20
  Malaysian HCNs 136
  managerial discretion 156–7
  model for factors affecting HCN integration 13–14
  nenko joretsu 82
  recruitment 63
  relationships with PCNs 122
  shushinkoyo 74–6
  Singaporean HCNs 138
  Thai HCNs 132–3
  training 88–9

Ichimura, S. 75, 215
Iida, T. 139–40
individualism–collectivism 15, 24–31, 55, 93, 125, 138, 156–7
Inohara, H. 45, 52–3, 60, 61, 63, 68, 77, 83–6
international human resource management (IHRM)
  the Achilles' heel of Japanese MNCs 7–11
  advantages of effective IHRM 1–2
  communication and IHRM 211
  control systems 109–10
  cultural aspects 15–22, 212–15
  during times of rapid international expansion 108
  effects on HCN integration 205–10
  ethnocentric, polycentric, regiocentric and geocentric 102–7
  as expatriates in their own country 120
  growing importance 2–5
  individualism v. collectivism 24–6
  in model for HCN integration 13–14
  patterns of MNC organizational development 98–102
  PCN training 122–3
  PCN repatriation and adjustment 123–4
  qualitative data 182–6
  quantitative data from HR managers 192–3
  quantitative data from HCN managers 193–8
  quantitative data from PCN managers 198–201
  racism 60
  scale for measuring 176–8
  staffing in MNCs in general 112–15
  staffing in Japanese MNCs 115–20
Ishida, H. 8

jinji-bu (personnel department) 60–1
Johnson, R. T. 18, 92

Kagono, T. 108, 208
Kalleberg, A. L. 93–5
Kashima, J. 146

Keeley, T. D. 112, 122, 153, 176
Kennedy, A. 19
Kilburn, D. 72
Kinoshita, A. 18
Kitayama, S. 25
Klein, E. 8
Kleinberg, J. 8
Kluckhohn, F. 16
Kobayashi, N. 101, 118, 122, 206
Kobrin, S. J. 114
Koike, K. 18, 33, 90
Kopp, R. 2, 4, 6, 10, 107, 109, 119, 177–8, 206–7, 218
Kotter, J. P. 141
Kunihiro, M. 144, 146, 212
Kurata, Y. 120

Laurent, A. 19, 21
LeVine, R. A. 16, 142
Lawler, J. J. 129–30, 132
Lebas, M. 109
Leung, K. 28
Lim, H. S. 92–3
Lincoln, J. R. 93–5
localization 5–7, 9, 112–13, 116, 217–19
Luthans, F. 94

Mannari, H. 59, 145
March, R. M. 159
Margerison, A. 80–1
Markus, H. R. 25
Marshall, L. 8
Maruyama, M. 22–5, 214
McAuley, I. 10, 92, 111, 131–3, 138, 155, 171, 204, 210
Mead, R. 21
Mechanic, D. 147
Mendenhall M. E. 121–2
Ministry of International Trade and Industry (MITI) 115, 118–19, 206
Ministry of Labour 68
Mishra, J. 4, 219
Miyamoto, M. 22
Miyashita, K. 36
Morris, J. 18
Mroczkowski, T. 81

Mukuda, M. 101, 120
Munchus, G. 67

Nakane, C. 42–4, 49–50, 70, 77, 85–6
Nanus, B. 141, 210
Negandhi, A. R. 116, 168, 170, 203–4, 206, 217, 212
nenko-joretsu (Japanese-style seniority system) 30, 32, 45, 65, 76–82, 96
Nicholas, S. 139
nihonjinron (discussions of the Japanese) 38–42, 141, 143–6, 177
Nishida, H. 122, 153, 211

Oddou, G. R. 121–2
Okada, K. 32–3, 35, 69, 77
Otterbeck, L. 111
Ouchi, W. G. 8, 34–6, 71, 89, 94
Oyama, N. 122, 150–2, 171, 205, 211

Palumbo, F. A. 37
parent country national (PCN)
  communication with HCNs 142–5, 150–4
  cultural adjustment 121–2, 132, 136
  domination of management positions 10, 91, 99, 103, 111–12, 115–20, 135
  overseas assignments 1–2, 6, 82, 102–7
  relationship with HCNs 8, 38, 50–1, 54, 91–3, 136, 138
  relationship with the parent firm 37
  repatriation and adjustment 123–4
  training 122–3
Pascale, R. T. 28, 94, 157, 159
Perlmutter, H. 23, 98, 102–7, 208
Pettigrew, A. M. 147–8, 154, 210
Plath, D. W. 66
Porter, M. E. 106

Index

Pucik, V. 4, 5, 10, 91, 112–14, 120, 169–70, 203, 206, 217, 219
Putti, J. 130

Ray, C. A. 19, 21, 109
reference group theory 139–40
Reich, R. 2, 217
Rohlen, T. P. 8, 49, 52
Russell, D. 36

Sammapan, N. 93
Sasaki, N. 9, 65, 99, 159, 162–5
Sato, H. 79, 81
Schein, E. 19–20
Schenk, G. J. 107
Schlender, B. R. 72, 165
Schuler, R. S. 4, 99, 102, 109, 206
Serapiro, M. G. 168
Sethi, S. P. 6, 10, 18, 26, 28, 35–6, 82, 102, 115, 147, 156, 158, 166–8, 203–5, 208
Shimada, H. 35–6, 66, 68, 81, 83, 86
Shimizu, R. 94
Shirai, T. 69
Shiraki, M. 118, 206
shushinkoyo (lifetime employment) 30, 32, 45, 64–76, 78–9, 81, 91, 96, 109
Shweder, R. A. 16, 142
sogo-shosha (general trading company) 99, 179–80, 182–85, 191
Sohn, J. H. 121
Stalk, G. 94
Strodtbeck, F. 16

Tachibanaki, T. 66
Takagi, H. 71

Takashita, T. 95
Takayama, H. 73
Thome, K. 10, 92, 111, 131–3, 138, 155, 171, 204, 210
Toba, K. 127
Tobin, J. J. 56
Toyo Keizai 130, 135, 139
Triandis, H. C. 24–5, 27, 214
Tsurumi, Y. 92, 115, 206
Tung, R. L. 8, 116–8, 121, 206

United Nations Center on Transnational Corporations (UNCTC) 3

van Houten, G. 115
van Wolferen, K. 87, 161

Watanabe, S. 66, 74
Weigenstein, J. 109
Wheeler, T. 133
White, M. 123
Whitehall, A. M. 28, 45
Wilkinson, B. 18
Wingrove, T. 6, 153, 210
Woronoff, J. 11, 37, 69, 167, 204

Yabe, T. 208
Yang, J. Z. 8, 18, 75, 88, 89, 90
Yoshihara H. 6–10, 24, 100, 112–13, 119, 153, 217
Yoshihara, K. 132
Yoshimura, N. 27, 48, 53, 57, 94, 164, 214–15
Yoshino, K. 38–42, 144
Yoshino, M. Y. 9, 58–9, 209
Yuen, E. 170, 203

Zeira, Y. 103, 218